D1321930

Boundaries and Identities:
Nation, Politics and Culture in Scotland

Editors: Catherine Di Domenico
Alex Law
Jonathan Skinner
Mick Smith

UNIVERSITY
of ABERTAY
PRESS

ISBN 1-899796-08-8

Designed and Typeset by Shona Norman BA (Hons), University of Abertay Dundee

Printed and bound in Scotland by the University of Abertay Press

Table of Contents

Preface & Acknowledgements

Scotland is undergoing rapid change. Her polity, economy, society and culture are becoming unrecognisable compared to even a few years ago. Above all, political devolution and the recent opening of the new Scottish Parliament in Edinburgh in 1999 have effected a changed image of Scotland. Within this fluid and developing context a two-day conference entitled 'Scotland's Boundaries and Identities in the New Millennium?' was convened at Dudhope Castle, Dundee on the 14th and 15th April 1998. The present collection of twelve papers is an edited compilation of articles drawn from the much larger number of original papers delivered at the conference.

The conference was organised by the Division of Sociology of the University of Abertay Dundee, partly to mark the fourth anniversary of the University being granted its charter. Formerly the Dundee Institute of Technology, the institution, which has been operating as a centre of learning and higher education since 1888, was celebrating its position as Scotland's newest University. The University is committed to the Scottish tradition of the 'democratic intellect' by encouraging wider access to higher education for those sections of society traditionally excluded. Individual student needs are at the heart of the philosophy of the University, where a stimulating and supportive learning environment encourages students to develop and reach their full potential. This philosophy thus both continues a cherished educational tradition and contributes to Scotland's new sense of itself.

Dundee provided an appropriate location for the conference as the city embodies a renewed emphasis on rejuvenation and redevelopment. Dundee nicely complements the changing national self-image of Scotland. Over the last decade Dundee has undergone a dramatic transformation by adopting strategies to revitalise its social, economic and cultural environment. Especially significant in this respect is Dundee's re-branding as the 'City of Discovery' in honour of Captain Scott's ship of that name which has become both a tourist attraction and a symbol of the city's aspirations. The concept of 'discovery' represents Dundee's commitment to its position as a centre of educational excellence and as an international leader of new technological initiatives, as in the computer games sector.

From this vantage point, the book attempts to reflect some of the debates taking place in and about Scotland. These include ideas derived from history, geography, politics, society, language and religion. They involve feelings of cultural pride, nationalism, ethnicity, community and family. Both senses of 'being' Scottish and 'belonging' to Scotland meld together a diverse range of identities, from past and present, local and national, urban and rural, refracted through the changing images of national, local and regional institutions and groupings. The analysis of Scottish identity is being re-appraised and re-fashioned through such debates and, in this way, the complexity of Scottish heritage should be better understood.

Each of the three sections of the book examines a critical area of Scottish boundaries and identities, with an introductory paper which aims to integrate the other four papers. The first section broadly focuses on political identity around the question 'Scotland, identity and the death of the nation-state?' The second deals with narratives of nation and identity and contains papers that share a common concern with what might be called 'storytelling'. These stories explore different aspects of Scottish identity and Scotland's past, present and future as a nation. The third section contains papers about tourism, heritage and community and how they impinge on notions of Scottish identity.

There are certain organisations and individuals without whose help and involvement this book would not have been possible. The conference was supported financially partly by the British Sociological Association and partly by the University of Abertay Dundee. Professor James McGoldrick, the Vice-Principal of the University of Abertay Dundee, originally put forward the idea of the conference and encouraged the members of the Division of Sociology to plan and organise the proceedings. This was accomplished with great commitment on the part of all, and especially by Dr Andrew Samuel who was given special responsibility for planning the conference. Professor Michael Swanston, Head of the School of Social and Health Sciences, added his support to the venture, as did members of staff from other Divisions within the School of Social and Health Sciences. We would like to acknowledge all their help. We would also like to thank all the conference participants and especially all those who presented papers. We are especially grateful to Professor David McCrone and Mr Jim Hunter who gave excellent keynote addresses. Thanks also go to Mr Ivor Lloyd, Head of Information Services, for his support and encouragement in producing this book and to Joan Penman and Shona Norman of Information Services for their work on its production and also Ms Tricia MacColl who copy-edited the book.

Catherine Di Domenico
Division Leader of Sociology
University of Abertay Dundee.

Biographies

Eleanor Bell is currently in the final year of her PhD at the University of Dundee. She is working on contemporary theories of ethics and representations of nationhood in contemporary Scottish literature.

Catherine Di Domenico is a senior lecturer and division leader in Sociology at the University of Abertay Dundee. Her research interests are in the sociology of development, Africa and Scotland.

MariaLaura Di Domenico recently completed an MRes in Scottish Studies at the University of Strathclyde, where she is at present undertaking research for a PhD on small-scale hospitality providers in the cities of Dundee and Inverness. Her research interests involve Scotland, tourism, urban identities, and small business and lifestyle choice.

Antonia Dodds is currently completing a PhD on the Scottish national movement at the University of Leeds. Her PhD provides an extended case-study of Scotland and probes theories of nationalism, and in particular on why national movements occur. More generally, her research interests involve Scotland, nationalism, and national identity.

Tim Edensor teaches cultural studies at Staffordshire University. He is the author of *Tourists at the Taj* and editor of *Reclaiming Stoke on Trent: Leisure, space and identity in the Potteries*. Other recent articles focus on walking in the city and the countryside, football in Mauritius, and tourism as performance. He is presently writing a book on national identity and popular culture.

Joy Gladstone lectures in tourism, heritage and the rural environment in the Leisure and Tourism Management Department at the Scottish Agricultural College, Edinburgh. She is also involved in training for the provision of sustainable rural tourism in Scotland.

Barbara Grabmann is a post-doctoral researcher currently involved in a research project called "rituals of memory", a comparison and systematisation of different forms of remembering the holocaust in Germany, France, Italy and Japan. Her research interests are in the areas of collective identities, ethnicity, nationalism, Scotland, Bavaria, museums, European integration and migration.

Ailsa Henderson recently completed her PhD in the Department of Politics at the University of Edinburgh. She is currently a post-doctoral fellow at the University of Toronto, Canada. She has several publications on national identity and political culture in Scotland and Quebec, in Scottish, Canadian and American journals.

Atsuko Ichijo is a lecturer at Gyosei International College in Reading and a visiting research associate at the European Institute, London School of Economics. She is also an editor of *Nations and Nationalism*. Her research interests include theories of ethnicity and nationalism, Scottish nationalism, European integration, Japanese nationalism, citizenship and representation of nations.

Alex Law is a lecturer in Sociology at the University of Abertay Dundee. He is interested in forms of national identity in everyday life.

David McCrone is a professor of sociology at the University of Edinburgh. His book *Understanding Scotland: the Sociology of a Stateless Nation* has become the benchmark for all subsequent debate on the sociology of Scotland. His recent work, which focuses on national identity and the comparative sociology of nationalism, includes *The Sociology of Nationalism: Tomorrow's Ancestors; The Scottish Electorate: the 1997 general election and beyond; Politics and Society in Scotland; Scotland – the Brand: the Making of Scottish Heritage.*

Angela Morris is lecturer in rural sociology at the Scottish Agricultural College, Edinburgh. One of her significant publications is *Scotland – the Brand: The Making of Scottish Heritage* co-written with D McCrone & R Kiely.

Graeme Morton is lecturer in economic and social history at Edinburgh University. He is interested in applying principles of civil society and governance to Scotland.

Jonathan Skinner is a lecturer in Sociology at the University of Abertay Dundee where he specialises in the sociology and social anthropology of leisure and tourism, and the sociology of health. After ethnographic work on the Caribbean island of Montserrat, he is now writing about the place of culture in counselling clients.

Mick Smith is a senior lecturer in sociology at the University of Abertay Dundee. His research interests are in environmental sociology, ethics, modernism/postmodernism and hermeneutics. He has published widely in journals such as *Environmental Ethics, Journal of Applied Philosophy, Ethics, Place and Environment* and *Hypatia* and a book *An Ethics of Place: Radical Environmentalism, Social Theory and Postmodernity* to be published by SUNY Press.

Kirsten Stirling is completing her PhD on *Woman as Nation in Twentieth Century Scottish Literature* at the University of Glasgow. She teaches in the English Department of the University of Lausanne, Switzerland.

Kirsti Wishart is a graduate of the University of St Andrews and recently completed a PhD there on Robert Louis Stevenson, R B Cunninghame Graham and John Buchan.

Section I

Introduction

Scotland, Identity and the Death of the Nation-state?

Alex Law

The end of the nation-state has been widely trumpeted. As a result of a pincer movement from without and within, the nation-state is no longer presumed to be the source of political power and popular allegiance that it once was. From without, the globalisation of the market economy, production and consumption has smashed down national barriers, apparently making it impossible for governments to control and regulate capitalism. From within, sub-national, regional and localised units of governance appear to make greater sense against impersonal global forces than out-dated, centralised and homogeneous 'great states'. Identities fragment into ever-lower uncommon denominators, governments cede greater power to civil society, and once inviolable national boundaries are surmounted by trans-national exchanges and networks (Castells 1997).

All this tends to understate the resilience of the world system of states and the demarcation of the world into national units. In fact, the image of modernity as a perfectly-ordered world of big nation-states, where *de jure* sovereignty and *de facto* autonomy coincided perfectly, is based on a myth. Clearly, some big states broke up while a number of small micro-states survived. Some states possessed considerable power to inflict their will on less powerful neighbours. And, cosy images of the rudderless postmodern subject notwithstanding, the ship of state is still in the business of preparing national populations for warfare. Numerous examples throughout the 1990s – from the Balkans to the Persian Gulf, at the Pakistan/Indian border, the murderous Indonesian brutality in East Timor – and at the start of the twenty-first century, as in the Russian bombing of Chechnya, indicate that this is unlikely to change.

State boundaries are not merely dissolving like acid in the wake of economic and technological forces. Jealous guard is maintained over real as well as fictive borders. Nowhere is this clearer than in immigration policy. In 1999, as New Labour prosecuted a 'humanitarian war' on behalf of Kosovan Albanian refugees, harsh new asylum legislation was being prepared to make Britain an unattractive destination for those fleeing from state violence elsewhere. Populations continue to be both corralled behind and kept outside of state borders. In a world of armed states, 'placeless' postmodern citizens do not yet exist.

Such geo-political coordinates form the backdrop to political change in Scotland. Rejected in Scotland at successive elections and ensnared in a narrowly Englished version of Britain and big-state nationalism, the long rule of the Conservative Party over Scotland (and the UK) came to an end in 1997. However, the incoming New Labour government immediately adapted itself to Tory policies in the assumption that market capitalism, left to itself, possesses magical qualities for creating wealth and jobs, despite a mountain of contrary evidence. The abiding priority of New Labour was to reassure affluent groups haunted by the spectre of tax increases. Egalitarian policies, it was argued, could only be smuggled past middle-income constituencies by quiet stealth. Yet stealth and appeasement will be incapable of undoing inequalities in Scotland, greatly sharpened by nearly three decades of unleashed market deregulation. The scale of social division in Scotland is staggering. According to official figures, over 40% of children in Scotland live in households with incomes of less than half the UK average (Scottish Office 1999), with up to 60% of Glasgow's population estimated to be living in areas of multiple deprivation (Mooney and Johnson 2000). Yet this barely rates a mention in official political discourse, except where it justifies a moralising rhetoric about 'social inclusion', community and empowerment.

Seemingly helpless against the market, New Labour instead attended to changing the British constitution. Neo-liberals like Marsden Pirie of the Adam Smith Institute argued that while the left was content to bask in the symbolism of constitutional change, the right retained the substance of free-market hegemony. David McCrone's chapter ends by asking whether a Scottish Parliament matters. His focus is less on grossly unequal material conditions in Scotland than on identity and attitudes. Building on earlier studies (Brown et al 1998, Surridge et al 1999), he makes use of survey data to paint a picture of national identity in Scotland. Attitudinally, Scots, he argues, are more left-wing, socially liberal and less British than other parts of Britain. In other words, to be Scottish is less to do with blood, religion or class, than to broadly subscribe to social democratic values. How this set of national values squares with New Labour conservatism and electoral loyalty in Scotland to the Labour Party – the two are not necessarily identical – it may be too early to say. At least the elections and the referendum show that the political situation in Scotland, and indeed the UK, is changeable. National identity and the elements that compose it also fluctuate according to conditions. As McCrone says, 'there is nothing fixed and eternal' about national identity, and nor is it 'some kind of a priori essentialised given, a badge which we treat independently of how it operates'. Some idea of the role of socio-economic conditions, the state and mass communications in constituting national identity seem to be necessary here to prevent the rational kernel of McCrone's argument sailing too close to verities about the rudderless post-modern subject.

Through a comparison of Scotland and Quebec, Ailsa Henderson's chapter examines the roles of the respective nationalist parties in 'politicising national identity'. The chapter establishes that Quebecers identify less with the Canadian state than with their province, just as many Scots prioritise a sense of Scottishness over Britishness. Interestingly, in the case of Quebec state definitions are used – relative attachment to province versus Canada – while in the case of Scotland national identity is employed – Scottish versus British. An important difference exists between state and national identity, which the chapter alludes to, but makes the crucial distinction between political and cultural national identity. Vaguely inclusive, cultural national identity is contrasted to an exclusive, enunciated political national identity. Much of this analysis will prove highly contentious. The idea of a pre-political, cultural national identity is highly problematic. Cultural identity is assumed to be prior to political identity at a number of points: 'the political use of pre-existing cultural markers', 'the politicisation of cultural national identity', political parties 'manipulate cultural identity into a political tool'. I will discuss just two issues central to the construction of political national identity.

First, in what sense can 'cultural nationalism' be said to be inclusive while political nationalism is understood to be exclusive? Henderson clearly sees this as a novel departure from conventional categories of nationalism. But are not all national discourses, 'cultural' and 'political', or 'ethnic' and 'civic', always premised on exclusion and inclusion somewhere along the line? It is always civic identity that is typically described as a 'reflexive movement', while ethnic identities mobilise 'latent' characteristics (Billig 1995). Our two sub-nationalisms are, of course, of the nice, civic variety. Some idea seems necessary here of how Quebec became part of the Confederation, through conquest, military oppression and regular attacks on French rights. Political nationalists are kept distinct from 'non-nationalists'. Henderson has in mind as political nationalists only those parties that separate themselves from the mundane nationalism of the big-states within which they are presently contained. Greater British or Canadian Nationalisms are thus exempted from the charge of manipulating and politicising 'culture'.

Second, how is identity understood? Henderson claims that the question of identity is largely absent from current political debate in Scotland while 'interest' is foregrounded. Perhaps, as McCrone's chapter argues, this all depends on what is meant by 'identity'. Partly, this may have to do with the three assumptions that are made explicit. One, identity is self-defined at an individual level. Two, national identity is only one part of complex self-identity. Three, cultural national identity is flexible. In Quebec, national identity became politicised through an exclusive focus on the French language, which all the main parties in Quebec share. In Scotland, the major political parties are split on the national issue, with the SNP seeking to be exclusively associated with 'the national interest'. Attention is thus drawn to differences in the ways in which the constitutional status of Quebec and Scotland is framed.

Those individuals who 'feel themselves outside the nation in Scotland' are said to be excluded because of their values and not because of language or ancestry. Recent research on Scottish identity tends to broadly confirm this, although where appropriate social cues, especially accent, are absent relatively relaxed social interaction can be disrupted (Bechhofer et al 1999). As Volosinov (1973: 20) stressed, although we may share the same language, each ideological sign is 'multi-accentual', subject to 'an extraordinary sensitivity to all fluctuations in social atmosphere'. Identity can never therefore be pre-ideological or understood by abstractly counter-posing interests to values, initially locked-up in the inner psychic structures of the individual's head and then expressed outwardly as cultural identity, which nationalists then tap into to create widespread national sentiment.

Antonia Dodds' chapter gives an example where a national movement did *not* emerge as an expression of national consciousness: nineteenth century Scotland. Even as the nineteenth century witnessed the emergence of national movements across Europe, Scotland failed to provide one. Five factors explain this absence according to Dodds: incorporated elites; a corporate British identity; local administrative autonomy; adequate reform within British state framework; culture and economics did not divide into separate nations. Ultimately, Dodds argues, economics must be relegated as an explanatory cause of nationalism and cultural identity and state power foregrounded. How can economics be separated from state or culture-identity? Dodds uses Hroch's mobilisation model of emergent national movements, which tends to radically disassociate culture and politics, first culture, then agitation, then mass movement, with an especially privileged role for nationalist intellectuals.

Against these straight lines of development might be posed Trotsky's notion of combined and uneven development, where the amalgam of the archaic and the modern created the conditions in nineteenth century Europe for the rise of national movements. Scotland, by the mid-nineteenth century, was already modernised and, since the late eighteenth century, subject to unified state authority (Davidson 2000). Scotland developed at a ferocious tempo after the 1780s, creating extreme unevenness, both within Scotland and globally. This precipitated the early creation of the first distinctly working *class* political movement, Chartism, which was *not* exclusively Scottish (Mitchell 1999), at a time when plebeian Europe agitated around *national* movements. Again, the state and socio-economic development needs to be reintroduced to the analysis of nationalism. As Anderson (1983: 45) makes plain, it is only with the rise of print capitalism that *state* languages began to be instilled into territorially-defined vernacular communities. This process was political-administrative from the beginning. Only in the nineteenth century does popular linguistic nationalism appear.

Atsuko Ichijo's chapter deals more explicitly with the state form. She examines the apparent contradiction between heightened Scottish Nationalism (separatism) and European integration (trans-state identity) since 1979. This is done through interviews with members of the so-called 'Scottish intelligentsia', although little is said about how these individuals were selected as significant opinion formers in Scotland. Through these voices an anti-English frame of reference is employed to measure Scottish attitudes towards Europe. Pre-1997 Europe seemed to offer legal-juridical protection against the so-called 'democratic deficit'. This can, of course, be read in other ways which de-emphasise nation and foreground class. Nation can also be a surrogate for class politics. Anti-Thatcher politics became a touchstone of 'national authenticity' in Scotland. This was arguably less to do with some abstract democratic principle than with defending the admittedly flawed material of the (UK-wide) welfare state.

Three visions of Europe are outlined: as a force for independence/ autonomy; a force for a social-democratic politics; and a substitute for Empire. Although these visions provide useful frames, alternatives, such as Europe as a greater white, capitalist fortress, technocratic Europe or militarised Europe, are downplayed or subsumed. But this of course depends on who you speak to as part of a national 'intelligentsia'. Andrew Neil or Tommy Sheridan would, I suspect, offer contrary viewpoints. Why do the respondents want to see 'a more confident nation' or a 'national renaissance' within Europe? Are these national self-images not self-justifying? In answer, Ichijo employs the civic/ethnic distinction, a dualism criticised elsewhere for naturalising national identity as an either/or affinity, to values or blood.

In this brief introduction, some issues have been raised that might be further explored. Nevertheless, taken together, these chapters provide a challenging range of perspectives for locating political boundaries and identities in Scotland in the second Christian millennium.

References

Anderson B 1983 Imagined Communities: Reflections on the Spread and Origins of Nationalism. London, Verso

Bechhofer F, McCrone D, Kiely R, Stewart R 1999 'Constructing national identity: arts and landed elites in Scotland. Sociology 33:3, 515–34

Billig M 1995 Banal Nationalism. London, Sage

Brown A, McCrone D, Paterson L 1998 Politics and Society in Scotland, 2nd edn. London, Macmillan

Castells M 1997 The Rise of the Network Society. Oxford; Cambridge, MA, Blackwell

Davidson N 2000 The Origins of Scottish Nationhood. London, Verso

Mitchell M J 1999 The Irish in the West of Scotland, 1797-1848: Trade Unions, Strikes and Political Movements. Edinburgh, John Donald

Mooney G, Johnstone C 2000 Scotland divided: Poverty, inequality and the Scottish Parliament. Critical Social Policy

Scottish Office 1999 Social Inclusion: Opening the Door to a Better Scotland. Edinburgh, The Scottish Office

Surridge P, Brown A, McCrone D, Paterson L 1999 The Scottish Electorate. London, Macmillan.

Volosinov V N 1973 Marxism and the Philosophy of Language. Cambridge, MA, Harvard University Press

Who Are We?
Understanding Scottish Identity

David McCrone

The late twentieth century, with its language of 'ethnic cleansing', is an epoch in which ethnicity and nationalism have come into their own. The editors of a recently published anthology on ethnicity wrote: 'Ethnicity, far from fading away, has now become a central issue in the social and political life of every continent. The 'end of history', it seems, turns out to have ushered in the era of ethnicity' (Hutchinson and Smith 1996:v). Whether we look at the Balkans, Chechnya, Nagorno-Karabakh, central Africa, or closer to home in Northern Ireland and Euzkadi (the Basque country), some of the most emotionally charged and seemingly intractable political disputes appear to be 'ethnic' in origin.

Many students of nationalism also argue that ethnicity and nationalism are closely linked. For example, Walker Connor begins his collection of essays on 'Ethnonationalism' by justifying why he did not simply call it 'nationalism'. The answer he gives is that 'there is no difference if nationalism is used in its pristine sense' (1994:xi). Unfortunately, he continues, this is rarely the case. Why it should be 'unfortunate' is debatable, but it is a fairly widespread sentiment. Nationalism without ethnicity is judged not to be quite the right thing.

Nationalism in Scotland

The analysis of nationalism in Scotland provides a good, apparently negative, instance of this. In recent years, much has been made of the fact that what underlies Scottish nationalism is a 'sense of place' rather than a 'sense of tribe' (Smout 1994). In other words, Scottishness is based on living in a common territory despite clear and abiding social, religious and geographical differences. The nationalist party, the SNP, prides itself on the 'mongrel' character of the Scots, and has argued that residence in Scotland, not blood-line, will confer citizenship if and when political independence is achieved.

Some writers have drawn the implication of this 'territorial' sense of nationality that it is a second-best definition, in the absence of a strong sense of ethnicity, that is, a sense of tribe. Steve Bruce, for example, has drawn lessons about Scotland from his work on Northern Ireland to argue that it is precisely because there is no single identity of a 'people' with common ancestors, common language, shared religion and a glorious history which prevented nationalism emerging in Scotland when it was doing so elsewhere in the nineteenth century. 'There is no modern demotic mythical history . . . and certainly nothing to compare to the shared history which informs the thinking of the majority of Ulster Protestants' (1993:11). As a result, 'If Scotland's intellectuals in the nineteenth century had wanted to promote Scottish nationalism, they would have been unable to do so' (ibid:11–12). This alludes to a now familiar argument that the 1707 Union 'solved' the problem of nationalism in Scotland by making the focus, at least of elite and progressive opinion, Britain (Kidd 1993). In this formulation, 'Scotland' ended in 1707; the future was British. If Scotland survived, it was a matter of the heart, not the head; of sentiment over reason.

Scotland, this wisdom went, had long been divided linguistically, geographically and religiously, which, coupled with the country's participation in British imperialism as a 'junior partner' rather than as a 'colony', has made nationalism a late, and not very convincing, developer. Bruce concludes that territoriality – civic nationalism – is too weak a base on which to erect the kind of atavistic passions generated by a sense of belonging to a 'community of the blood', as witnessed in the Balkans, Africa, and, indeed, Northern Ireland. While he accepts that, for example, religious divisions between Catholics and Protestants, or geo-linguistic ones between Highlanders and Lowlanders, are far less significant than previously, there does not seem to be enough of a common ethnicity for a full-blown nationalism worthy of the name to emerge in Scotland at the end of the twentieth century, which anyway, is a time in which the nation-state appears to be losing its powers. One finds echoes here of Hobsbawm's comment that the nationalist owl of Minerva flies at the dusk of the nation-state (1990:83).

In this conventional framework, Scotland is represented as divided and fragmented. For example, regional identities in Scotland are deemed to be stronger than national ones. After all, the conventional political wisdom is that Scottish devolution was lost in 1979 because various regions of Scotland did not trust the other: the north–the south; the east–the west; the Highlands–the Lowlands, and so on. We have heard less of this since the 1997 referendum, but it remains a shot in the locker of those who are hostile to genuine Scottish Home Rule. Tom Nairn has caricatured this position as follows:

> 'Scotland? which Scotland? – Highland or Lowland, Hugh Macdiarmid or the Sunday Post?': 'Scotland': if that word means anything – which I doubt - then surely it means different things in Grampian and Clydebank?' Scotland's internal contrasts (actually no greater than in most other nations) are thus weirdly elevated into mountain ranges of peculiarity – barriers exclusive of all possible consensus and common interest (Nairn 1997:185).

To complete the picture, let us examine how writers on nationalism view Scotland. First of all, nationalism in places like Scotland is seen as the result of contingent rather than necessary factors. Ernest Gellner (1978) had little to say, beyond, in his own words, a 'feeble' suggestion that nationalism in late twentieth century Scotland is contingent and instrumental. The discovery of North Sea oil, coupled with historical and cultural means for expressing identity, has allowed Scotland to try to renegotiate its relationship with the United Kingdom state which it joined in 1707.

Like Gellner, Benedict Anderson is more interested in the failure of nationalism to 'take' in Scotland in the nineteenth century. Anderson's explanation is that 'already in the early 17th century large parts of what would one day be imagined as Scotland were English-speaking and had immediate access to print-English, provided a minimum degree of literacy existed' (1996:90). The migration of Scottish intellectuals to England post-1707, together with open access to English markets, meant that a rising bourgeoisie had little need to mobilise nationalism for its political or economic ends.

Anthony Smith sees what he calls the 'third wave of demotic ethnic nationalisms' since the 1950s as specific to the political-cultural conditions of the well-established industrial states to which they belong. He judges them 'autonomist' rather than 'separatist', with particular emphasis on maintaining or developing cultural, social and economic autonomy, but remaining within the political framework of the state into which they were incorporated. They are persuaded of this by the economic benefits to be had, by which means Smith seeks to explain the devolution debate in Scotland in the 1970s: the triumph of economic self-interest over cultural sentiment. It also suits him to be able to show, in his desire to establish the pre-modern character of nationalism, that many of the recent movements post-1960s have been built on older ideals and identities. He comments: 'In all these cases [Wales, Scotland, Catalunya, Euzkadi, Brittany] a cultural renaissance, literary, linguistic, and historical, preceded the formation of political movements demanding ethnic autonomy' (1991:141).

Eric Hobsbawm who is undoubtedly the most hostile to neo-nationalism, commented that 'the characteristic nationalist movements of the late 20th century are essentially negative, or rather divisive' (1990:164). Most of this is directed at ethnic-linguistic forms such as in Wales and Quebec, where, he asserts; 'the stance of Quebec nationalism is that of a people in headlong retreat before historical forces which threaten to overwhelm it; a movement whose very advances are viewed in terms of potential weakness rather than as success' (165). Scottish nationalism, on the other hand, is, according to Hobsbawm, the outcome of adverse *political* processes. It is, he comments, 'plainly a reaction to an all-British government supported by only a modest minority of Scots, and a politically impotent all-British opposition party' (179), such a state of affairs no doubt to be redressed by the election of a Labour government, when support for nationalism will, he assumes, ebb away. Trends to date since May 1997 are not in Hobsbawm's favour.

Such a view touches on a favourite explanation for the rise of neo-nationalism, that it is not actually 'nationalism' at all, but something akin to 'regionalism', the mobilisation for instrumental ends of territorial identity, but stopping well short of separatism. Peter Alter, for example, comments that 'regionalism', 'resistance to the state's centre from peripheral areas' (1991: 135) results from inadequate political incorporation. The 'political nations' of France, Spain and the UK, he argues, were never completely unified or homo-geneous, and failed to develop the requisite conditions for a successful political system: a common political-cultural identity, a high degree of allegiance to the centre, and shared political aims. Parties like Plaid Cymru in Wales and the Scottish National Party (SNP) are mere 'regionalist organisations' 'not serious about complete political separation' (138), and 'regional economic differentiation as a generator of regionalism can also be fruitfully offered as a thesis to explain the situation in Catalonia and the Basque country' (141).

The sense that regions are playing the nationalist card for political reasons but without being true believers also fits into the general approach that territorial politics are at work. John Breuilly, for example, concludes that 'what has developed [in Quebec] as in the Basque and Scottish cases, is a rather tough-minded, frequently radical nationalism which is very different from the anti-modernist, rather romantic nationalist movements of 'peripheral' regions in many 19th century European countries' (1993:333). In other words, Breuilly sees these late twentieth century movements as quite different from their nineteenth century counterparts insofar as they have a much more 'political' orientation driven by largely economic concerns on the part of key social groups, especially upwardly mobile managerial and technical workers in these territories.

To sum up what has long been the conventional wisdom: Scotland's nationalism and national consciousness is deemed to be a weak and poor thing. Scotland lacks a strong sense of the ethnic; is regionally divided; belongs to the period before 1707 when it was an independent state, but not thereafter when its ruling elites went 'British'; and its late twentieth century form of nationalism is merely contingent, instrumental, political, and does not even warrant the name 'nationalism' but 'regionalism'. We might sum up this approach as seeking not so much to explain nationalism in Scotland as to explain it away.

National Identity in Scotland

Are the critics correct? Let us review what we know. Let us start with some straightforward evidence about national identity. Over the last decade we have built up a body of survey data using what has become known as the Moreno question (1995), named after the Spanish sociologist who invented a fairly simple five-point Likert scale which has been used fairly regularly in surveys and opinion polls. It is a simple question: which of these best describes how you see yourself? Scottish not British; more Scottish than British; equally Scottish and British; more British than Scottish; and British not Scottish. We can of course criticise it on methodological grounds: can we be sure that respondents interpret the categories in the same way? What if you feel that you respond differently in different circumstances? What we can say, however, is that the measure has a robustness to it. It correlates well and consistently with social variables such as social class, age, gender, educational achievement, and so on. The key to it, of course, is that most people in Scotland (and Wales for that matter) seem to grasp what the question is getting at: the relationship between national identity (Scottish) and state identity (British). For perfectly good reasons, most people in England do not get it. This was put especially well by Anthony Barnett in his recent book *This Time: Our Constitutional Revolution* (1997).

> What is the difference between being English and being British? If you ask a Scot or a Welsh person about their Britishness, the question makes sense to them. They might say that they feel Scots first and British second. Or that they enjoy a dual identity as Welsh–British, with both parts being equal. Or they might say. 'I'm definitely British first'. What they have in common is an understanding that there is a space between their nation and Britain, and they can assess the relationship between the two. The English, however, are more often baffled when asked how they relate their Englishness and Britishness to each other. They often fail to understand how the two can be contrasted at all. It seems like one of those puzzles that others can undo but you can't; Englishness and Britishness seem inseparable. They might prefer to be called one thing rather than the other – and today young people increasingly prefer English to British – but, like two sides of a coin, neither term has an independent existence from the other. (Barnett 1997:292-3)

Let me remind you that Barnett is a champion of constitutional change in the UK, a founder-member of Charter 88, someone who would like to see a UK federal state in which national identities (English, Scottish, Welsh and so on) sit more easily with state – British – identity. His sympathetic comments help to put things in context. I suppose we have grown quite used to 'for Britain, read England' but it is becoming a less tenable position. The historian Simon Schama has been commissioned by the BBC to write a 16-hour history of the 'British' Isles (my quotes – 'these islands' is a preferred option, as it does not assume continuing British ownership of the island of Ireland). Schama was quoted as saying: 'I want it to be a major contribution to the public discussion about how our history shapes our sense of Britishness, or of non-Britishness: of Scottishness, Welshness and Irishness' (*The Guardian*, 30 March 1998). No prizes for guessing who/what is missing. And lest we think this is a slip of his pen, he goes on to comment that he will end the series with his own essay on Britain in the twentieth century, an essay dealing with the debris of Empire, 'when the consolation for Suez is [wait for it] winning the world cup in 1966'! Mere words, you may say. Well, yes, but so is implying that 'people' are men. In terms of gender relations, we have properly recognised the power of/in language. Mere, let me remind you, means basic, fundamental.

Let me now turn to some data on nationality. These come from the British and Scottish Election Studies of 1997, and the subsequent Scottish Referendum Study later that year (Surridge et al 1998). They provide the most up-to-date data we have, and allow us in the first instance to compare national/state identities on this island of ours.

Table 1 National identity by country (X = Scottish/Welsh/English)

Percentage in column	Scotland	Wales	England
X not British	23	13	8
More X than British	38	29	16
Equally X and British	27	26	46
More British than X	4	10	15
British not X	4	15	9
None of these	4	7	6
Sample sizes	882	182	255

Source: British and Scottish Election Studies 1997.

These findings are broadly in line with previous ones. We can see that more than seven times more people living in Scotland give priority to being Scottish (either Scottish not British, or more Scottish than British) over being British. The ratio for Wales is just under 2 to 1; and in England, 'English' and 'British' are comparable at around 25% each. (Barnett's health warning applies, of course.)

Let us focus now on the Scottish data. The broad trends are given in Table 2.

Table 2 National identity in Scotland

Percentage in column	July 1986	Sept 1991	April 1992	SES 1992	SES 1997
Scottish not British	39	40	32	19	23
More Scottish than British	30	29	29	40	38
Equally Scottish and British	19	21	29	33	27
More British than Scottish	4	3	3	3	4
British not Scottish	6	4	6	3	4
None of these	2	3	1	1	4
Sample size	1021	1042	1056	957	882

Sources: July 1986: L. Moreno (1988); September 1991 and April 1992: The Scotsman; Scottish Election Survey 1992; Scottish Election Survey 1997.

Again, we see that the ratios for those prioritising Scottishness over Britishness are between 7:1 and 9:1. We will return to how to interpret these data more fully at a later stage. The point I want to leave you with here is that we need to see these responses in the political-cultural context in which they were made (note, for example, that the 1986 and 1991 surveys show very high levels of 'Scottish only' responses, but that those for the later 1990s are lower).

Politics is, I think, the key. Let us examine identity by vote (Table 3).

Table 3 National identity by vote in 1997 General Election

Percentage in column	Con	Labour	Lib-Dem	SNP	All
Scottish not British	10	25	13	32	23
Scottish more than British	26	39	42	44	38
Equally Scottish and British	45	26	28	18	27
British more than Scottish	7	4	6	2	4
British not Scottish	7	3	5	2	4
None of these	4	3	5	1	4
Sample sizes	96	363	96	132	882

Source: Scottish Election Survey 1997.

Defining oneself as predominantly British is not at all a feature, even among Conservative voters. Note too that only one-third of SNP voters say they are Scottish not British.

How does identity relate then to preferred constitutional option? Do those preferring independence do so because they think of themselves as Scottish only?

Table 4 National identity by preferred constitutional option

Percentage in column	Independence	Home Rule	No Change	All
Scottish not British	40	18	12	23
More Scottish than British	40	43	23	38
Equally Scottish & British	14	27	47	27
More British than Scottish	2	5	7	4
British not Scottish	2	4	5	4
None of these	2	3	6	4
Sample sizes	231	449	150	882

Source: Scottish Election Survey 1997.

The answer, as shown in Table 4 is of course, 'no'. Just as many wanting independence (40%) retain some (albeit minor) sense of being British as well as Scottish. Plainly, we are dealing with some complex interrelationships here. We cannot explain national identity in terms of social class either (Table 5).

Table 5 National identity by social class (Registrar General's Categories)

Percentage in column	I and II	IIIn-m	IIIm	IV and V	All
Scottish not British	13	19	32	31	23
More Scottish than British	36	41	40	37	38
Equally Scottish and British	33	26	21	26	27
More British than Scottish	7	4	4	3	3
British not Scottish	8	4	1	1	3
None of these	3	5	2	3	4
Sample sizes	222	206	172	223	882

Source: Scottish Election Survey 1997.

Religion does not help us to discriminate in terms of national identity either (Table 6).

Table 6 National identity by religion

Percentage in column	Catholic	Protestant	Other/none	All
Scottish not British	23	19	28	23
Scottish more than British	38	41	35	38
Equally Scottish and British	26	31	23	27
British more than Scottish	5	4	4	4
British not Scottish	5	3	4	4
None of these	3	2	6	4
Sample size	125	395	362	882

Source: Scottish Election Survey 1997.

Let me explore how people in Scotland decide who is a Scot or not. The answer is, on the face of it, pretty straightforward, as shown by Table 7. Respondents were asked: how important or unimportant is each of the following to being truly Scottish?

Table 7 Components of Scottishness

Percentage in column	Birth	Ancestry*	Residence
Very important	48	36	30
Fairly important	34	37	35
Not very important	14	22	23
Not at all important	3	4	10
Do not know	1	1	2

*Ancestry is defined as having Scottish parents or grandparents.

In other words, for most people living in Scotland, birth, ancestry and residence are the main markers of Scottishness, probably in that order (with 82% saying birth is very or fairly important, 73% ancestry, and 65% residence). So far, so obvious, you might think. However, before I take you back to a more conceptual discussion of national identity, let me use this fairly basic information of birth, ancestry and residence as definers of Scottishness (there are, of course, others such as language, religion etc, but I want to keep it simple for the moment).

You may have noticed that in North America, 6 April is Tartan Day. I am sure that many found this more than a bit uncomfortable. It seemed, at least from this distance, to arouse that old *bête noir* of Tom Nairn's, the tartan monster and its excesses. Be that as it may (and how can we tell?) it raised nicely the question of who is a Scot. That dubious statistic of 15 million Scots abroad reared its head. However that calculation is done, it does raise the issue of what defines Scottishness. I guess that much of our native discomfort with Tartan Day is that many of us living in Scotland do not care very much for an ancestral, an ethnic, definition of Scottishness. 'My mother's a McTavish' does not do a lot to measure the commitment and contribution to Scotland in our scale of values these days.

I use this example because it captures nicely the potential for different ways of defining a Scot. Is it someone who is born here, whose granny actually was a McTavish, and who lives and works here? If the answer is 'yes', then it shows that we have not had to define ourselves too closely, because we are not confronted with different, even competing, ways of being Scottish. Let me try to lay out some of the possible dimensions. I have invented these labels, and you are free to use your own. Whatever you want to call them, I hope you agree that they represent different ways of being Scottish.

Let us construct a typology from these three dimensions: birth, lineage, and residence, and apply it to Scotland. For example, one can be born or not born in Scotland; of Scottish lineage or not; and resident in Scotland or not (necessary in any emigrant society, given the 'émigrés' who feel they have some blood claim). This gives us some 'types' as follows:

Table 8 Types of Scot

	Born in Scotland		Not born in Scotland	
	Scottish lineage	Not Scottish lineage	Scottish lineage	Not Scottish lineage
Living in Scotland	Pure' Scots	'Real' Scots	'Returning' Scots	'New' Scots
Not living in Scotland	'Expatriate' Scots	'Accidental' Scots	'Heritage' Scots	N/A

The names themselves have mnemonic rather than analytical value, but they allow us to lay out alternative ways one can be 'Scottish'. Today, these 'types' of Scots rarely conflict with each other; we would be hard pushed to claim that there is a clear hierarchy of ways to be Scottish. Nevertheless, alternative ways have been employed in writing about Scotland. In the 1980s and 1990s, we have heard much of the importance of the 'civic', that is, territorial definition of who is a Scot: you are Scottish because you live and work in Scotland. The Scottish National Party, for example, has made significant play of what they term 'new' Scots, that is, people whose Scottishness is defined solely in residential and not in terms of birth or lineage. 'New' Scots can be English-born, or of Asian extraction (if not born in Scotland), thus overcoming the anti-nationalist jibe that nationalism is inherently racist and ethnicist. Scotland as a 'mongrel' nation, to use the novelist William McIlvanney's term, is deemed by nationalists to be a positive and celebratory feature, and used in the late 1980s and early 1990s against extreme forms of nationalism as practised by militant groups such as Settler Watch and Scottish Watch. The SNP itself is also subject to counter-attack on the grounds that one of its most prominent supporters the actor Sean Connery does not actually live in Scotland but in Spain, thereby undermining its residential qualification for Scottishness.

There is no political or cultural reason for people to have to choose whether birth is more important than residence, for example. One could imagine a situation perhaps where lineage and/or birth might outweigh residence. German citizenship is a case in point. People of Turkish origin, even those born in Germany until 1999, had no claim to citizenship. On the other hand, those of German origin in the former USSR with proven lineage links have the right to settle in Germany. This is the expression of *ius sanguinis* rather than *ius soli* (Brubaker 1992). Similarly, in Bosnia, lineage seems to have overtaken residence and even birth as proof of 'real' Bosnian-ness and hence political trust-worthiness (Malcolm 1994). Thankfully, in most western democracies the geo-political significance of these distinctions is absent.

Here we are connecting into more familiar distinctions between 'civic' and 'ethnic' criteria of nationality. While mainstream and liberal (including nationalist) opinion in Scotland favours the former over the latter, there is some evidence that for most Scots lineage and birth – the essence of ethnicity – matters more, insofar as they ever think about it. And that is the point. For most people as they go about their daily lives, this is not a puzzle they have to solve. No political decisions have to be made about who gets what according to nationality. The geo-politics of Scotland in the late twentieth century does not demand that one criterion has to be prioritised over another.

What will happen now that there is a Scottish Parliament? We might speculate that territoriality (ie where one lived) might come to define more strongly who is a 'Scot' compared with one's birth and lineage. During the 1997 Scottish referendum campaign the opposition to a parliament sought to make some capital out of the fact that 'Scots' living in England (in other words, defined by their birth and lineage) were excluded from having a say in the vote. The so-called 'Gary McAllister question' – why was the captain of the Scottish football team excluded from having a say in the country's future? [answer: he did not live in Scotland] – failed to catch on. The journalist John Lloyd echoed similar sentiments after the Scottish referendum when he suggested that émigré Scots (like himself) might increasingly be distanced from an evolving, more political, sense of being Scottish which a parliament would help to foster and amplify. In other words, Scottishness might well take on a stronger civic than an ethnic dimension. The Catalan nationalist leader Jordi Pujol commented: 'a Catalan is whoever lives and works in Catalunya'

(Conversi 1997:215). We might be seeing a 'civic' rather than an 'ethnic' definition of Scottishness emerging under the new political dispensation. The few surveys we have do suggest that people born in England who do live in Scotland are much more likely to 'go native' in political terms than their 'ethnic' counterparts south of the border (Dickson 1994).

Understanding National Identity

I want now to explore with you the ways in which the new political context might be shaping what we mean by Scottishness, but first let me be more explicit about what I mean by national identity in conceptual terms. Plainly it is a label, a badge, but we cannot take it at face value. I am attracted to Anthony Cohen's comment that the language of ethnicity (we can use nationality in this context too) 'refers to a decision people make to depict themselves or others symbolically as the bearers of a certain cultural identity' (1993:197). Ethnicity has to do with the politicisation of culture. 'Thus, it is part a claim to a particular culture, with all that entails. The statement made ... in Northern Ireland, 'He's a Prod' – is clearly not merely descriptive: it has an added value, either negative or positive, depending on who is speaking to whom' (Cohen 1993:197). This is an appropriate point to refer back to Steve Bruce's observations. Labels like Catholic or Protestant (or for that matter, Scots and English) are not neutral descriptive labels but need to be interpreted in the context of the social and cultural claims which are being made.

The point here is not that nationalism, for example, is the mobilisation of objective and longstanding differences in ethnicity, but the mobilisation of those which actors deem to be salient. In other words, cultural differences like language, religion, even skin colour, are not primary and definitional characteristics, but are social identifiers which are the result, the product, of struggles in the first place. Being able to show that there is ethnic homogeneity in a given territory – or, rather, that people living there believe themselves to be homogeneous – is the outcome of political and social processes, not their explanation, their cause. Writers on the Balkans, for example, tell how neighbours who lived in a fair degree of harmony for decades, even centuries, suddenly developed great hatred for each other on the grounds that they are

Serb, or Bosnian or Croat. This activity cannot be explained in terms of long-standing and deep-seated ethnic rivalries, but those which the combatants choose to remember, construct or activate as a result of the changing political context. Before the outbreak of the Balkan war in 1991, it was supposed that the different peoples of the region living quite literally side by side had nothing to fight about. As Eriksen observes:

> Ethnic boundaries, dormant for decades, were activated; presumed cultural differences which had been irrelevant for two generations were suddenly 'remembered' and invoked as proof that it was impossible for the two groups to live side by side. It is only when they make a difference that cultural differences are important in the creation of ethnic boundaries (1993:39).

In Barth's words: 'To the extent that actors use ethnic identities to categorise themselves and others for purposes of interaction, they form ethnic groups in this organisational sense' (1981:202-3). The key point here is that there is no one-to-one relationship between ethnicity and cultural identifiers. What matters is which ones key actors regard as significant, for which purposes, and under which conditions. Barth continues: 'some cultural factors are used by the actors as signals and emblems of differences, others are ignored, and in some relationships radical differences are played down and denied' (1981:203).

Related to the variation in the potency of cultural markers is the issue of boundaries. It is the social boundary which defines the group in question, not the cultural stuff which the boundary contains. Where social interaction is defined as taking place within or across these boundaries, then the group's identity will be maintained, reinforced or dissipated. It will not be necessary for the cultural content of two adjacent groups to alter significantly – indeed, they may grow more similar. What matters is the interaction across a meaningful boundary (not only geographical, but also social and cultural) which may weaken or strengthen. For example, it is not difficult to show that in most respects the people who live in Scotland and England have grown more similar in economic, social and cultural terms. What matters sociologically, however, is how they define themselves vis-à-vis each other.

The missing link here is 'identity'. We find that we cannot discuss ethnicity and nationality without focusing on processes of identification, on the active negotiation which people take part in as they construct who they are and who they want to be. In Hall's words:

Identity is not as transparent or unproblematic as we think. Perhaps instead of thinking of identity as an already accomplished fact, with the new cultural practices they represent, we should think instead of identity as 'production', which is never complete, always in process, and always constituted within, not outside, representation. This view problematises the very authority and authenticity to which the term 'cultural identity' lays claim' (1990:222).

While it is true that identities are constructed by participants in the course of social and political action, they are not entirely of their own making. We work within cultural representations, as Stuart Hall points out: 'We only know what it is to be "English" because of the way "Englishness" has come to be represented, as a set of meanings, by English national culture. It follows that a nation is not only a political entity but something which produces meanings – a system of cultural representation.' (1992:292) Try substituting 'Scottish' and 'Scottishness' in this comment, and see what you come up with.

Hall argues that national culture is a discourse, a way of constructing meanings which influences and organises our actions and our conceptions of ourselves. The idea of the nation is a 'narrative' (Bhabha 1990) whose origin is obscure, but whose symbolic power to mobilise the sense of identity and allegiance is strong.

Problematising identity in the late twentieth century suggests that identity should be considered less as a categorical self-concept, and more as a process. In Stuart Hall's words:

Though they seem to invoke an origin in a historical past with which they continue to correspond, actually identities are about using the resources of history, language and culture in the process of becoming rather than being; not 'who we are' or 'where have we come from' so much as what we might become, how we have been represented and how that bears on how we might represent ourselves. Identities are therefore constituted within, not outside representation. (1996:4)

In other words, identities should be seen as a concern with 'routes' rather than 'roots', as maps for the future rather than trails from the past. To put it another way, identity, as Bauman points out, should be treated as a verb not a noun, 'albeit a strange one to be sure: it appears only in the future tense' (1996:19). Identity, he says, is 'a name given to the escape from [that] uncertainty'.

National identities become more problematic as conventional state-identities are corroded by forces of globalisation which shift the classical sociological focus away from the assumption that 'societies' are well-bounded social, economic and cultural systems. What replaces conventional state-identities is not 'cultural homogenisation' in which everyone shares in the same global post-modern identity because they consume the same material and cultural products. Rather, as Stuart Hall observes, 'We are confronted by a range of different identities, each appealing to us, or rather to different parts of ourselves, from which it seems possible to choose'(1992:303).

Following Said (1995), we can see that who 'we' are and who 'they' are become inextricably linked. The 'West' is defined in terms of the 'Orient', as well as vice versa. Hall provides the link between 'ethnic' and 'national' identities with which we began. In an English context, for example, the other actually defines who 'we' are: 'The English are racist not because they hate the blacks, but because they don't know who they are without the blacks' (1996:345). [Again, try substituting Scots for English, and English for blacks. You get: The Scots are racist not because they hate the English, but because they don't know who they are without the English'.]

In other words, they have to know who they are not in order to know who they are. 'The other is not outside but also inside the self, the identity. So identity is a process; identity is split. Identity is not a fixed point but an ambivalent point. Identity is also the relationship of the other to oneself' (Hall 1996.). Nor is this process unique to ethnic/national identity. 'Constructing difference' with regard to gender, class, and so on involves a relational opposition (but not necessarily antagonism) to the other. Hence, constructing an essential, and exclusive, sense of cultural self cannot avoid embedding the 'other', whether one is talking about black/white, Scottish/English, and so on. The 'difference' involves the 'same'.

Well, you might say, all this is operating above the level of individual consciousness, is it not? In the last few years there has been a growing interest in 'personal' nationalism, whose starting point is Renan's dictum of the 'daily plebiscite', the everyday affirmation of national identity (Rennan 1882). Michael Billig, for example, has drawn our attention to what he terms the 'banality' of nationalism so that 'the flags melt into the background as 'our' particular world is experienced as *the* world' (1995:50). The most obvious expression of this is the daily pledge to the flag which takes place in American schools. He comments:

> The ceremony is a ritual display of national unity. Children, in knowing that this is the way in which the school day starts, will take it for granted that other pupils, the length and breadth of the homeland, are also beginning their day similarly; and that their parents and grandparents, if schooled in the United States, did likewise; they might even suppose that all over the world the school day starts thus. (Billig 1995:50).

Billig's account is a useful antidote to the view that nationalism is a top-down phenomenon practised on a gullible public for political reasons. The everyday affirmation of national identity is an active process, reinforced by the banal symbolism of national identity, most obviously the national flag. Only where that flag is seen as problematic, or where there is an alternative national emblem – as in Northern Ireland where the British and Irish flags are key icons implying competing national identities – does it fail to work its magic. Often, we cannot read off the meaning simply from the fact that different flags fly. For example, to Scottish Nationalists, flying the Saltire (St Andrews Cross) may signify a counter-nationalism to that of the British state, whereas to Unionists, it implies that being Scottish and being British are complementary not competing identities.

With regard to nationality, or 'nation-ness', these are the day-to-day interactions and practices which produce inherent and usually unarticulated feelings of belonging, of being 'at home' (Verdery 1993). In other words, the 'nation' is an aspect of the political and symbolic order as well as a world of social interaction and feeling. In Anthony Cohen's phrase, the individual is represented as the nation writ small, and the nation as the individual writ large. 'Individuals "own" the nation; the nation conducts itself as a collective individual' (1994:157). And again,

> It is to say 'I am Scottish', when Scottishness means everything that I am: I substantiate the otherwise vacuous national label in terms of my own experience, my reading of history, my perception of the landscape, and my reading of Scotland's literature and music, so that when I 'see' the nation, I am looking at myself. (Cohen 1996:805)

This is the personalisation of nation-ness, which makes it appear natural, inevitable and taken-for-granted, except in the case of the Stone of Scone, its 'glamour' does not work automatically. Neither is it reducible to a single dimension. We mentioned earlier that in Scotland a 'sense of tribe' (defining Scottishness in terms of blood, genealogy) is perhaps weaker than a 'sense of place' (in terms of residence, territory). Scotland's best-selling tabloid newspaper the *Daily Record* has run a campaign using car stickers proclaiming 'I am a real Scot from [place]' which speaks to this. 'Real-ness' is defined by residence in any town or city in the country. As the historian Christopher Smout has pointed out, it is enough to come from the town of Bathgate, for example, rather than to have a grandmother who came from Bathgate (Smout 1994). By implication, best of all to have a granny who came from Bathgate, and to come from Bathgate yourself.

Politics and Identity

In the final part, I want to explore the relationship between politics and identity through the medium of the Scottish and British Election Surveys for 1997, coupled with the Scottish Referendum study six months later. We have here complex data sets which allow us considerable scope to examine this relationship. For some years I have been interested in the ways Scottishness comes to be defined and mobilised through political behaviour and values. There has long been a strong strand of opinion (hark back to Hobsbawm's comment about how Scottish nationalism is simply an expression of anti-Toryism in a different political guise) which views Scottish differences as being epiphenomenal (a good Marxist expression which Hobsbawm would recognise). One version of this is to say that Scots voted anti-Tory because Scotland has a higher proportion of social groups (eg more working class people and council tenants) who are anti-Tory. If we control for these 'social structural' differences, the Scottish/English differences would disappear. I have tested this out on a few occasions (McCrone 1992, Bechhofer and McCrone 1993) and found it as an account to be wanting.

The 1997 election studies have allowed Alice Brown, Lindsay Paterson, Paula Surridge and myself to explore this in a more systematic way (see also Brown et al, 1996). The results are detailed in our book *The Scottish Electorate*,

1999. I want to give you the overall picture because I think the results are quite dramatic and conclusive.

In the 1997 Scottish Election Study (carried out in the months after May, but before the actual referendum in September) we asked respondents about their likely vote in the referendum. People supported the setting up of a Scottish Parliament because they had clear expectations of what such a body would do in areas of policy such as health, welfare, education, employment and so on. In other words, the referendum outcome was not a reflection of people's social location (their social class, gender, age, religion etc). Nor, surprisingly, was it a simple expression of national identity as such. In other words, people did not vote yes/yes as an expression of their Scottishness. Those who thought of themselves as British, and even English (though the numbers are small) also tended to vote yes/yes. I should qualify what I said about not expressing national identity as such. In fact, it seems that people were expressing their Scottishness by opting for policy reasons relating to economic and social welfare. In other words, 'being Scottish' meant being in favour of public spending on services, being in favour of greater redistribution of wealth, even nationalisation.

Well, one might reply, is not it the case that the British population generally has been broadly and stubbornly in favour of social democratic policies throughout the last twenty years, in spite of Conservative rule? Indeed, and it is important to say that Scotland and England do not differ all that much in policy terms, at least not enough simply to explain what are very sizeable differences in voting patterns. Nevertheless, there are striking differences especially with regard to education (on selection in schools, and to private schooling in particular). There is not much evidence that these differences between Scotland and England as regards policy are the result of social structural factors, but it is plain that nationality does make a significant difference in these respects.

From our work on the election survey we can say that, compared with others in this island, Scots are more 'socialist' (on a socialist-laissez-faire scale); more 'liberal' (on a liberal-authoritarian scale); and less 'British' (on a 'proud to be British' scale). The evidence seems to be that while Scottish 'liberalism' can be explained by and large in terms of social structural differences, only a small part of Scottish 'socialism' can be, and none of the negative attachment to 'British nationalism' can be. To express this another way, even

29

after we control for social structure, people in Scotland are still more left-wing/ socialist than those in the rest of Britain. Nor is this an artefact of comparison. Scotland is more 'socialist' and less 'British nationalist' than any other region/nation of Great Britain. In other words, feeling Scottish is significantly linked to left-wing values.

One of the main reasons for this, it seems, is that the dominant political discourse, notably the domination of Scottish politics in the last decade or so by Labour and the SNP, has both helped to shape political values and opinion, while also being a reflection of these values. We know, for example, from both 1992 and 1997 data that there is little by way of political values and attitudes that distinguishes the typical Labour and SNP voter. That is why both parties are locked into a pretty vicious political battle: they are both competing for the same broad and sizeable swathe of Scottish public opinion, and in turn this helps to shape the political discourse of Scotland at the present time.

Further proof of this interpretation is that the Conservative party in Scotland did so badly – even among its 'natural' voters. One striking statistic is that just as many or few of Scotland's middle classes voted Tory in 1997 as England's semi- and unskilled working classes. In other words, the Scottish Tory debacle of 1997 resulted from the fact that they went through the floor of their 1992 result and into the proverbial cellar. They were not simply getting to the floor first in 1992. As regards the mainstream of Scottish public opinion (which is, as we have seen, socialist, liberal and non-British national), the Conservative party are so out of line on these policy issues that they are deemed to be an 'English' party. In other words, national identity and policy preferences interact with each other to produce a 'left-wing Scottish' agenda which doubly disadvantages the Tories in Scotland. None of this, of course, is set in stone, but it does mean that shedding their 'English' image will require the Conservatives to reposition themselves back into the mainstream policy agenda in Scotland. Whether the Tories like it or not, the Scottish electorate believes that being Scottish is being left-of-centre and liberal. Being left-of-centre and liberal in England (or Wales), of course, does not mean being Scottish, but north of the border that link between nationality and the policy agenda is very clear. In other words, if you define yourself as Scottish, you tend to have certain values and policy attitudes; and if you have certain values and policy attitudes, then you are more likely to define yourself as Scottish.

There is nothing fixed and eternal about this. Political agendas have long shaped and in turn been shaped by national – and other social – identities. For example, the long hegemony of the Tories in Scotland in the first half of this century was the result of their appeal to a Unionist-Imperial-Protestant version of Scotland, which in turn they helped to shape, and in turn benefit from electorally. This vision of Scotland was both the cause and the effect of Tory hegemony. Similarly, over the last two decades or so, a socialist-nationalist-secular vision of Scotland has predominated, which both Labour and the SNP (and to an extent even the Liberal-Democrats in their own way) have been both the producers and the beneficiaries. (Note in passing that Catholics in Scotland are marginally more likely than Protestants to describe themselves as Scottish not British. There is no barrier to Catholics feeling Scottish these days.)

National identity, of course, is simply one identity among many. We know, for example, from both 1992 and 1997 that people in Scotland are more likely than their English counterparts to adopt a working class identity. Twice as many people (48% to 24% in 1997) give preference to their national identity over their class identity, when asked whether they identify more with a same-nation, different class person or with a same-class, different nation person. We also have the intriguing finding that the middle class in Scotland are much more likely than people in England to describe themselves as 'working class'. Taking father's and own objective class into account, where own class is working class, there is little difference between Scotland and England in the propensity to self-assign to working class. However, where own class is middle class, there is a distinct Scottish effect (of the order of 14 percentage points difference between the two countries) to self-assign as working class regardless of whether one's father was working class or middle class. This suggests that in Scotland father's class is a strong predictor of self-assigned class, whereas in England own class is stronger.

Where does this leave my argument? I want to convey the message that we should not treat national identity as some kind of a priori essentialised given, a badge which we treat independently of how it operates. We know from our own personal experiences that we will mix and match who we are and who we want to be, and present according to the circumstances we find ourselves in. We do not carry the weight of nationality on our backs like some kind of historic burden. That has been the thrust of much writing on national identity in recent years. It is my contention that we need to approach it in a new way, to attribute to people much greater capacity to shape and form these things. Clearly, this is a complex process for sociologists to understand, and as I have tried to show in this paper, there is an obvious interaction between our beliefs, values and attitudes about politics and society on the one hand, and how we identify ourselves especially in national terms on the other. They shape each other; the process is dynamic.

It also follows that people can be much more innovative, even promiscuous, about identities. To take one example, you will have noticed in Table 1 that 23% of respondents in the Scottish Election Survey said they were 'Scottish not British'. We asked the same question (to different people) in the Scottish Referendum Survey some six months later, and it had risen to 33%. Had 50% of Scots suddenly changed their nationality? Of course, not. The Referendum event was seen by them to be a time for forefronting Scottishness, just as the British political agenda at UK general elections has the propensity to put the focus on British issues too.

Does having a Scottish Parliament matter? Our analysis indicates very clearly that what people want from a parliament relates to policy preferences. It is not simply a vehicle for expressing Scottishness per se. Nevertheless, the parliament is likely reinforce national identity precisely because it pursues a policy agenda in which it is likely to find the division of powers unduly restrictive. If the parliament fails to make an impact on matters such as running the economy or managing social security which are reserved for Westminster, then it is in a position to claim that it requires further powers at the behest of the Scottish electorate. In other words, standing up for Scotland's interests may well require seeking more powers for a Scottish Parliament, and if this evolves incrementally towards independence then our evidence is that a clear majority of people in Scotland will not object. Matters of policy, identity and constitutional politics are entering a new and uncharted era.

Acknowledgements

I am indebted to my colleagues Alice Brown, Lindsay Paterson and Paula Surridge with whom I worked on the Scottish Election Study, and the Scottish Referendum Study, and to ESRC who funded both studies. I am also indebted to Frank Bechhofer with whom I have worked on a number of research projects on identity. We are grateful to ESRC and to The Leverhulme Trust for their financial support with this research.

References

Alter P 1991 Nationalism. London, Edward Arnold

Anderson B 1996 Imagined Communities:reflections on the origin and spread of nationalism. (Revised edition). London, Verso

Barnett A 1997 This Time: our constitutional revolution. London, Vintage

Barth F 1981 Ethnic Groups and Boundaries. In: Process and form in social life: Selected essays of Fredrik Barth: vol. 1. London, Routledge and Kegan Paul

Bauman Z 1996 From Pilgrim to Tourist: - or a short history of identity. In: Hall S, DuGay P (eds) Questions of Cultural Identity. London, Sage

Bechhofer F, McCrone D 1993 The Scotland-England Divide: politics and locality in Britain. In: Political Studies, XLI.

Bhabha H (ed) 1990 Nation and Narration. London, Routledge

Billig M 1995 Banal Nationalism. London, Sage

Breuilly J 1993 Nationalism and the State. (Revised edition). Manchester University Press

Brown A, McCrone D, Paterson L 1996 Politics and Society in Scotland. London, Macmillan

Brubaker R 1992 Citizenship and Nationhood in France and Germany. Harvard University Press

Bruce S 1993 A Failure of the Imagination: ethnicity and nationalism in Scotland's history. In: Scotia, XVII.

Cohen AP 1993 Culture as Identity. In: New Literary History, 24(1)

Cohen AP 1994 Self Consciousness: an Alternative Anthropology of Identity. London, Routledge

Cohen AP 1997 Nationalism and Social Identity: who owns the interests of Scotland?. In: Scottish Affairs, 18

Connor W 1994 Ethnonationalism: the Quest for Understanding. New Jersey, Princeton University Press

Conversi D 1997 The Catalans, The Basques and Spain. London, Hurst

Dickson M 1994 Should Auld Acquaintance be forgot? a comparison of the Scots and English in Scotland. Scottish Affairs, no.7

Eriksen TH 1993 Ethnicity and Nationalism: anthropological perspectives. London, Pluto Press

Gellner E 1978 Nationalism, or the New Confessions of a Justified Edinburgh Sinner. In: Political Quarterly, 49(1)

Hall S 1990 Cultural Identity and Diaspora. In: Rutherford J (ed) Identity: Community, Culture and Difference. London, Lawrence and Wishart

Hall S 1992 The question of cultural identity. In: Hall S, Held D, McGrew T (eds) Modernity and Its Futures. Cambridge, Polity Press

Hall S 1996 Introduction: who needs identity? In: Hall S, DuGay P (eds) Questions of Cultural Identity. London, Sage

Hobsbawm EJ 1990 Nations and Nationalism since 1780: programme, myth and reality. Cambridge University Press

Hutchinson J, Smith AD (eds) 1996 Ethnicity. Oxford University Press

Kidd C 1993 Subverting Scotland's Past: Scottish Whig Historians and the Creation of an Anglo-Scottish Identity, 1689-c.1830. Cambridge University Press

McCrone D 1992 Understanding Scotland: The Sociology of a Stateless Nation. London, Routledge

Malcolm D 1994 Bosnia: a short history. London, Macmillan

Moreno L 1995 Multiple Ethnoterritorial Concurrence in Spain. In: Nationalism and Ethnic Politics 1(1)

Nairn T 1997 Faces of Nationalism. London, Verso Books

Renan E 1882 'What is a Nation?'. Reprinted in Bhabha H (ed) 1990 Nation and Narration. London, Routledge

Said E 1995 Orientalism: Western conceptions of the Orient. Harmondsworth, Penguin

Smith A 1991 National Identity. Harmondsworth, Penguin

Smout TC 1994 Perspectives on the Scottish Identity. In: Scottish Affairs, 6

Surridge P, Paterson L, Brown A, McCrone D 1998 The Scottish Electorate and the Scottish Parliament. In: Understanding Constitutional Change, special issue of Scottish Affairs

Verdery K 1993 Whither 'Nation' and 'Nationalism'? In: Daedalus, 122(3)

Constructing Identity in Scotland and Quebec:
Political Parties and Civic Values in the Nationalist Discourse*

Ailsa Henderson

The official opening of the Scottish Parliament provides a useful opportunity to reflect on the success and struggles of other regional or sub-national Parliaments, particularly those where nationalist parties seek to form a government. Comparisons between Scotland and Quebec have been plentiful since the 1997 General Election, when it appeared that for the first time in 300 years Scotland would acquire its own Parliament. Given the frequency with which politicians on either side point to the other as proof of success or failure, the extent to which Quebec provides lessons for the establishment of the Scottish political system warrants attention. For nationalists, the electoral strength of the Parti Québécois provides evidence that nationalist parties can govern prudently while at the same time calling for greater autonomy in key areas of jurisdiction. For those less enamoured of separatism, the presence of a nationalist party bent on increasing political autonomy presents a serious danger to the ability of the government to function and thus poses a threat to the economic and social well-being of all within its borders. As Scottish politicians, on either side of the nationalist divide, each use Quebec to prove their case, a deeper examination of the differences and similarities between the two cases seems prudent. (For the purposes of brevity, this paper refers to home rule parties in Scotland as nationalist. The extent to which this is an accurate reflection of policy lies outwith the scope of this work.)

In the development of a national political programme nationalist leaders project and encourage a sense of national identity in order to sustain

---

* A version of this paper 'Political Constructions of National Identity in Scotland and Quebec' was published in *Scottish Affairs*, 29, Autumn 1999 and is reproduced with permission.

the necessity of the project. The political use of pre-existing markers of cultural identity clarifies the components of that identity, allowing it to be harnessed as a potent political force. In order to examine how a nationalism politicises identity this chapter first defines its terms, placing particular emphasis on the difference between cultural and political identity. Nationalist parties and the governments they form compose merely one organised group among many that might exert influence over civic values. The media, the Church, unions, protest or civic groups, may each rely on conceptions of national identity in their interaction with the nationalist project. This chapter, however, limits its analysis to the influence of nationalist parties on politicising national identity.

Comparative coverage of the 1997 and 1995 referenda and subsequent elections in Scotland and Quebec suggest that the two political situations lend themselves to comparison. (Keating 1996) While probably motivated by the timing of political events as much as the similarities between the two programmes, the differences between the two nationalist projects and an analysis of how these different tactics affected their respective political situations provide for a greater understanding of the relationship between civic values and national identity. The nationalist programmes in Scotland and Quebec operate within British parliamentary models, the latter an adapted federal system to suit the particular cultural needs of the 'two founding nations'. The debate surrounding the existence of two, three, or ten founding nations in Canada, while integral to an understanding of the federal system, is beyond the scope of this chapter. (For an analysis of French Canadian evaluations of the benefits of Confederation see Silver 1982). The case study thus chronicles the events and circumstances in two varying approaches to internal challenges to the British parliamentary model: one which has reacted to particularity from the beginning and at several subsequent opportunities; and the other, which has sought to resist change, adapting only when public outcry has prompted action. (For a recent examination of the British State's attempts to deal with nationalist demands from Scotland, see Nairn 1998. For a more complimentary view of the British State's ability to adapt, see Paterson 1994.)

For the purposes of this chapter, three basic assumptions for the point of departure for the use of national identity are made. The first two factors provide a workable definition of national identity from the available literature while the third factor provides the main underlying assumption of this paper, that cultural identity and political identity are different in their construction and in their relative levels of inclusiveness. According to the first assumption, national identity represents the self-defined sense of belonging to an 'imagined' community that occurs through the incorporation of national values. (Anderson 1991, Turner 1987 and 1991, Tajfel 1981 and 1982). In the acquisition of values promoted by organised groups within society citizens acquire a sense of national consciousness. Just as the process of socialisation introduces individuals at an early age to norms of acceptable behaviour, the competing message of national socialisation promotes the civic values that allow individuals to integrate within the nation (Almond and Verba 1963). Although the process of identification may not be a conscious and reflexive one made in the face of appeals to uniquely civic membership, identity, ultimately, is self-defined in the face of nationalist messages from a variety of sources. Nationalist actors and their opponents vie for the attention of individuals by each providing interpretations of the past development and future prospects of the nation. The recent battle of think tank reports debating the future economic stability of an independent Scotland provides a relevant example. Often made on the basis of collective, group characteristics such as language or place of residency, appeals to individuals as voters and potential party members constitute the preferred option of democratic nationalist parties. The historical accuracy of the message matters less than public perception of fact. Or, as Richard Finlay states: the factual invalidation of myths in weighty academic tomes does not and never has invalidated them as complex icons of cultural, social and political belief (Finlay 1987). Whether such messages are a plea for membership, in the case of a reflexive civic movement, or an attempt to mobilise ethnic, latent characteristics, depends on the construction of identity and type of nationalism.

The resulting second tenet asserts that national identity is not a single overarching construction of self but part of a series of multiple and often conflicting identities. Self conception related to gender, employment status, family environment and class compete with national identity in affecting attitudes, values and behaviour (Hall 1992 and 1996). The strength with which national identity is felt, in addition to its relationship with alternate identities, varies in reaction to different stimuli throughout a lifetime. No direct relationship exists between the strength of national allegiance and age, nor does national identity assume a constant and primal role in determining decisions. (Martin 1998, Reid 1996, Brown et al 1999).

The third assertion points to the inherently vague and malleable nature of cultural national identity. National leaders point to the presence of national culture and history but rarely enunciate the specifics of these two pillars. An emphasis on distinctness accompanies the promotion of generally positive national traits such as tolerance or democracy, values which no member could contest. One Quebec Liberal Party policy paper on identity, for example, makes reference to the shared Quebec values of individual freedom, pluralism and a willingness to decrease social inequalities. (QLP 1997). Citizens left to define their own conception of culture and interpretation of history thus may all feel included in the nation. When invoked in the name of a political project, however, national identity distinguishes itself from cultural identity. In the politicisation of cultural national identity, in particular by political parties, the vision of national identity emerges, if not as a checklist of national characteristics, then certainly as a consensus of values. The potency of national identity thus relies less on content than on the treatment it receives from organised groups within civil society. If cultural identity represents the vague, inclusive aspect of national allegiance, politicised national identity is the more exclusive, enunciated force. The potency of cultural identity lies in its ability to appeal to a wide variety of people, whereas the power of political identity hinges on the potential for mobilisation in the name of a political project. In their efforts to advance the nationalist cause political parties in Scotland and Quebec have manipulated cultural identity into a political tool, articulating a framework of civic values and national characteristics that justify greater political autonomy. In so doing, they have created an exclusive, and admittedly powerful identity at the expense of non-nationalists in Quebec and Scotland. In a departure from the oft employed categories of civic and ethnic nationalism, this examination of national identity claims that inclusion and exclusion operate within all national discourses. The extent of this exclusion, whether it is based on inherited characteristics or selected values, or felt by individuals who exclude themselves in the face of publicly inclusive notions of belonging, varies according to the treatment of national identity by nationalist actors.

Measuring National Identity

A s a result of these three characteristics, national identity proves difficult to measure. Most work using national identity as an independent variable exerting influence over partisan preference or voter turnout rely on a variation of Luis Moreno's five-point identity scale. (Moreno 1988) Developed while comparing national identity in Scotland and Catalonia, Moreno's scale requires respondents to describe their sense of allegiance given the following options: Scottish not British, More Scottish than British, Equally Scottish and British, More British than Scottish, British not Scottish. Used in the 1997 British Election Survey and Scottish Election booster survey, the results from similar questions have been used in several papers presented at a fall 1997 conference for the Centre for Research on Elections and Social Trends (CREST). (See *Scottish Affairs* 1998). Such a categorisation lends itself to straightforward quantification and cross-national comparison. Despite the importance of creating data to test relationships between variables, what Moreno's scale gains in applicability it lacks in description. The scale fails to identify the strength with which national feelings are held, what such self-identification actually means to the individual, and leaves hidden the components of identity itself. What, for instance, are the distinguishing characteristics of the Scottish or Québécois national identity? How is the identity of an individual who self-identifies as solely Scottish different from the identity of an individual whose self-definition allows for a minimal sense of Britishness? If used in isolation, Moreno's categories, while valuable in their ability to demonstrate the effect of national identity on political behaviour, fail to provide a sense of context to national identity; what it is about national identity that affects subsequent behaviour. Although Canadian newspapers have been quick to commission opinion polls using the Moreno identity scales, the election surveys in Canada rely on a different instrument to measure the varying levels of identity within the country. Asking respondents to indicate their level of attachment to their province and country on two scales of 1 to 100, while avoiding the binary opposition of the British scale, provides little insight into the motivations of belonging. As previously argued, identity is not a thing and should not be treated as such. That said, in attempts to mobilise identity behind a political project, nationalist parties encourage the creation and acquisition of a definable identity package that provides citizens with the tools to interpret their past, present and future. For those who exclude themselves from national identity a reluctance to align oneself with the associated values and characteristics of the nation matters as much as the notion of belonging itself. Although both scales provide an accurate reflection of belonging, their continued use in isolation inhibits a solid understanding of identity in Scotland and Quebec. This chapter seeks to supplement available quantitative data by examining the content and treatment of politicised national identity in Scotland and Quebec. To this end it examines recent polls measuring national identity before presenting the civic values engendered in the content and treatment of national identity.

Table 1 Sense of belonging in Canada and Quebec (Well 1998). Percentage claiming a moderate to intense sense of belonging

	Quebecers		Other Canadians	
Date	To Canada	To Quebec	To Canada	To Province
1998	54	68	88	70
1997	57	75	90	71
1996	54	74	93	74
1995	58	87	95	81
1994	57	73	88	75

Ekos 1998. Sample size 3000 (Quebec 1004).

A recent poll in the English-language daily in Montreal produced the figures shown in Table 1. The results demonstrate that while Quebecers record similar levels of allegiance to their province as other Canadians in their respective provinces (apart from a high of 87% in the referendum year), their sense of belonging to Canada is less than that of other Canadians by an average of 35%. It is worth noting that Quebecers do not appear to be supporting sovereignty because of a profound belief in the infallibility of the provincial government. Rather than holding unreasonable expectations, Quebecers view their government in the same light as other Canadians view their respective provincial legislatures. Support for autonomy in Quebec appears to stem more from a lack of attachment to the federal entity than a stronger sense of belonging in Quebec. Additional poll results highlight the relationship between attachment to province and attachment to Canada. In a post-referendum examination of attitudes in Canada, pollster Angus Reid also asked whether individuals felt less attached to Canada than they did a few years ago.

Table 2 Sense of attachment in Canada and Quebec (Reid 1996). Percentage agreeing with the statement 'I feel...'

Identity	Country of Residence		
	Canada	Quebec	Rest of Canada
Profoundly attached to Canada	86	62	95
Profoundly attached to province	89	91	88
More attached to province than to Canada	46	66	40
Less committed to Canada than a few years ago	31	53	23

Angus Reid 1996. Sample size 3603 (Quebec 650).

As these results indicate, the declining attachment to Canada among one in two Quebecers accompanies a similar decline among one in five Canadians outside Quebec. Similarly, two in five Canadians outside Quebec feel more attached to their province than to Canada. The poll results demonstrate a clear trend of allegiance away from the larger entity towards the local. This trend is obvious throughout Canada although more pronounced in Quebec.

Scottish poll results, gathered in the recent British Election Study, provide for an equivalent regional comparison as seen in Table 3.

Table 3 Identity in Britain. Percentage agreeing with the statement 'I feel...'

Identity	Country of Residence		
	Scotland	Wales	England
X not British	23	13	8
More X than British	39	29	16
Equally X and British	26	26	46
More British than X	4	10	15
British not X	4	15	9
Other	4	6	6

British Election Study 1997. Sample size: Scotland 882; Wales 182; England 2551.

The results highlight a lack of allegiance to the British identity in Scotland. Only 8% prioritise their British identity while 62% prioritise their Scottishness.

This imbalance compares with 42% in Wales and 24% in England who feel greater allegiance to their region rather than the State. The often assumed role of language in entrenching a distinct sense of language, while beyond the scope of this chapter, warrants further attention given identity distribution in Wales. In their analysis of the 1997 Welsh referendum Richard Wyn Jones and Dafydd Trystan indicate that although all linguistic groups shy away from prioritising their Welsh identity exclusively, the resulting distribution of identity preferences highlights the influence of language in the Welsh debate (Wyn Jones and Trystan 1999). Language, both by virtue of its role as a pillar of identity in Quebec, and the protection it has received from successive Québécois governments since the 1960s has exerted a much stronger influence on identity in Canada. The first part of this paper ends, then, having produced a clear definition of national identity, a summary of the problems of identity measurement, and a brief examination of the patterns of identity in Scotland and Quebec. An analysis of the content and treatment of national identity by nationalist parties in both locations will deepen the understanding of the processes underlying political uses of national identity.

Historical Constructions of National Identity

Civic values promoted through the historical development of the nation in Scotland and Quebec appear remarkably similar. In both case studies, the survival of institutions following the loss of political independence allowed for the maintenance of a civil society that served as the guardian of identity. National identity in both case studies obviously has roots extending beyond the eighteenth century. For the purposes of this chapter, the timing of the two events, and the similarities in their influence on civil society, provide a convenient starting point. (For an analysis of identity prior to 1707 see, for example, Broun et al 1998). Much as the 1707 Treaty of Union allowed for the survival of the distinct Scottish education system, legal system and Presbyterian Church of Scotland, the 1774 Quebec Act preserved the role of the Catholic Church, civil code and French language in Britain's colony. Current nationalist parties rely on these institutions, and use them to foster a sense of collectivism and civic duty, proudly democratic and egalitarian.

These parties also refer to values and descriptors of the nation's population that extend beyond these basic founding values. The pre-eminence of culture and language in political constructions of Quebec identity, in addition to recurrent references to the Québécois people, link the individual to the process of national building. The result is a defined collective in search of self determination fuelled by feelings of its distinctiveness. Different approaches in Scotland, in particular attention to the state of democracy in the current system, suggest that the emphasis is one of an unjust situation that must be rectified rather than a people suffering an injustice. The final section of this chapter examines how these parties have aligned certain values and institutions with a politicised national identity. In so doing, it concentrates on two issues, the role of identity versus interest in the nationalist programme, and the extent to which individuals feel included or excluded by notions of national identity.

Modern national identity in Quebec finds its foundations in the civic institutions that existed following the British Conquest of Quebec in 1760 and in the more recent political developments of the last four decades. The Church, civil law and the French language, as protected in the 1774 Quebec Act were to become the foundation of Québécois identity until a change in emphasis during the period of modernisation in the 1960s. Long considered as the genesis of the modern nation, the break with France once received much attention from academics who debated the negative psychological and social development of the province (Brunet 1969). Only ten years ago political scientist Léon Dion noted 'We Quebecers are uncertain of our identity and haunted by the fear of a tragic destiny' (Dion 1988). While that interpretation has changed in favour of a more conventional vision of society and democracy in Quebec, awareness of a minority position continues. In the wake of the failed sovereignty referendum in 1995, former Premier Jacques Parizeau closed his now famous speech by saying 'Never will it be so important to have a Parti Québécois government to protect us till the next round'. The speech is notable largely because Parizeau announced the sovereignty option had been defeated by 'money and the ehtnic vote', a move which did little to endear the sovereignist leader to many of the cultural communities within Quebec (Parizeau 1995). In post-Conquest Quebec, a decapitated French society saw the Church as the logical height of civil society, affording it a sense of authority and legitimacy that might not otherwise have existed. The Church thus defended the interests of Quebecers in the face of a foreign State power and defined their sense of identity. Well into the twentieth century, to be Canadien was to be Catholic much more than it was to be French.

Just as national identity in Quebec depends on an examination of national pillars across time, Scottish national identity has its roots in the civic institutions that survived following the Acts of Union in 1707. The legacy of Scottish history preceding the Union provided Scotland with a sense of nationhood predating significant European presence in North America. National heroes, military defeats and clan life are credited with the development of an identity with a strong sense of social cohesion and an awareness of 'other'. The presence of Calvinist doctrine, a strong education system and collectivist civil code is credited with creating an identity infused with a firm sense of equal opportunity for all, success for the hard working, and social responsibility for the less well off. Just as it is credited with the promotion of fatalism and acceptance, the Church of Scotland made great strides in advancing the democratic intellect of Scottish identity. Created by John Knox, the General Assembly of the established Church offered opportunities for church members to debate and vote on issues related to doctrine, practice, and national life. That process has continued today in the activities of the Church and Nation committee (Forrester 1993).

That the two nations enjoyed similar institutional protection following their respective losses of sovereignty, should not obscure the influence of factors inherent in that loss which served to produce two particularly distinct civil societies. Faced with similar minority positions Scotland and Quebec each placed particular emphasis on collective identity and action. The circumstances of the Conquest and Acts of Union, however, dictated the importance of these civic values. The military defeat imposed on New France could not have had the same effect as a voluntary political partnership even in the face of public opposition to the arrangement. The immediate political integration of Scots within the British parliamentary system, despite limited electoral franchise, provided the nation with a focus of assimilated political activity unmatched in Quebec. Although far from immediate, political opportunities for Francophones in Quebec existed within a relatively distinct sphere of activity. (Even after the union of the two Canadian provinces in 1841 residents of current-day Ontario and Quebec sent their own representatives to the united legislature.) While political participation was eventually an option in both Scotland and Quebec, the context and outlet of that activity was notably different.

Modern Constructions of National Identity

The rise of modern, organised nationalist movements does not mark the beginning of dissatisfaction with the constitutional solutions reached following the British Conquest and Acts of Union. Resistance to Canadian Confederation and the British State has a long and rich history beyond the scope of this chapter (McNaught 1988, Lynch 1992). Democratic parties highlighting national particularity and the goal of greater political autonomy, by virtue of their efforts to gain members and voters, are afforded greater attention by individuals and the media, thus bringing what might otherwise represent a narrow cultural movement into the mainstream political discourse. The following section highlights two particular aspects of identity, the definition of national membership and the salience of identity to the nationalist cause, to further analyse the division between cultural and political national identity.

The growing secularisation of Quebec society throughout the 1950s prompted a series of policies from the newly-elected Liberal government in 1960. The proceeding Quiet Revolution witnessed the end of the Catholic Church as a marker of Quebec identity in favour of the French language. With the slogan 'Maitres Chez Nous' (Masters In Our Own House) the Liberals, under Jean Lesage, sought to engage the means of the State for the protection of a distinct Quebec identity. Or, to paraphrase Gerard Pelletier, the absolutism of the Church was replaced with an absolute quest for State sovereignty (Pelletier 1988). The creation of the Office de la Langue Française during the Liberals' first term was heralded as the 'tangible and omnipresent expression of the conscience of French Canada' (Handler 1988). A series of language bills followed, all designed to ensure the use of French in Quebec public life. Documents such as the 1977 Language Charter and the 1978 White Paper on Culture Development, which recognised the French language as the 'central component of a solitary national identity around which

Quebecers of all ethnic origins could be expected to rally' have drawn derision from Anglo–Quebecers and other Canadians. (Handler 1988, Richler 1992, Scowen 1991) In short, the 1960s heralded the use of language as a key to membership in the national community in Quebec. While this construction of identity allows for non-Francophones to attain membership should they learn French, the identity is inherently exclusive. The values present in the historical construction of Quebec national identity thus depend on the importance of the Church, State, French language and lastly the civil code. Much as the previous factors have contributed to a sense of collectivism in society, the civil code above all, with its emphasis on society as a cohesive unit, and the resulting Charter of Human Rights and Freedoms, which governs relations among citizens in addition to those between citizens and the State, contributes to a sense of duty and responsibility within Quebec.

The economic prosperity of the British Empire and the administrative control gained through the creation of the Scottish Office in 1886 led to favourable interpretations of the Union (Paterson 1994). Well into the 1950s the British unitary State was seen as the best political option by many Scots. In 1951 the Unionist Conservative party still enjoyed 50% of the popular vote in Scotland. According to the SNP's description of its own origins: 'Generally speaking, the 1950s were not a particularly productive period for the National Party. A major reason for this is that Scotland was a much more 'British Country' than it is now, with a relatively low level of teaching and awareness of Scottish culture and history' (SNP 1995a). Social transformations of the 1960s, including the increased freedom of the Scottish media, coincided with a declining British presence in Scotland (Lynch 1992, Brown et al 1996). The discovery of oil and declining industry in the 1970s provided the Scottish National Party with an opportunity to frame the debate in national terms. The higher dependence on the public sector and nationalised industry in Scotland, rarely a fertile ground for Conservative support, in addition to the Labour government's insistence on the 40% rule in the 1979 devolution referendum allowed the SNP to portray the Conservatives as an anti-Scottish party both in its position on the political spectrum and policy regarding Scottish devolution (Mitchell 1990). Thus, just as Quebec identity changed focus from Church-led to language-led, (French Canadian to Québécois), Scottish identity began to assert itself as separate from British identity, from British (Scottish) to Scottish.

Political Constructions of National Identity

The different constitutional structures in Scotland and Quebec have dictated that nationalist political parties assert themselves and pursue their goals differently. The early recognition of administrative autonomy in Scotland has provided a generally accepted recognition of national status. Despite the presence of a provincial government and role as the de facto representative of French Canada recognition of Quebec's nationhood is much less accepted in the rest of Canada. The consensus that exists among Quebec political parties, and among British parties operating in Scotland, bypasses a debate about particularity that drives much of the debate between Quebec and the rest of Canada. This lack of recognition has affected the way in which Quebec nationalists have constructed the boundaries and membership of the nation. That there is still much convincing to be done by Quebec suggests that full acknowledgement of Quebec's distinct society could move the debate away from social characteristics and closer to the value driven debate in Scotland.

The Preamble to the 1995 Bill respecting the sovereignty of Quebec lists several recent key events:

We were hoodwinked in 1982 when the governments of Canada and the English-speaking provinces made changes to the Constitution, in depth and to our detriment, in defiance of the categorical opposition of our National Assembly.

Twice since then attempts were made to right that wrong. The failure of the Meech Lake Accord in 1990 confirmed a refusal to recognise even our distinct character. And in 1992 the rejection of the Charlottetown Accord by both Canadians and Quebecers confirmed the conclusion that no redress was possible...

Because starting with the Quiet Revolution we reached a decision never again to restrict ourselves to mere survival but from this time on to build upon our difference;

Because we have the deep-seated conviction that continuing within Canada would be tantamount to condemning ourselves to languish and to debasing our very identity;

Because the respect we owe ourselves must guide our deeds;

We the people of Quebec, declare it is our will to be in full possession of all the powers of a State... (Quebec 1995)

The preceding statement has sparked a controversy among the cultural communities in Quebec, largely due to the use of 'We' in the preamble. This statement, which not only outlines the defeats of a people but defines several characteristics of the population, excludes those without a 'deep-seated conviction' in separation, those whose primary identity is to Canada, and those who feel there is little difference between Quebecers and other Canadians. Lastly, the preamble clearly juxtaposes the use of 'Quebecer' with 'Canadian', suggesting that an individual should posses one primary identity or the other, but not both. The preamble contrasts starkly with the lack of any similar statement of intent in the Scotland Act. The closest any post-referendum document comes to such a pronouncement is found in the final report of the Consultative Steering Group in which Scottish Office Minister and CSG Chair Henry McLeish states '... the establishment of the Scottish Parliament offers the opportunity to put in place a new sort of democracy in Scotland, closer to the Scottish people and more in tune with Scottish needs' (CSG 1998.) With the sole mention of Scottish needs, traditionally dictated as much by geography as by cultural difference, the statement emphasises the absence of identity from the current political debate in Scotland.

Of the three main political parties in Quebec, the Quebec Liberal Party, the Parti Québécois and the Bloc Québécois, all make two important connections regarding the traditional pillars of Québécois national identity: first, that language is the cornerstone of culture; and second, that culture is the cornerstone of identity. Or, according to the 1994 PQ platform 'culture is the essence of a people, the very expression of a feeling and belonging to a collectivity ... French is the primary vehicle of Quebec cultural identity' (PQ 1994). Similar statements emanate from the PQ government and Liberal Party. According to the Ministry of Culture and Communications, French is not just a language and instrument of communication, it is 'un milieu de vie, une façon d'être, de penser, d'écrire et de créer pour tous les Québécois'(Ministère Culture 1998) The Liberal Party similarly commits itself to the 'protection et le developpement du fait français et des institutions qui marquent l'identité québécoise' (QLP 1997). All parties define membership according to language and the less articulated notion of culture. References to social cohesion also feature in political constructions of identity in Quebec. Seen as a means of integration for new arrivals to Quebec and an opportunity to enable traditional

Quebecers to understand their own culture, the education system receives particular attention from nationalist parties. In a document entitled 'Reaffirming the Mission of our Schools' the task force on Quebec's curriculum declares the education system 'must teach common values ... must help young people growing up in a culture to assimilate their identity, assimilate the cultural tradition of society ... that French and national community are the cornerstones of identity' (Task Force 1997). Or, as the Parti Québécois states: 'The education system is the cradle of society, a unique place for the transmission and development of culture. Values, beliefs, attitudes and cultural references, as well as a sense of belonging to Quebec society, are shaped within it' (PQ 1994). Attention to the collective surfaces also in such diverse areas as law and sport. Considered a document based on individual rights, the Canadian Charter of Rights and Freedoms is portrayed as alien to the collectivist spirit of Quebec society (Legault 1992). Legault claims part of the misunderstanding between Anglophones and Francophones in Quebec lies in the inability of Anglophones to understand that individual rights are not held in the same regard by Francophones. Similarly, information provided by the current PQ government on Quebec society maintains recreational activities not only combat social isolation, but present opportunities for expressing cultural identity (Quebec 1998). Attempts to instil a sense of civic duty stems from this collectivist vision of society. According to the Ministry of Citizen Relations and Immigration: 'Le ministère veut encourager une plus grande participation des citoyens à la vie collective et favoriser le développement de l'appartenance à la société québécoise' (Ministère Relations 1998). In support of this principle the Ministry issues awards for participation in collective life.

On most constructions of national identity both provincial parties agree. The Parti Québécois and Quebec Liberal Party support the need to defend the distinct character of Quebec and the necessity of national identity in the struggle for greater political autonomy. For its part, the federal Bloc Québécois has attempted to portray Quebecers and the sovereignty movement as a modern political force; 'the sovereignty movement is inclusive, forward-looking, respectful of others, tolerant and peaceful' (BQ 1998). And, later in the same document:

> Quebecers do not claim to be better than Canadians. They simply believe that they are different, as they do not share the same language, the same culture, nor the

same social and economic visions ... The Quebec people show a deeply rooted commitment to and respect for liberty and equality. They are tolerant, peace-loving and concerned for the well-being of their fellow man. A resolutely outward-looking people ... an open-minded people.

As in the preamble to the 1995 sovereignty bill the preceding statement provides two telling definitions of who is a Quebecer, and who is a Canadian, and why the two are mutually exclusive. Because the languages spoken by Quebecers and other Canadians are set in opposition, so too are the identities set out for English and French speakers. The suspicion that they have been con-sidered outsiders within their own province has long bothered non-French speakers in Quebec (Johnson 1991). The document thus excludes these individuals while professing to be inclusive. The attempt reinforces the efforts of all three parties in Quebec to define membership in the national collective along linguistic lines while reinforcing the inclusive, democratic and socially responsible aspects of that community. The results of these policy positions is a content marked by a strong sense of history fuelled by recent political events and a sense of difference marked by a distinct language, culture and resulting civic values. The values promoted throughout the nationalist discourse provide models of social behaviour for those within Quebec's borders. If the construction of national identity in Quebec is exclusive, it is in the emphasis on the characteristics of the majority population. This exclusion is emphasised through the nationalist agenda which seeks to right the democratic wrongs suffered by this majority population. That all these traits form part of a broad consensus for the three main political parties strengthens the accepted wisdom of the political debate, and the construction of national identity within the province.

Values, rather than social characteristics, form the litmus test of identity in Scotland. The prevalence of egalitarianism and the perception of a democratic intellect, in combination with recent political events, have compounded to foster a sense of identity marked by a coexistent low self-belief and political indignation (Beveridge and Turnbull 1989.) As shown earlier, treatment of national identity by political parties, organised groups and the media has sought to counteract this claim while promoting the belief that the current lack of democratic control for Scotland is an affront to national identity. As much as the political debate in Quebec has concentrated on the role of culture and language, and a resulting identity, nationalist actors in Scotland have reinforced the desire for Scotland's needs and interests to be protected. The difference is one of identity versus interest. While the two are not necessarily mutually exclusive, nor mutually antagonistic, the difference in emphasis of the two programmes explains why nationalists in Scotland are not labelled as exclusive to the same extent as nationalists in Quebec. The difference between the two programmes is not one of civic nationalism versus ethnic nationalism, but rather points to differences in emphasis and tactics within the general rubric of civic nationalism.

Another significant distinction from Quebec is the lack of consensus among political parties in Scotland. Despite the spirit of cooperation among the three parties which supported devolution during the 1997 referendum campaign, partisan differences parallel contrasting interpretations of the need for change. All four major parties point to different aspects of the current situation that require attention, and all four offer different methods to address these problems. Unlike in Quebec, where both the Liberal Party and the Parti Québécois agree that greater autonomy and respect for difference would represent positive change, the Scottish political spectrum offers an assortment of constitutional options including unionism, federalism, devolution and independence. Each constitutional option is associated with a point on the left-right continuum, forcing Scots to make two commitments, one political, the other constitutional, at once. In his 1996 speech to his national conference, Scottish National Party leader Alex Salmond set out his party's place in Scottish politics and decried the arrogance of Labour, noting its 'contempt for the traditional values and lack of respect for the common weel' (Salmond 1996). One year earlier he attacked Prime Minister John Major's Conservatives claiming 'the cohesive nature of the Scottish state system presents a political obstacle in the way of the Conservative Party and its anti-Scottish elitist dogma' (Salmond 1995a). In each case, the effort was to align the SNP closer to the traditional values and interests of Scots than its two opponents. These statements, in addition to various references to the London levy, higher business rates and council tax in Scotland, Trident, the Stone of Destiny and the poll tax demonstrate the efforts of the SNP to align the strong tradition of democracy and egalitarianism with the left of the political spectrum, effectively excluding the Conservatives from any claim to Scottish national identity. Labour, in its efforts to portray itself 'as the real national party of Scotland', announced that the 'Tories were confirmed as representing and acting for a smaller and smaller elite, having failed Britain and turned against Scotland' (Labour 1997). In addition to these efforts, SNP policy regarding the House of Lords and references to the 'archaic, anti-democratic and sometimes farcical Westminster parliamentary system' reinforce the perception that a unitary state does not meet the democratic needs of Scotland's interests, breeds a sense of dependence and impotence, and weakens confidence and distorts self-image. For example, 'the notion of a revising chamber with a membership present by accident of birth or by political patronage is deeply repugnant to the Scottish sense of democracy' (SNP 1995). Current SNP MSP George Reid's comment that 'Independence by itself is far less important than what Independence is actually for' implies that the promotion of confidence and self-worth are important components of the nationalistic drive for greater political autonomy (Reid 1995).

The place of education in Scottish national identity, while stronger than that in Quebec, occupies a slightly different role. In Quebec, education serves as a tool of identity, reinforcing a sense of difference. Scottish education, however, provides a pillar of identity itself. Valued in its creation of a literate society and tool as a social leveller, the education system is credited with offering more than a sense of Scottish particularity. In its recent update to the Higher Examination Core requirements for History and English, the Scottish Qualifications Authority notes that there is no obligation to use Scottish texts in the syllabus for English, and only four of the twenty-two history modules cover Scottish history. In reference to this lack of Scottish material, Alex Salmond warned that an education system fails a nation 'if it does not instil within our young people a sense of their history, for it is from that that will often spring the determination to create a better tomorrow'. The quotation continues 'We should be ashamed that it has taken Hollywood to give so many Scots back our history, and put the name and fame of Wallace on the lips of every schoolchild in our country' (Salmond 1995a).

References to civic values, 'the passion for improvement, education, family and tradition ... equality of access and opportunity for all', pervade the SNP's general policy papers (Salmond 1995b). The promotion of these values coexists with promises from all the major parties to look after the interests of

Scotland at Westminster. According to the SNP, only the nationalists possess the additional factor of 'being the only party which, always, can put Scottish interests first' suggesting that the three others, in efforts to maintain British-wide appeal, will be less vigilant in their defence of Scottish concerns (Reid 1995). This claim, in addition to the traditional pillars of identity, has produced a sense of Scottish identity driven less by culture than the perception of political injustice. The Westminster Parliament, its unitary style of government, and the former Conservative government are depicted as anti-Scottish in their economic and political viewpoints. (SNP 1996) It is unlikely that Conservative voters in Scotland feel less Scottish than their Labour counterparts, despite how they respond to the binary choices offered in opinion polls. Data from recent Election surveys suggest that Conservatives are more likely to feel equally Scottish and British and less likely to prioritise their Scottishness than supporters of other parties (Brown et al 1996). Just as Anglophones in Quebec may feel a greater allegiance to their province than to Canada, however, the exclusive message of nationalist actors affects the values accepted as markers of national identity.

Conclusions

Given the similarity of civic values promoted by nationalists in Scotland and Quebec, the differing process through which each movement has sought to politicise national identity produces the largest divergence between the two case studies. In linking culture, language and identity, political parties in Quebec have defined the boundaries of their community as well as the sphere of acceptable political activity. By linking self-perception to politics, political participation reinforces membership in the national community. In Scotland, the political spectrum has polarised according to the national issues. Conservatives arguing for the union are seen by nationalists as denying their Scottish identity.

The treatment of national identity in Scotland and Quebec differs according to two dimensions, the importance of identity versus interest in the nationalist programme, and the perceptions of inclusion and exclusion within the nation. As mentioned earlier, this chapter does not seek to assign nationalism in Scotland and Quebec to categories of civic or ethnic movements. Both nationalist programmes operate in societies with a strong respect for fundamental human rights. To label either movement as exclusive is not to elicit comparisons with oppressive regimes or programmes where non-members fear for their safety or other equally undesirable implications of exclusion. Rather, this paper argues that in the presence of nationalism or nationalist programmes, identity is constructed in such a way as to provide identifiable characteristics to mark the boundaries of the nation. The implications of this definition of identity are intended to allow individuals to make conclusions about their own sense of belonging within the nation. Overt exclusion in both cases, does not exist. The basis upon which individuals may choose to evaluate their claims to belonging present varying opportunities for inclusion. In Quebec, the primordial importance of the French language as an identifiable pillar of national identity presents serious problems for unilingual Anglophones who were born, raised and continue to live within the provincial boundaries. The perception that there are hierarchies of belonging, however, stems from the way the nation has been defined, rather than abstract notions of civic or ethnic nationalism. With the establishment of two key groups within its organisation, New Scots for Independence, and Asian Scots for Independence, the SNP has sought to defend itself from charges that it possesses an exclusive view of Scottish national belonging. Despite the claims from other political parties that the SNP is anti-English, the lack of Scottish identity is rarely linked to personal characteristics. Instead, it is in its definition of Conservative party members, unionists, and those who would place themselves on the right of the political spectrum as anti-Scottish that the SNP contributes to its definition of Scottish identity. If individuals are wont to feel themselves as outside the nation in Scotland, it is more likely because of the political values that they hold rather than on account of their language or ancestry.

If both nationalist programmes define their visions of the nation in such a way that individuals may choose to exclude themselves, why has Quebec received much greater attention on this front? The answer, alluded to earlier, stems from the role of identity versus interest in the nationalist agenda. Exclusion from a separatist-defined vision of identity matters in Quebec, because identity is the cornerstone of constitutional change. Calls for greater autonomy in Scotland, however, stem from the alleged inadequacies of the current power-sharing arrangement between Scotland and the Westminster Parliament. Whether this emphasis on interest will give way to greater identity-centred debate upon the official opening of the Holyrood Parliament remains to be seen.

References

Almond G, Verba S 1963 The Civic Culture: political attitudes and democracy in five nations . Princeton, Princeton University Press

Anderson B 1991 Imagined communities: reflections on the origin and spread of nationalism . London, Verso

Beveridge C, Turnbull R 1989 The Eclipse of Scottish Culture. Edinburgh, Polygon

Bloc Québécois 1998 Québec ... on the road to nationhood. Quebec, BQ

Broun D et al 1998 Image and Identity: The Making and Re-making of Scotland Through the Ages, Edinburgh, John Donald

Brown A et al 1996 Politics and Society in Scotland. Basingstoke, Macmillan

Brown A et al 1999 The Scottish Electorate: the 1997 General Election and Beyond. Basingstoke, Macmillan

Brunet M 1969 Les Canadiens après la conquête 1759-1775 de la revolution canadienne à la revolution americaine. Montréal, Fides

Consultative Steering Group of the Scottish Parliament 1998 Shaping Scotland's Parliament. Edinburgh, Scottish Office

Dion L 1988 'The Mystery of Quebec'. In: Daedalus 177(4)

Finlay R 1997 'Heroes, Myths and Anniversaries in Modern Scotland'. In: Scottish Affairs 13

Forrester DB 1993 'The Church of Scotland and Public Policy'. In: Scottish Affairs 4:67-81

Government of Quebec 1995 An Act Respecting the Sovereignty of Quebec.

Government of Quebec 1998 Quebec Society. www.gouv.qc.ca

Hall S 1992 'The question of cultural identity'. In: Hall S, Held D, McGrew T (eds) Modernity and Its Futures. Cambridge, Polity Press

Hall S 1996 'Introduction: who needs identity?' In: Hall S, DuGay P (eds) Questions of Cultural Identity. London, Sage

Handler R 1988 Nationalism and the Politics of Culture in Quebec. Madison, University of Wisconsin Press

Johnson W 1991 Anglophobia: made in Quebec. Montreal, Stanké

Keating M 1996 Nations Against the State. Basingstoke, Macmillan

Labour Party 1997 www.labour.org.uk

Legault, J 1992 L'invention d'une minorité, Quebec, Boréal

Lynch M 1992 Scotland A New History. London, Pimlico

McNaught K 1988 Canada. Toronto, Penguin

Martin P 1998 'Identity Groups and Values: Dispositions and choice on the question of sovereignty in Quebec'. (Unpublished Paper). American Political Science Association

Ministère de la Culture et des Communications 1998 Langue. www.gouv.qc.ca

Ministère des Relations des Citoyens et Immigration 1998 Les Relations Civiques . www.mrci.gouv.qc.ca

Mitchell J 1990 Conservatives and the Union: a study of Conservative party attitudes in Scotland. Edinburgh, Edinburgh University Press

Moreno L 1988 'Scotland and Catalonia: the Path to Home Rule'. In: McCrone D, Brown A (eds) The Scottish Government Yearbook. Edinburgh, Unit for the Study of Government in Scotland

Nairn T 1988 'Virtual Liberation or: British sovereignty since the election'. Scottish Affairs, Special Issue: 13-37

Parizeau J 1995 Post-Referendum Speech. Montreal, PQ

Parti Québécois 1994 Des Idées pour mon pays: programme du Parti Québécois. Québec, PQ

Paterson L 1994 The Autonomy of Modern Scotland. Edinburgh, Edinburgh University Press

Pelletier G 1988 'Quebec: Different but in Step with North America'. Daedalus 177(4)

Quebec Liberal Party 1997 Recognition and interdependence. Montreal, Quebec Liberal Party

Reid A 1996 Renewing Canada. Toronto, Angus Reid

Reid G 1995 10th Donaldson Lecture. Edinburgh, SNP

Richler M 1992 Oh Canada Oh Quebec: requiem for a divided country. Toronto, Penguin

Salmond A 1995a Address to the Annual National Conference. Edinburgh, SNP

Salmond A 1995b William Memorial Lecture. Edinburgh, SNP

Salmond A 1996 Address to the Annual National Conference. Edinburgh, SNP

Scottish National Party 1995a SNP History: 1921 to the present day. Edinburgh, SNP

Scottish National Party 1995b Citizens not Subject. Edinburgh, SNP

Scottish National Party 1996 Anti-Scottish Tories. Edinburgh, SNP

Scowen R 1991 A Different Vision: the English in Quebec in the 1990s. Don Mills, Maxwell Macmillan

Silver AI 1982 The French Canadian Idea of Confederation 1864-1900. Toronto, Toronto University Press

Tajfel H 1981 Human Groups and Social Categories: studies in social psychology/. Cambridge, Cambridge University Press

Tajfel H 1982 Social identity and intergroup relations. Cambridge, Cambridge University Press

Task Force on Curriculum Reform 1997 Reaffirming the Mission of Our Schools. Quebec, Government of Quebec

Turner JC 1987 Rediscovering the social group: a self-categorization theory. Oxford, Blackwell

Turner JC 1991 Social Influence. Milton Keynes, Open University Press

Well P 1998 'Sovereignty Star fading: Poll'. In: The Gazette 2 April

Wyn Jones R, Trystan D 1999 'The 1997 Welsh referendum vote'. In: Taylor B, Thomson K (eds) Scotland and Wales: Nations Again? Cardiff, University of Wales Press, 78

The Exception to the Rule:
Nineteenth Century Scotland and the Causes of National Movements

Antonia Dodds

Scotland presents an intriguing case-study to the student of nationalism because it provides an exception to the European norm. It has a clear and strongly-felt national identity, yet it failed to produce a national movement in the nineteenth century, when nationalism was sweeping across Europe from the Baltic to the Balkans, despite the presence of many factors, such as a distinct language and culture, territorial integrity and history, and some economic under-development, that elsewhere in Europe led to a national movement. However Scotland has produced a vibrant national movement in the late twentieth century, resulting in the restoration of its parliament after almost three hundred years. As we enter the next millennium we are entering a new era of Scottish politics. Yet one of the main questions remains as yet unanswered: does devolution present an end in itself, or is it merely a step along the road to independence?

This paper contends that an exploration of the factors which explain Scotland's failure to produce a national movement last century will help both to elucidate the causes of European secessionist national movements in general, and to shed light on the trajectory of Scotland's own twentieth century national movement. Scotland raises important theoretical questions about the causes of national movements, and the relationship of the state to the nation. Its coming political settlement – devolution in the UK, or independence, its relation to the EU – presents a test-case for the future of small nations in Europe and for the relationship between the state and nation.

This paper will start by outlining some of the most common theories explaining the appearance of a national movement found in the literature on nationalism. It will then examine nineteenth-century Scotland in the light of them, and argue that one factor alone is not sufficient to explain the rise of a national movement; rather, the interaction between certain key factors is necessary to explain the rise of this phenomenon. Some comparisons will be drawn with other small European nations which did produce national movements in the nineteenth century, such as Latvia. The paper will conclude with a brief examination of the relevance of the key factors to contemporary Scotland.

Causes of National Movements

There are numerous theories in the academic literature to account for the rise of national movements, which prioritise different explanatory factors. Three main factors will be reviewed here: culture and national identity, the role of elites, and the role of the economy.

To state the obvious, without a nation there can be no national movement, and most nationalist theory assumes (with apologies to Jane Austen) that a nation in possession of an identity must be in want of a state. Most definitions of the nation include the element of shared culture, most frequently, but not necessarily, language; for example, Seton–Watson's definition, 'a nation is a community of people, whose members are bound together by a sense of solidarity, a common culture, a national consciousness' (Seton–Watson 1977:1). Or Smith's definition (1991:14): 'A nation can therefore be defined as a named human population sharing an historic territory, common myths and historical memories, a mass, public culture, a common economy and common legal rights and duties for all members'. However, as these definitions suggest, the nation cannot be defined by purely objective criteria: there is a subjective element whereby the nation exists when a sufficient quantity of its members think of themselves as belonging to the nation. This does not mean, however, that a nation must exist before the national movement can occur – national movements can and do create and spread a popular concept of national identity, as in Hroch's phase B (see below) – but nor yet can nations always be successfully created at the behest of a state or national movement (two notable failures being, last century, 'North Britain', and this century East Germany). Nor does this imply that the actual content of the national identity is static, or even objectively quantifiable. National identities are notoriously hard to quantify, and certainly develop over time. However, what is important is that there exists a sense of shared identity both across space (the territory of the nation) and time (linking the present to the past and the future). A D Smith (1991) has tried to combine the 'modernist' approach of theorists such as Ernest Gellner (1983) who see the nation as essentially modern with the 'primordialist' approach which sees nations as ancient by arguing that ethnic groups – what he calls 'ethnies' – will develop into nations in the modern era, and that nations will 'mine' ethnies for material on which to base their claim to nationhood, but that not all ethnies will make the transition. Certainly national movements frequently draw on the (real or imaginary) past to create a national identity, and it would seem logical to assume that nations with more material to draw on would be more successful in creating their national identity.

Benedict Anderson (1991) has argued that national identity was not originally political. It developed in the older European states through print-capitalism which spread a standard language and shared concept of community in a spontaneous and un-willed manner, without a political agenda, and often the boundaries of areas which shared a national identity did not coincide with political boundaries (although in some cases such as England the national identity occurred within a stable state). As Anderson points out, early national movements (eg eighteenth century Ireland, USA) did not base their claims to independent nationhood on linguistic or cultural elements but on democratic and political arguments. However, in the nineteenth century – often referred to as the 'Age of Nationalism' – the idea that state and nation should be congruent became widespread (due to the spread of the Romantic movement, and, according to theorists such as Gellner [1983], the processes of modernisation), and this idea is still one of the key bases of political legitimacy in the modern world. This fueled both minority nations' desire for statehood and existing states' own national movements aimed at creating a culturally homogeneous and loyal nation-state. It is this very link between nation and state, the assumption that a nation with a national identity will desire political self-determination, which is at the core of many definitions of nationalism, such as Gellner's 'Nationalism is primarily a political principle, which holds that the political and the national unit should be congruent' (Gellner 1983:1).

The nineteenth century was the great age of national movements. Miroslav Hroch (1985, 1993) has divided national movements into a three-stage process, which sees both the cultural and political phases as essential, but separate, and which prioritises the role of elites in stimulating the national movement.

Phase A involves academic interest in the peasant culture (codification of language, creation of high literature where none existed, etc); in phase B a group of activists consciously try to spread the idea of the nation; and in phase C the national movement takes on a mass dimension. Although it is not at first political, national culture can rapidly become politicised in the face of attempts at cultural homogenisation from the imperial centre, such as Russification in the Baltic provinces at the end of the nineteenth century (see Plakans 1981) This can still be seen in present-day Latvia, where the widespread belief amongst ethnic Latvians is that political independence is necessary to preserve Latvian culture, and cultural elements are of fundamental importance in politics. For example, the naturalisation laws require a high degree of sufficiency in the Latvian language. This has often been criticised as a barrier preventing the many ethnic Russians (mainly Soviet-era immigrants) from becoming Latvian citizens. In October 1998, however, a referendum on easing the citizenship process (including the language element) was passed, which may reflect a growing confidence on Latvia's part that her culture is no longer perceived as being under threat from Russian dominance. It also reflects Latvia's desire to join the EU – the question of the stateless minorities had been one of the barriers to EU membership.

Hroch is very aware of the process of establishing national identity, but he does not question its relationship to politics: he assumes, like many other writers, both theorists of nationalism and nationalists themselves, that the successful outcome of a national movement is political self-determination, ie full independence. For example, the Latvian historians Spekke and Sprudzs portray the national movement of the nineteenth and twentieth centuries as leading inexorably to the only logical outcome, independence. 'The revolt was a link in the chain of historical development which finally led to definite and formulated demands for independence' (Spekke 1951:312). Sprudzs writes of the academic and politician Bilmanis that he struggled 'to prove that the independence of Latvia... was not an "accident of history", but the logically inevitable end result of the course of history in that part of Europe' (Sprudzs 1968:19). The Flemish national movement is therefore unfinished as full independence has not been achieved. Hroch (1985) divides his three phases of the national movement (A, scholarly study of the national group; B, the period of 'patriotic agitation'; C, the mass movement) into four types, depending on when they are played out against two historical stages: stage 1 (the struggle against feudalism and the rise of the bourgeoisie); and stage 2 (after the victory of capitalism, and the rise of the working class). The four types of national movement are: type 1, integrated, where the transition from phase B to C occurs during the transition from stage 1 to 2, eg Czech and Estonian; type 2, belated, where the transition from B to C occurs well into stage 2, eg Slovak and Lithuanian; type 3, insurrectional, where all three phases A, B, and C occur during stage 1, eg Bulgarian and Macedonian; type 4, disintegrated, where phase B occurs well into stage 2, and phase C is yet to occur, therefore the national movement has yet to achieve the third, mass phase, eg Flemish.

There is a substantial literature on the process of the formation of national identity, but most assumes that national identity and political independence go hand in hand.

The concern of this paper, however, is not with exploring the primordialist versus the modernist debate on the origin of nations, but with examining nineteenth century Scotland, which had a popularly (and subjectively) felt national identity which failed to turn into a political nationalist movement despite having more material than many other European nations on which to build such a movement.

The second main explanatory factor, the role of the elite, is a primary concern of Hroch's. National movements of course need leaders (Hroch's main focus is on the social background of the elites in national movements), and the intellectuals and elites are also key players in the formulation and dissemination of national identity. If elites are effectively co-opted into the imperial structure they will, presumably, be less liable to agitate for a national movement to gain input into the political system and to create their own administration. One of the reasons for the American War of Independence was the Americans' lack of representation in Westminster. Colley (1992:136) comments that eighteenth-century American elites, unlike Scottish elites, did not have access to state employment (because the American administration was too small) and this also was a factor in the push for independence. Anderson (1991:93) points out that native elites in the British Empire – except, notably, the Scots – were frequently banned from access to jobs at the imperial centre, even when they had been anglicised, partly due to the emergent 'official nationalism' at the imperial centre (itself a reaction to peripheral nationalism). The Scots did have access to the imperial structure, and their elites were thus effectively co-opted.

The third factor, the role played by the economy, is probably the most commonly heard argument for or against modern nationalism, in particular in the debate over whether secession will be better or worse for the economy, and the many economic explanations for the rise of the SNP. The SNP and Labour campaigns in the run-up to the 1999 Scottish Parliamentary Elections focused heavily on the economics of independence and, following the announcement of the SNP's 'Penny for Scotland' policy, issues of taxation; debate on identity, sovereignty, and the more emotional aspects of independence was notably lacking. Michael Hechter (1975) and Tom Nairn (1981) both present economic theories for the rise of national movements. Both argue that capitalism and economic development spread in an uneven manner, privileging some areas over others, and that the comparatively under-developed areas will give rise to a national movement. With reference to the nineteenth century, Hechter outlined his thesis of 'internal colonialism' to explain the survival of separate core and peripheral identities during the age of industrialisation; it is thus a comment on Gellner's approach to nationalism as a means of cultural homogenisation undertaken by the state to aid in the transition to industrialisation. In his 'internal colonial' model of development, the centre dominates and exploits the periphery, subjugating the periphery's economy to the centre's, and thus ensuring a cultural division of labour, in turn ensuring the survival of the periphery's identity. He applies this theory to the British 'Celtic Fringe', to explain the survival of peripheral identities, and, presumably, the basis for their national movements (at least Ireland's). Tom Nairn's famous theory of 'uneven development' (Nairn 1981), states that capitalism occurs at different rates across the globe. Peripheries are dominated and exploited by centres; they wish to avoid this, and catch up economically, and political self-rule is the best way to achieve this. These approaches offer a very instrumental view of nationalism, which is seen as a useful means of achieving economic development, rather than an end in itself. Hechter's original approach is more suited to Ireland than to Scotland; Scotland failed to produce a national movement in the nineteenth century because, as Nairn argues, it did not suffer economically at the hands of the centre.

Scotland in the Nineteenth Century

How then do these three factors, national identity, elites and the economy, relate to Scotland in the nineteenth century?

That there was a clear national identity can be in no doubt. Staunch Unionists such as Sir Walter Scott defended the right of Scottish banks to print their own notes; public subscription created the Wallace Monument at Stirling; mid-century campaigns argued for the correct use of 'Britain', not 'England', and for the correct use of Scottish heraldry; Scotland became increasingly fashionable for tourism, fueling a rise in consumer demand for things 'Scottish' (what Nairn 1981 has dubbed the 'Tartan Monster'); and towards the end of the century Burns clubs sprung up across the globe. Although the Enlightenment was not a national movement as such, it put Edinburgh proudly at the cultural centre of Europe at the start of the nineteenth century. Moreover, Scotland had more cultural material than many other European nations on which to base a national movement; it had, amongst other things, a patriotic literature extending back to the middle ages (including John Barbour's *The Bruce*, Blind Harry's *Wallace*, and the *Declaration of Arbroath* of 1320, as well as the later works of Henryson, Dunbar, Lyndsay et al), unlike Latvia, which had only its dainas (folksongs) from which to create a Latvian history and literature. Known as the 'Latvian second bible', the dainas were essential to the national movement, because, since Latvia had no written history, it was in them that the 'national awakeners' found the descriptions of Latvian culture and history, and Krisjanis Barons, the man who did much of the classification, is a national hero. They were collected and codified from the mid-nineteenth century onwards. In fact, one of the first collectors of Latvian folklore was a Scot, Robert Jamieson, who had started collecting Scots folklore but had covered the same ground as Walter Scott, so had taken a position as a tutor in Riga, where he developed an interest in Latvian folklore (Birznieks 1992). Many of the activities undertaken during a national movement such as that in Latvia had already occurred in Scotland: for example, the collection of ballads and folksongs (by Sir Walter Scott and others), there was an active press and media (whereas in Latvia the first novel in Latvian was not written until 1879); there were national museums; and, of course, ancient universities (compare the struggle in Wales to establish a university). Scotland had in fact passed through Hroch's phase A before most other small European nations.

However, Scots in the nineteenth century had a dual national identity. Scottish national identity was able to sit within an Imperial British identity; the one did not preclude the other. There was no inherent contradiction in being a nationalist and a Unionist, as Graeme Morton has shown with his concept of Unionist-Nationalism (Morton 1996). Unlike the countries of Eastern Europe, the existence of a national identity did not lead to a national movement, and Scotland therefore presents a good example of a split between national identity and political nationalism. Why was this?

There are three aspects to the answer of this question: Scots contributed to the creation of a British imperial identity; Scots identity in Scotland survived the Union; and a process of homogenisation went on within Scotland which eroded the distinct cultural identity of the Highlands. First, as Linda Colley has shown, a British national identity was created during the eighteenth century based on war with France, Empire, trade and Protestantism (Colley 1992). This new British identity was not synonymous with an English identity, but was shaped by both English and Scots.

> As I have argued, Scots were not just passively assimilated. They did not invariably become honorary or, according to one's point of view, dishonourable Englishmen. They brought their own ideas and prejudices to bear on the business of being British. (Colley 1992:131)

In addition, the Empire provided much trade, so that being British paid off: patriotism and profit went together, and the newly created Great Britain was seen as a 'useable resource'. So much so that by the time of the American War of Independence many Scots towns took the opportunity to demonstrate their loyalty to Britain by opposing American independence.

Second, Scots identity survived intact. The Union ensured the survival of the Kirk, legal system and education system, and many commentators (Harvie 1994, Kellas 1992 inter alia) have argued that the survival of these elements of Scots civil society preserved and disseminated a Scottish identity. Scottish national symbols continued to be used, but they were seen as complementary to English national symbols, not incompatible. The Chartists, for example, marched with banners representing William Wallace alongside Magna Carta, all representing freedom from tyranny, rather than with a particularly nationalist overtone (Smout 1986). Nor did the Union enforce cultural assimilation. A certain degree of assimilation went on (such as anglicisation of the language), but it was voluntarily undertaken by Lowland Scots eager to achieve in the new Great Britain. Scottish national culture was not perceived as a threat by the British state, and there was little interference in cultural affairs, in contrast to many other European countries. For example, the state did not prevent the erection of the Wallace monument, even if *The Times* was scathing about it (Hanham 1969:79) in contrast to the Habsburg Empire, which prevented the Czechs from erecting a monument to Jan Hus in Prague in the 1890s (Paterson 1994). Scotland was not systematically subject to cultural homogenisation or oppression, as many other European nations were under imperial rule, and did not therefore produce a nationalist backlash.

Third, in the areas where there was a very distinct culture which had suffered a conscious homogenisation following the 1745 Jacobite rebellion – namely the Gaelic-speaking Highlands – and where a nationalist movement might have been expected to arise (compare Ireland), the absence of local elites and the fact that it was a regional, not a national identity, explain the lack of a national movement. The Scots identity which triumphed at the Union was predominantly Lowland; and many of those responsible for the Highland Clearances were themselves Lowland Scots; while the power of the clan chiefs was broken after Culloden and the aristocracy became rapidly anglicised. In fact anglicisation of the Highlands had started well before 1745 in an attempt to bring the area more firmly under the rule of the crown: for example, James VI's Statutes of Iona of 1609 stipulated that the eldest children of clan chiefs had to be educated in English on the mainland (Lynch 1992:241-2), and bodies such as the Society in Scotland for Propagating Christian Knowledge (founded 1708) were aimed at eradicating the Gaelic language. The SSPCK is described by Harvie as 'the spearhead of the attack on Gaelic culture' (1994:46, see also Withers 1982). The Highlands would thus suggest that the presence of a distinct cultural and territorial identity is not on its own sufficient to produce a national movement, even when combined with economic underdevelopment and exploitation; the identity and economic ills need to be perceived as national, not merely regional, which in this case of course they were not, perhaps owing to the lack of an intelligentsia to create a concept of a Highland nation. Walter Scott created a romantic vision of the Highlands in novels such as *Waverley* and *Rob Roy*, but it was a vision of the past, not the future, and it was not in opposition to the Union; Nairn describes him as a 'valedictory realist' (1981:114ff). There was no figure comparable to the Irish Parnell in Scotland. By the end of the eighteenth century – helped by factors such as the removal of Jacobitism as a real political force, growing tourism and the publication of Macpherson's Ossianic poems – a sanitised Highland culture had become acceptable enough to be appropriated by Lowland intelligentsias as part of Scottish national identity. See Leneman (1987a, 1987b) on the role played by the Ossianic poems in making the Highlands acceptable to Lowland Scotland; also Trevor-Roper (1983) on the development of the tartan industry and the 'invention of tradition' during the period.

The lack of a charismatic leader such as Parnell brings us to the second of the explanatory factors, the role of the elites. Scots elites, unlike the Catholic Irish for most of the century, had access to state employment; they could and did compete with the English for top jobs in Britain and throughout the Empire, which provided career opportunities unknown in Scotland, and they did not have to become 'English' to do so. Nation-building energies went into the British-Imperial project rather than into Scotland itself. By contrast, in Latvia, upward social mobility was possible (although given that Latvians were peasants, not common), but it required changing one's identity, language, culture, and often religion, and assimilating to the German- or Russian-speaking communities: going into the army was known colloquially as 'becoming Russian' (Plakans 1981). Many of the key leaders in the Latvian Awakening of the 1850s had found themselves in a position of being about to assimilate to the German- or Russian-speaking intelligentsias, and had undergone some sudden 'conversion' to Latvian nationalism, thus becoming the first members of the Latvian intelligentsia (see Plakans 1974, 1981). Scots elites, unlike Latvians, did not need to assimilate culturally; they could be simultaneously Scottish and British, no doubt in part because of the similarity between Lowland Scots and English culture. Christopher Harvie (1994) in fact devotes more time in his chapters on the nineteenth century to Scots' exploits in the Empire than to the political movements within Scotland itself (such as the National Association for the Vindication of Scottish Rights; see Hanham 1969). Emigration, to England or further afield, also provided an outlet to those who were stifled at home; in turn, this 'brain drain' made a national movement less likely by removing many of the most able from Scotland.

The third explanatory factor is the economy. Hechter's internal colonialism theory can apply at various points – in the immediate effects of the Union on the Scottish linen trade – or to the Highlands in the nineteenth century, in particular the Clearances. But it does not fit Scotland as a whole (it fits Ireland somewhat better). By the middle of the eighteenth century, and into the nineteenth, Scotland was profiting from the free trade brought by the Union and from the access to colonial markets in the Empire. Its growth rate outstripped England's at the end of the eighteenth century, and this economic success continued on into the nineteenth century. Nor does Hechter's associated theory of cultural imperialism hold water: according to Hechter, an area which suffers internal colonialism would resist cultural homogenisation, and the cultural division of labour would preserve the peripheral identity, while in an area which is economically developed, cultural assimilation to the core would eventually occur. Scotland experienced a high degree of economic and industrial development (and a degree of voluntary assimilation) but also preserved a national identity distinct from that of the core, partly through the preservation of its distinct institutions. Moreover, as far as the Highlands are concerned, the important fact is that the 'colonisers' were in the main Lowland Scots. The economic cleavages did not overlay national cleavages, and the Highlands lacked an intelligentsia to lead a nationalist movement.

Tom Nairn's thesis provides a better fit for Scotland because it argues that economic development is uneven, and the comparatively under-developed areas will produce a national movement in an attempt to 'catch up' with the developed cores. Hence, he argues, the lack of a national movement in nineteenth century Scotland despite the presence of a national identity, was precisely because nineteenth century Scotland was at the forefront of economic and industrial development. Put simply, Scottish economic success made a national movement unnecessary, because the elite did not need to take a nationalist stance to achieve economic ends. This is not to imply, however, that there was no poverty in Scotland – far from it – but the extreme poverty experienced by the working class did not influence the political agenda to the degree to which it can do now (although there was working-class political agitation, such as Chartism), since there was no universal franchise. In an age when central government had little or no intervention in the economy, especially in Britain where industrialisation was not state-led, there was not the same expectation that the government was responsible for the economic well-being of all. As R H Campbell argues: 'Whatever the reality of an economic case for nationalism in Scotland before 1914, none was imagined' (Campbell 1980:146).

All of the above theories are useful, but none are alone sufficient to explain the rise of national movements. There is a danger in trying to account for a national movement with only one factor, or trying to find one monolithic global cause for national movements. Nairn's theory of 'uneven development' (where a less developed periphery will strive for self-determination in order to develop its economy), for example, is certainly a factor in explaining nineteenth century Scotland, but it does not alone account for the sustained rise of modern nationalism, or for the national movements in nineteenth century Catalonia, Finland, and elsewhere, which were more economically developed than their respective centres (see Karner 1991 on Finland, and Pi-Sunyer 1985 and Medrano 1995 on Catalonia). Stressing only one factor, such as the economy, can lead to ignoring others, such as the role played by national identity. Nor do theories of national identity usually take into account the relationship between the 'national' identity and the imperial identity. In fact, the theoretical literature on nationalism can be quite simplistic in its tendency to seek for a single explanatory factor (such as economics in the case of Hechter and Nairn). Looking at less theoretical and more historical work done on Scotland, other factors emerge which are also relevant to explain the lack of a national movement.

Additional Factors: the Preservation of Autonomy

National movements often gain support from overlapping or merging with other social movements or adopting popular policies which are not necessarily nationalist per se, such as land reform, or liberalism and civil rights. In Ireland, the Home Rule party won 60 out of 103 Irish seats in the 1874 election, and '...the most successful candidates were those who mixed home rule with a programme which included the aims of the Catholic union and land reform.' (Boyce 1995:196) In Latvia the relationship between the social democrats and the nationalists (although not entirely solved until independence in 1917) strengthened the national movement, as social democracy helped make nationalism a mass movement, and conversely by adopting some nationalist ideas, the more affluent Latvians could be won over to the social democracy which was otherwise aimed at the urban proletariat and landless agricultural workers. Ultimately the move to independence may have been inspired by the desire to attain the much needed land reforms (which were extensive, as half of the land had been held by the Baltic German nobility). In Ukraine, the success of the Ukrainian Socialist Revolutionaries in 1917–21 has been explained not by a popular sense of nationalism but by their proposed land reforms (Takach 1996).

In Scotland on the other hand, these aims were achieved in a British context. The Great Reform Act of 1832 had a revolutionary effect upon the Scots franchise, which had been proportionately far lower than the English: during the years 1832–5, it increased from 4500 to 65 000. The Reform Act went a long way towards reconciling the middle classes to the (British) state, and working class movements such as Chartism and later the Labour Party were developed on a UK-wide basis. In Ireland, however, the British Labour Party put down only shallow roots, thus leaving those issues for the growing nationalist movement. Land reform in the Scottish Highlands was gained in 1886, shortly after the Irish Land Act was passed, and giving very similar rights to tenants. However the four MPs of the Crofters' Party (the political wing of the Highland Land Law Reform Association) who had been elected in 1886 were soon afterwards co-opted into the Liberal party and did not thus turn the land reform issue into a nationalist movement (Hunter 1974), unlike in Ireland where the granting of land reform in fact catapulted Parnell, the leader of the Land League, into power, thus giving more momentum to Irish nationalism. There was specifically Scottish political agitation, most notably in the National Association for the Vindication of Scottish Rights of the 1850s, but this saw the answer not as secession but as greater equality within the Union, in the form of better political representation at Westminster, and the restoration of a Secretary of State for Scotland (See Hanham 1967, 1969 and Morton 1996). The NAVSR was an important but short-lived movement which gathered wide support from across the political spectrum, the major town councils, the Convention of Royal Burghs, and Tory romantics (but not from Scots politicians). It was committed to the Union but wanted Scotland and England to be equal partners. After many meetings and pamphlets it disappeared due to the outbreak of the Crimean War and the Indian Mutiny, and perhaps also due to the heterogeneity of its members. Its aims were eventually achieved, although not by the NAVSR itself.

In addition, as Paterson (1994) has argued, Scotland preserved a high degree of autonomy despite the loss of its Parliament. Not only was its civil society preserved in the form of the kirk, education system and legal system, but due to the nature of the British government, local government had far more effect on the daily lives of most Scots than central government, and local government was, of course, Scots. When national institutions were introduced and the state's influence over people's daily lives grew, the institutions were often administered on a Scottish basis. The laissez-faire nature of the British state benefited Scotland because it allowed industrialisation and, particularly, civil society to develop without much state control, and in a localised and spontaneous manner, in contrast to later industrialising nations in which the state played a larger role. Paterson (1994) maintains that despite the lack of a Parliament, Scotland had in the nineteenth century a level of autonomy which was greater than that of other small European nations such as the Czechs, and comparable to that of Norway or Finland.

Furthermore, it is often implicit in the literature on nationalism that a national movement is only successful if independence is aimed at and attained. Hroch (1985) places Scotland in his fourth, 'disintegrated', ie 'incomplete' category, and theorists such as Nairn (1981) say that Scotland did not have a national movement in the nineteenth century because there was no political agitation for independence. Certainly, Scotland did not have a political nationalism aimed at independence in the nineteenth century. Yet many of the European national movements did not aim at independence until the end of the century when it became clear that they could not achieve their goals within the existing imperial status quo. Most members of the Latvian movement desired cultural rights and a federal government within the Russian Empire until the eve of independence. The Czechs wanted political liberties, free trade, cultural rights and a federal empire, and again, most activists did not seek outright independence until the end of the nineteenth century when it became clear that they could not achieve their aims within the Habsburg empire (Palacky had argued for a federal Austrian empire of equal nations: see Klima 1993). In addition, international events bear on the success of national movements: Latvia achieved independence (only to lose it twenty years later) because Russia was distracted by civil war, and it suited the West to have a 'buffer zone' in the Baltic (some help was given by Britain and France). Paterson (1994) comments that Scotland did not need a political nationalism because it had already achieved the aims (such as cultural rights, political liberties, access to the imperial centre) that the national movements of other small European nations desired. Independence was not originally one of those aims, but was adopted as a goal when the other aspects could not be achieved without it. To assume therefore that a national movement will automatically desire independence (and that if independence is not an aim then there is no national movement or no nationalism) can be a case of twentieth century theorists putting the cart before the nineteenth century horse. There have been some recent revisions of Scotland's 'missing nationalism', for example Morton (1998), who suggests that Scotland did have a nationalism, but an early form of civic rather than ethnic nationalism which is only now being recognised.

To summarise: Scotland's failure to produce a nationalist movement aimed at secession in the nineteenth century was due not to a lack of national feeling but to five main factors: the co-optation of elites; the preservation of a high degree of local political self-determination; cultural and economic cleavages did not coincide with national boundaries; the creation of an over-arching (British) identity; and the fact that most social and democratic demands were answered within a British framework. In short, the main reason for the lack of a coherent national movement in Scotland must be then that the main factors which cause a national movement were satisfactorily dealt with within the British state.

Conclusion: Present-day Scotland

I wish to end by briefly raising a few relevant points from these findings to present-day Scotland, as there is now, unlike last century, a strong, popular national movement which includes a cultural renaissance, the devolution movement resulting in the re-establishment of the Parliament in 1999, and a pro-independence movement. How do the factors outlined above relate to the current national movement? There is only space here to outline a few key avenues for further research. The survival of a Scottish identity, albeit an evolving and pluralistic identity, is one major element. As Colley (1992) suggests, with the end of Empire, and the rise of multi-cultural Britain, many of the factors on which British identity were built have gone. Protestantism is no longer sufficiently important to enough people, or cohesive enough, to serve as a truly national identity; the opportunities provided by the Empire are no longer there; free trade is increasingly answered by the European Union rather than the United Kingdom, hence the logic of the SNP's 'Independence in Europe' policy. The rise of the Scottish national movement may be seen as a reaction to the end of a viable British identity following Britain's post-war decline and the end of Empire. The new cultural and political confidence in Scotland and the increasing strength of Scottish national identity are revealed by, for example, the increase in interest in Scottish history and culture, as well as survey data on national identity in Scotland. British identity (notwithstanding recent attempts to repackage Britain as 'Cool Britannia') is now far weaker, and Scottish national identity far stronger, although the two have not yet become incompatible. For example, see Smout (1994) who argues that Scottish and British identities are complementary rather than competing.

Britain's post-war economic decline certainly played a part in the rise of the SNP in the late 1960s and 1970s, yet is not on its own sufficient to explain that rise, as areas of England suffering an equally severe depression did not produce a nationalist movement. The SNP tend to focus on economic arguments – the referendum on independence was bottom of their list of election pledges in their manifesto for the 1999 Scottish Parliamentary Elections – partly because due to the historical divide between Scottish national identity and political nationalism, all the political parties claim a Scottish identity and the SNP cannot base its mobilisation only on grounds of identity. Yet without the national identity and sense of the nation there could be no nationalist party. And (as indicated above) national movements tend to gain support by adopting aims which are not specifically nationalist, in this case, economic aims. The continued success of the SNP, however, does not appear to be clearly linked to the decline in Scotland's economic performance per se; rather, the economy is presented by the SNP as one factor (others being Scotland's say in the EU, a more responsive democracy, and so on) which would flourish best under Scottish independence. For example, in the 1990s when the Scottish economy has improved, support for the SNP has also increased – and in any case the state's ability to control the economy is dwindling given the increasingly globalised nature of the economy.

The economy is undoubtedly a factor in explaining the current national movement, but only one of many, and will not alone provide the answer. The changing role of the state is also an important factor: in the twentieth century it has become far more centralised and exerted more power over the daily lives of its citizens (even in the context of a global economy). This has eroded the local autonomy so important to nineteenth century Scotland and has challenged the distinctively Scottish nature of decision-making in Scotland. Hence, in order to achieve a comparable level of autonomy, a parliament has become necessary. The next few years will show whether a devolved parliament provides a sufficient level of autonomy, or whether tensions between Edinburgh and London over such areas as macro-economics and foreign policy will make independence necessary. In addition, the Parliament will deepen democracy in Scotland in ways which are either not, or not yet, achievable through Westminster. These include remedying the 'democratic deficit' whereby the Government and therefore the Scottish Secretary of State belongs to the ruling Westminster party which may not be the majority party in Scotland, and adopting Proportional Representation (the AMS system) rather than First Past the Post for the election of MSPs. Thus, whereas in the nineteenth century increased demands for democracy generally took the form of enlarging the franchise, and were met albeit reluctantly by the British state, in the late twentieth they are concerned with accountability of the ministers who run Scotland. Similarly, the shift of New Labour away from socialism is already producing tension between London and the Scottish ('old') Labour Party; it may be that Scots political aims are beginning to be unanswerable within a UK context.

I would therefore suggest that the economic approach which is often taken to Scottish nationalism is not on its own sufficient, in particular now given the changing nature of the global economy, but that Scottish nationalism is better examined from a twin perspective, namely identity (both Scottish and British) and the powers of the state (Scottish, British, and European), and how these factors interact. The outcome of Scotland's national movement will not automatically be independence, if the current devolution settlement can fulfill Scottish aspirations for political autonomy while maintaining a viable British identity. Most polls in the last few years, and the results of the May 1999 elections show that a majority of Scots do not currently desire full independence, although the creation of the Parliament has not, as Labour had hoped, lessened support for the SNP, but has rather enabled the SNP to be the main Opposition. However, the very existence of the Scottish Parliament makes Westminster less important to Scotland and therefore weakens one of the few remaining aspects of British national identity, as well as increasing Scottish identity through developing a new Scottish political culture. Moreover, the establishment of the Parliament has opened up areas of potential conflict between Holyrood and Westminster, such as macro-economics, foreign policy, and, topically, tuition fees, which make the move towards independence more likely now than in the pre-devolution period.

The Scottish case has, in turn, implications for the theory of nationalism in the relationship between national identity and political independence. Having been an example of the way in which national identity and political nationalism can be distinct, the two seem to be reconverging, but within a wider European cultural and political context. The settlement that Scotland evolves in the coming years will be a test case for the future of small nations in Europe.

References

Anderson B 1991 Imagined Communities. Verso, London and New York

Birznieks I 1992 'Robert Jamieson: a Scottish folklorist in Riga'. In: Journal of Baltic Studies vol XXIII no 1, Spring 1992

Boyce D G 1995 Nationalism in Ireland. Routledge, London

Campbell R H 1980 'The Economic Case for Nationalism: Scotland'. In: Mitchison R (ed) The Roots of Nationalism: Studies in Northern Europe. John Donald Publishers, Edinburgh

Colley L 1992 Britons: Forging the Nation 1707- 1837. Pimlico, London

Esman M J 1977 'Scottish Nationalism, North Sea Oil, and the British Response'. In: Esman M J (ed) Ethnic Conflict in the Western World. Cornell University Press, Ithaca and London

Gellner E 1983 Nations and Nationalism. Blackwell, Oxford

Hanham H J 1967 'Mid-Century Scottish Nationalism: Romantic and Radical'. In: Robson R (ed) Ideas and Institutions of Victorian Britain. G Bell and Sons Ltd., London

Hanham H J 1969 Scottish Nationalism. Harvard University Press, Cambridge Massachusetts

Harvie C 1994 Scotland and Nationalism: Scottish Society and Politics 1707-1994. Routledge, London and New York

Hechter M 1975 Internal Colonialism: The Celtic Fringe in British National Development, 1536 - 1966. Routledge and Kegan Paul, London

Hroch M 1985 Social Preconditions of National Revival in Europe : a Comparative Analysis of the Social Composition of Patriotic Groups among the Smaller European Nations. Cambridge University Press, Cambridge

Hroch M 1993 'From National Movement to the Fully-formed Nation: the nation-building process in Europe'. In: New Left Review 198, March-April 1993

Hunter J 1974 'The politics of highland land reform, 1873-1895'. In: Scottish Historical Review, vol 53

Karner T X 1991 'Ideology and Nationalism: the Finnish move to independence, 1809 - 1918'. Ethnic and Racial Studies 14.2, April 1991

Kellas J G 1992 'The Social Origins of Nationalism in Great Britain: the Case of Scotland'. In: Coakley J (ed) The Social Origins of Nationalist Movements: the Contemporary West European Experience. Sage Publications, London

Klima A 1993 'The Czechs'. In: Teich M, Porter R (eds) The National Question in Europe in Historical Context. Cambridge University Press, Cambridge

Leneman L 1987a 'The Effects of Ossian in Lowland Scotland'. In: Carter J J, Pittock J H (eds) Aberdeen and the Enlightenment. Aberdeen University Press, Aberdeen

Leneman L 1987b 'Ossian and the Enlightenment'. In: Scotia vol XI

Lynch M 1992 Scotland: A New History. Pimlico, London

Medrano J D 1995 'Catalan Nationalism, 1876-1936'. In: Divided Nations: Class, Politics and Nationalism in the Basque Country and Catalonia. Cornell University Press, Ithaca and London

Morton, G 1996 'Scottish Rights and "centralisation" in the mid-nineteenth century'. Nations and Nationalism 2:2 1996

Morton G 1998 'What if?: The Significance of Scotland's Missing Nationalism in the Nineteenth Century'. In: Broun D, Filay R J, Lynch M (eds) Image and Identity: The Making and Re-making of Scotland Through the Ages. John Donald Publishers Ltd, Edinburgh

Nairn T 1981 The Break-Up of Britain: Crisis and Neo-Nationalism. New Left Books, London

Paterson L 1994 The Autonomy of Modern Scotland. Edinburgh University Press, Edinburgh

Pi-Sunyer O 1985 'Catalan Nationalism: some Theoretical and Historical Considerations. In: Tiryakian E A, Rogowski R (eds) New Nationalisms of the Developed West: Toward Explanation. Allen and Unwin, Boston

Plakans A 1974 'Modernization and the Latvians in Nineteenth-Century Baltikum'. In: Baltic History. Ziedonis A et al (eds) Association for the Advancement of Baltic Studies, Columbus, Ohio

Plakans A 1981 'The Latvians'. In: Thaden E C (ed) Russification in the Baltic Provinces and Finland, 1855-1914. Princeton University Press, Princeton

Seton-Watson H 1977 Nations and States: an Enquiry into the Origins of Nations and the Politics of Nationalism. Methuen, London

Smith A D 1991 National Identity. Penguin, London

Smout T C 1986 A Century of the Scottish People 1830-1950. Collins, London

Smout T C 1994 'Perspectives on the Scottish Identity'. Scottish Affairs no 6, Winter 1994

Spekke A 1951 History of Latvia: an Outline. Zelta Abele, Stockholm

Sprudzs A, Armins R (eds) 1968 Res Baltica: a Collection of Essays in Honor of the Memory of Dr Alfred Bilmanis (1887-1948). A W Sijthoff-Leyden, Leyden

Takach A 1996 'In search of Ukrainian national identity: 1840 - 1921'. In: Ethnic and Racial Studies 19.3, July 1996

Trevor–Roper H 1993 'The Invention of Tradition: The Highland Traditions of Scotland'. In: Hobsbawm E, Ranger T (eds) The Invention of Tradition. Cambridge University Press, Cambridge

Withers C W J 1982 'Education and Anglicisation: the Policy of the SSPCK toward the Education of the Highlander, 1709-1825'. In: Scottish Studies 26

Scottish Identity in the Age of European Integration

Atsuko Ichijo

A s widely recognised, 1979 was one of the most significant turning points in the recent history of Scotland. The referendum result, despite the 'yes' vote outnumbering the 'no', failed to satisfy the so-called '40% rule' which dictated that in order to implement the Scotland Bill, it would have to be approved by more than 40% of the total electorate (for the referendum result, see Appendix). Because of the outcome of the referendum, the then Labour government was brought down and in May of the same year, the Conservatives came to power. The Scottish National Party (SNP) lost all but two seats at Westminster and its share of votes was almost halved. The Scotland Bill was scrapped by the Thatcher government and Scottish nationalism appeared to be on the decline. (See Mitchell (1996) and Clements et al (1996) for a chronology of events leading up to and following the 1979 referendum).

Although the SNP's electoral performance from 1979 up to the late 1980s remained low-key, Scottish nationalism did not disappear, and Scottish identity was neither completely subsumed by British identity nor fragmented into more local identities. Instead, Scottish identity was redefined and strengthened throughout the 1980s. The evidence of this heightening sense of being Scottish can be found in various aspects of contemporary Scotland, in particular in culture. Writing, painting, theatre and also folk and pop cultures seem to have experienced some kind of revival as can be seen in the success of James Kelman and Irvine Welsh in novels; the emergence of a new group of Glasgow painters including Steven Campbell; the renewed rigour in Scottish drama shown in Liz Lochead's work and the movement for the establishment of a Scottish national theatre; the rise of the number of folk clubs (Shoupe 1995) and the emergence and success of Gaelic pop culture most prominently personified in the rock band Runrig. In addition, many argue that there has been a renaissance of the study of Scottish history. There was a surge of interest in Scottish history and politics before the 1979 Referendum, reflecting the general mood of Scotland. Despite the disappointment of 1979, more articles, books and PhD theses have been written in the field of Scottish history than before (Lynch 1992: xv). It is not just a matter of quantity, however, there has been a rigorous re-examination of the once dominant Whig interpretation of history, an attempt to shed a different light on the study of Scottish history.

Against this background a significant event took place in Scottish politics: the adoption of the 'Independence in Europe' policy by the SNP in 1988. This was an extraordinary move for a nationalist party to take since what it meant was to recognise the legitimacy of an entity which might limit the sovereignty of an independent state. Moreover, the SNP was long known for its anti-European stance; it had campaigned fiercely for a 'no' vote at the 1975 EEC Referendum. The reason for its opposition to British EEC membership was a fear that Scotland would be further marginalised within what was perceived as a huge capitalist bloc. This was the kind of response one could naturally expect from a nationalist party. Common sense tells us that Scottish Nationalists ought to be against the project of European integration. In the 1980s, however, one of the once most prominent opponents to the project of European integration, Jim Sillars, joined the SNP and started making a case for the 'independence within Europe' policy (Sillars 1986). This time, Sillars portrayed the European Community as a framework that would guarantee Scottish independence rather than as an entity which would undermine the value of Scottish statehood. The policy was finally endorsed by the Party's Annual Conference in 1988, and the SNP's conversion to the pro-European stance was complete.

It was not just the SNP that was becoming pro-Europe. Scottish society has, since the late 1980s, come to be known for its pro-European tendencies. The SNP, now one of the most pro-European parties in the United Kingdom, has been forcefully arguing that the Scots are more European than the English, citing historical facts which suggest a closer relationship between Scotland and Europe before the Union of 1707. Other events, such as the warm reception of the European Union (EU) summit in Edinburgh in 1992, are often held as evidence of the alleged pro-Europeanness of the Scottish public (Ascherson 1993: xix-xxvii).

Moreover, many opinion polls have shown that the Scots are marginally more enthusiastic about and noticeably more reluctant to be against the EU than the English (Ichijo 1998: Ch.VII). At the same time, the Scots seem to have become more nationalist (with a small 'n') in politics, as seen in the increased level of support for devolution, and to some extent, independence. Following the widely observed practice in Scotland, I use the term 'nationalists' to refer to those who want to have some kind of constitutional change. The 'Nationalists' are, then, the supporters of the SNP. Above all, the results of the 1997 referendum finally affirmed the establishment of a Scottish Parliament and its tax raising power (for the result, see Appendix). In short, since the late 1980s the Scottish people seem to have become both pro-Europe and nationalist. This, however, strikes as being a contradiction in terms. Are these positions, pro-Europe and nationalist, not incompatible since the project of European integration would eventually nullify the sovereignty of the member states? Should nationalists be against anything that may compromise their aspiration? Why is it possible for contemporary Scots to be both Scottish nationalist and pro-Europe at the same time? These are the questions this paper addresses.

In order to identify and explore ideas about the relationship between Scotland and Europe which were in circulation in contemporary Scotland, I carried out a series of in-depth interviews with members of the Scottish intelligentsia. Here, intelligentsia refers to a certain group of people who have received a university level education, are in the business of producing or articulating ideas about Scotland and are consciously disseminating their ideas to the public. Scottish intelligentsia became the focus of this research because of the propositions of the sociology of knowledge which hold that knowledge is socially constructed and that intellectuals and intelligentsia are assigned a special task of producing and circulating knowledge. The sample was drawn using the snowball method, covering a wide spectrum of political persuasion and after conducting thirty-six interviews, I identified three main views about the relationship between Scotland and Europe, which I term the Scoto–European relationship. In the rest of paper, I would like to discuss the findings and my analysis of these views.

Europe as a Tool to Distinguish the
Scots from the English

Before turning to what I call the three visions of the Scoto–European relationship that have emerged from the interviews, I would first like to elaborate a certain type of answer my respondents gave, which, I believe, should be separated from these visions. This can be observed in the following statements.

> Hostility to Europe is an English experience. It is really, hardly found here. We want to be European. (JH: poet, literary critic)

> People are fed up with Britain and London rule and cannot think Europe would be any worse. Some way, they think it would be better. (AM: solicitor)

What is being said here is that Europe is good for Scotland because it is not England, and that the Scots like Europe, again because it is not England. This is obviously not a view of the relationship between Scotland and Europe. It is, however, a reaction which reveals how contemporary Scots tend to see the world, and therefore, suggests the overall framework within which ideas about Scotland are being produced. What emerges here is that Europe, in its vague and all-encompassing sense, functions as a reference point from which contemporary Scots can distinguish themselves from their southern neighbours, the English. Europe, in this context, stands in opposition to England without assuming any particular meaning. It is 'something out there', something that could conveniently replace England.

But why Europe? How has it become a preferred reference point? One of possible reasons is the so-called 'democratic deficit' in Scotland (Miller 1981). This refers to the political situation in the UK, especially from 1979 until 1997, when, despite the majority of the MPs returned to the House of Commons by the Scottish electorate coming from opposition parties, there had been a Conservative government. Put differently, the Scottish people were ruled for eighteen years by the party for which the majority did not vote. This has led to a strong association between the Conservative Party and the English in the minds of the Scottish people. Furthermore, those who spectacularly displayed their doubts about European integration were often Tory Cabinet

Members, Tory back benchers and Prime Ministers themselves. Although not all the Conservatives are Euro-sceptics and not all the Labour and Liberal Democrat MPs are pro-Europe, under the 'democratic deficit', it is helpful for the Scottish people to adopt the English-are-Tories-and-therefore-Euro-sceptics theory in order both to make sense of and put some order into the current situation, and to think about what they are and what they should do. Consequently, if the English are Euro-sceptic, the Scots are, by definition, pro-Europe. Partly in response to this political development in the UK, Europe has become a handy tool and a neutral reference point for the Scots to use to assert that they are different from the English.

Vision One: Europe as a Means to Achieve Independence/More Autonomy

One of the most popular views on the relationship between Scotland and Europe is that the European Union serves Scotland as a means of achieving independence, or, to some, obtaining a greater degree of autonomy for Scotland. This is a vision which does not necessarily contradict the conventional view of the relationship between nationalism and the process of European integration; the nationalists could argue that they are taking a very pragmatic approach towards the fulfillment of their goals. This view is clearly expressed in the following statement:

> We see the European Union as a strategic method of winning independence. That is you can have maximum political change with the minimum economic disruption.
> (GW: solicitor, former SNP Chariman/President)

So, for the Nationalists, the EU is an instrument to secure Scottish independence and they are prepared, if necessary, to sacrifice some aspect of the sovereignty of an independent Scotland. The Nationalists now argue that in this increasingly interdependent world, 'Independence in Europe' is the only realistic option available to Scotland. Jim Sillars, for instance, goes out of his way to argue that the absolute sovereignty of an independent state is a thing of the past, something that does not exist in the contemporary world (Sillars 1986: 182-3). Even the devolutionists often refer to the decision-making process within the EU as more suitable for Scotland, since it is designed to reflect minority views better than the Westminster system.

They are also keen on being a 'region' of Europe, which would enable Scotland to enter into direct negotiations with EU institutions or other regions and member states. But for the devolutionist, this would only be possible through Scotland's own parliament. Otherwise, negotiations would have to be conducted by the London government, which, to devolutionists and Nationalists alike, would not secure the best deal for Scotland. European integration, thus, would ensure and even necessitate a greater Scottish autonomy The importance attached to the European dimension is clearly expressed in Scottish Constitutional Convention's report, *Scotland's Parliament, Scotland's Right,* (1995).

Why is gaining independence or a greater degree of autonomy presented to be so important for the Scots? Many of my respondents think that the roots of the problems contemporary Scotland faces lie in the lack of confidence or self-respect on the part of the Scottish people. At the same time, opinion polls have repeatedly shown that the majority of the Scots want some kind of constitutional change. Taking these two into an account, an idea, or perhaps, a conviction that problems in Scottish society could be tackled and redressed by certain constitutional change has emerged. Some respondents argue that under the current arrangement Scottish distinctiveness is not properly respected. One of the examples is that the Scots are now unjustifiably, according to these respondents, labeled as 'subsidy junkies'. This, of course, destroys the pride and confidence of the Scottish nation, which leads to apathy and the decay of social fabric, for instance. The Unionists in Scotland still think that the union of Scotland and England can be maintained with some adjustments (Massie 1995) but others look to the European Union to secure the renaissance of the Scottish nation. According to many of my respondents, it is important for the Scots to regain the confidence that any proper nation should possess. A more confident Scotland, they argue, would stop blaming England for its problems and be able to cooperate with England more positively to bring about a better future.

An interesting point to note here is that within this vision the EU is very often described as a 'Confederal Europe', a loose grouping of independent states, not as a 'Federal Europe', ie, a United States of Europe. The type of

Europe Scottish Nationalists lend their support to as a means of achieving their goals is not the type of Europe the Euro-sceptics are opposed to, that is an entity which is driven by supranationalism to establish its own identity either as a superstate or supernation in order to subsume existing national states. For this reason, Scottish Nationalists, in general, are not so willing to discuss certain issues such as the Euro, since this is where their idea of a Confederal Europe comes in a head-on collision with the vision of a Federal Europe. The Transition to Independence Committee, a working group set up by the SNP to scrutinise the logistics of implementing the 'Independence in Europe' policy ruled that the issue of a single currency was 'out of its remit'. The Scottish Constitutional Convention did not discuss the Euro since it was one of the responsibilities to be retained by the UK government. Other images of Europe, such as Europe as a capitalist bloc or Europe as an undemocratic bureaucracy, are acknowledged by the respondents. However, they are more often than not portrayed as something that an independent or devolved Scotland would fight to safeguard its right, and do not attract further consideration in this vision of the Scoto–European relationship. The image of Europe in this vision is, therefore, carefully constructed so that it would not weaken the nationalist agenda.

In addition to this selective image of Europe, there is another factor which makes this view acceptable to contemporary Scots: the history of Scotland's links with continental Europe, to which almost all the respondents refer in describing their ideas. Many respondents claim that the Scots are traditionally pro-Europe because of their history. The Auld Alliance with France which goes back to the thirteenth century, together with the trade link with Scandinavian countries, Baltic countries, France and Low countries, and the intellectual and religious links with Holland are the three most frequently cited episodes used to support their argument for a special Scottish affinity with continental Europe (Scott 1992, Smout 1995). The argument goes as follows: history shows that the Scots were very closely involved with the Continent before the Union of 1707, which serves to demonstrate that the Scots are historically very European. Even if the Scots are currently not so enthusiastic about Europe, it is only because they have forgotten Scotland's old links with the continental countries which were broken by its participation in the British Empire. Once this history is remembered and fully appreciated, the Scots would naturally feel more comfortable in Europe and be good

Europeans. According to my respondents, such historical facts can only strengthen the case for the traditional Scottish affinity with Europe, which, in turn, should cultivate the readiness on the part of the Scottish people to accept this vision of the Scoto–European relationship.

Vision Two: Europe as a Socio-economic Space where a More Just Scotland is Possible

Another vision of the Scoto–European relationship is based on the different understanding of the European Union and a different aspect of the idea of what the Scottish nation is. In this view, Europe represents something progressive; the project of European integration is not a mere capitalist conspiracy but is about social democracy, concern for peripheries and minorities, and the welfare of people in Europe. This reflects relatively recent developments in the process of European integration such as the operation of the European Regional Development Fund (ERDF), the establishment of the Council of the Regions and the drafting of the Social Chapter. Europe, to some respondents, therefore, represents social democratic values as opposed to free marketeering. What effect does this understanding of Europe have on the views of the Scoto–European relationship? One of the respondents offers a clue:

> ... many of these who vote for the SNP without being committed to nationalism are not just voting tactically. Their thinking is based on the idea that you might be able to have a more just society in Scotland. (TB: historian)

Behind this statement lies the concept that Scotland is a nation with a long history of egalitarianism, concern for the community and commitment to the welfare state. These Scottish values, which have been nurtured through the tradition of humanism of medieval Scotland (Allan 1993, Broadie 1990), the legacy of the Presbyterian reformation, as seen in the egalitarian structure of the Kirk, the much cherished parish school system, the 'democratic intellect' (Davie 1961 and 1986, Walker 1994) and so on, are, according to the respondents, under threat. This threat to Scottish values, they believed, arose from the ideology that dominated the UK of market-oriented, aggressive individualism, as personified by Mrs Thatcher. (For the question of what Thatcherism is and what impact it has had on Scotland, see Mitchell and Bennie 1995). Within the framework of Europe where social democratic values are upheld, the Scots would be allowed to realise their ideal Scotland, something they cannot achieve within the current framework of the UK. Europe, therefore, would be good for Scotland because it would provide a space where the Scots could build their society based on these communal values and where such an effort would be received with empathy. The following is an example of the Scottish self-understanding:

> I suppose I feel more comfortable being grouped around with economic prosperity, being able to, in an egalitarian way, help other less prosperous nations to improve the quality of living and reduce poverty and malnourishment. (DM: lecturer in Media Studies)

What is interesting in this vision is that it tends to emphasise the civic aspect of the Scottish nation. This is not a place for an elaborate examination of ideal types of civic and ethnic nationalism, and a short account of the main features of each type should suffice. The defining characteristic of civic nationalism is its conceptualisaiton of a nation as a territorial and associational entity. A nation in civic nationalism is understood to be a group of people living in a common territory under the same government, choosing to work together to pursue a common purpose. The membership of a civic nation is therefore voluntary, and one major characteristic of civic nationalism is its inclusiveness. In contrast, in ethnic nationalism, a nation is regarded as an organic entity whose membership is largely defined by 'blood', ie genealogy, language, customs and so on. Ethnic nationalism is therefore mystical and exclusive (Smith 1992: 79-84). If the Scots are a people who are proud of the social values that are reflected in their social institutions as opposed to the lineage or some specific cultural markings such as a language, what they pursue is not ugly ethnic nationalism but respectable civic nationalism. This is, of course, favoured by the Scottish elite because this is the only way to dismiss the allegation that nationalism is a dark force, something that is strongly associated with ethnic cleansing and endless violence. Some of the respondents also point out that the moderate and constitutional nature of Scottish nationalism is well received by the EU as a model to counter the threat of ethnic, or 'bad' nationalism. In this instance, the Scottish elite and the Eurocrats share an interest in the promotion of a civic version of nationalism in the modern world. Moreover, the fact that they have a common interest would ensure, conveniently for the Scots, a warm acceptance of the Scots in the EU.

Two points should be made regarding this vision of the Scoto-European relationship. First, this is essentially a moral argument, in which gaining independence or a greater degree of autonomy is considered to be a secondary matter, that is, a means of bringing about a better society. The message of this vision is the assertion of the moral superiority of the Scots over, in particular, the English by showing the Scots to be a people with high moral standards who care for community more than money. They are also prepared to contribute to Europe and the world in the combined effort to encourage social progress. Second, Europe, in this vision, is seen as a moral community with a set of values which counter the aggressive type of capitalism as manifested most notably in England. Another factor is that Europe is not seen as an entity driven by supranationalism to overtake existing national states. Moreover, since sovereignty is not the central issue in this vision, this argument could sit easily even within a 'Federal Europe' so long as it is presented as a necessary condition to bring about social justice across Europe.

Vision Three: Europe as a Substitute for the Empire

Thirdly, there is a view of Europe replacing the British Empire. This raises a question; what was the Empire for Scotland? On a rather abstract level, for a long time it used to offer the Scots a focus or frame of reference for their understanding of the world. The Scots were, in the heyday of the British Empire, a 'mother nation' with the status of a 'race of Empire builders' and the best of the Scottish characteristics were demonstrated (Finlay 1997: 9-15). With the decline of the Empire, however, the Scots need an alternative framework, and Europe can serve as one. On a more practical level, the Empire provided the solution for Scotland's problem of being a poor nation with an educated, talented and motivated population. Scotland used to send out these talented people elsewhere in the world as administrators, engineers, soldiers and so on, thus allowing these individuals to realise their potential and to leave significant footprints all over the world. For example, the historian Charles Dilke pointed out that in the British settlements, 'for every Englishman you meet who has worked himself up to wealth from small beginnings without external aid, you find ten Scotchmen' (Finlay 1997: 28). Scottish participation in colonial India was disproportionate and Henry Dundas, the then President of the Board of Control for India, warned the new Governor of Madras, Sir Archibald Campbell, in 1787:

> It is said with a Scotchman at the head of the Board of Control and a Scotchman at the Government of Madras, all India will soon be in their hands, and that the country of Argyle will be depopulated by the emigration of Campbells to be provided by you at Madras. (Lenman 1981: 82)

It is also estimated that between 1850 and 1939, almost a third of the colonial governor generals were Scots (Finlay 1997: 29). Taking part in the Empire offered Scots a kind of role in the international arena which a small nation like Scotland might not otherwise have played on its own. The EU, in this vision, is presented as a substitute for the Empire because of its guaranteed freedom of movement within the EU territory; the Scots are free to go out and explore the possibility of success in the member countries. What is more, since the EU is a club of independent states, there is no negative implication of imperialism while pursuing one's career within the EU. In this sense, the EU is a politically correct alternative to the Empire which could provide a new stage for Scottish talent; a new frontier and a bigger role to play in the world.

Unlike the old Scottish link with the Continent, memories of Scottish success in the Empire have not been completely buried. Older generations still remember that their history lessons at school were 'all about the Empire and the successful Scots' (GB, economist). There is ample historical experience to assure the respondents, and the Scottish people as a whole, that the Scots would be as successful in Europe as they were in the Empire. According to the respondents, by embracing European integration wholeheartedly, the Scots can revive their tradition of venturing abroad to make the most of their talents, thereby revitalising the Scottish nation whose talent remains dormant at home because of the lack of opportunities. Moreover, the rediscovery of the close Scottish ties with Europe before the Union strongly suggests that the Scots are likely to prosper in the framework of the EU and also gain a reputation for being good Europeans (Smout 1995). It is all the more important for Scots, therefore, to dissociate themselves from the English, who have gained a rather unfavourable reputation in Europe.

Conclusion

The three visions of the Scoto–European relationship identified and analysed so far are nationalist ones. They are of a nationalist nature in the sense that they are concerned with establishing and maintaining the identity and autonomy of the Scottish nation, not because they are the calls for independence for Scotland. For the definition of nationalism, I follow the one put forward by Anthony D. Smith (1992). As already noted, Europe in these visions is not conceived as a manifestation of supranationalism. In the first vision, this aspect of Europe is deliberately ignored to present a coherent argument about the virtue of being pragmatic nationalists. In the remaining two, since sovereignty is not the main issue, not much attention is paid to it. That is why contemporary Scots can be both nationalist and pro-Europe; the supposed contradiction between the two positions does not exist. This does not, however, mean that European integration is not a form of supranationalism; it may well be. But the Scottish nationalists in their pursuit of their goals either refuse to acknowledge the possible supranational nature of Europe or feel little need to attend to it. This reveals more about the multi-faceted nature of nationalism than it does of European integration.

There are two more points to be addressed at this juncture. The first is that what lies at the core of all three visions of the Scoto–European relationship is, in fact, Scotland's relationship with England. This is perhaps logical since these visions are formed and proposed in the overall framework, discussed earlier, which defines Europe as a replacement of England. It is most clearly expressed in the first vision where Europe is considered to be merely a means of achieving the goal of bringing about a more equal relationship with England. Europe in this vision is a tool to redress Scotland's relationship with England which my correspondents believe to be deteriorating fast by bringing Scotland's formal status to a level equal to England. The second vision also addresses Scotland's relationship with England from a moral perspective.

Asserting Scottish moral superiority over the 'greedy' English is a way in which the Scots, a smaller nation, could overcome the English dominance, in every sense, in the UK. In the third vision, the issue is not clearly addressed. Nonetheless, the idea of Europe as a substitute for the British Empire is built on the memory of the golden age of Scotland, in which the Scots were, in many ways, more successful than the English. The third vision is a call for the return to those days when the Scots were equal, and even superior to the English in many respects. This is another way of amending what is perceived as an unequal relationship between Scotland and England.

That these three visions are actually about the Anglo-Scottish relationship is evident by the fact that 'Europe' is left unarticulated in these visions. Each of them addresses a particular aspect of this multi-dimensional idea of 'Europe'; Europe is the institutional framework of the European Union, or a space where social democratic values are respected. Europe is an open, international but orderly market. In other words, Europe is like a canvas onto which the Scottish intelligentsia project their own images of Scotland and Europe. The image of Europe presented in these visions is, therefore, vague enough to allow a lot of room for interpretation.

The second point is the role of history in forming an idea about a nation and maintaining a national identity. Although it is not possible to discuss this in detail, each vision about the relationship between Scotland and Europe is built on certain historical experiences of the Scottish people. Different episodes are mobilised to justify different visions, but the emergence of the seemingly pro-European attitudes among contemporary Scots has been made possible because these visions are based on history. The Scots have a long and well-documented history to which the intelligentsia can refer in order to form a new vision for Scotland. Since Scottish history – in the form of official history and shared memories – is long and eventful, it can provide a considerable amount of evidence for the claims made on behalf of the Scottish nation. For some, for example, the Declaration of Arbroath is proof that the Scots are inherently democratic and that they have been democratic ever since 1320. That the Scottish nation was formed as a result of mixing many peoples, the Picts, Scots, Angles, Norse, Normans, etc, can back up the assertion that the Scots are a mongrel nation and therefore civic and inclusive. History is also open to interpretation. The Reformation, for instance, could be the basis of the case for Scottish individualism, arguably the most prominent feature of nineteenth century Scotland; now in the late twentieth century, it underpins the alleged social democratic character of the Scottish people.

The same mechanism works for the idea of Europe. Because the idea of Europe has evolved a long way, it has acquired a variety of images. Europe is still Christendom to some people; it is synonymous with civilisation for other people; it can mean the land of progress and science or the land of democracy; it has acquired a new face, the free market as the project of European integration has progressed, and it is now also the land of social democratic values. (For the evolution of the idea of Europe, see Delanty 1995 and Wilson and Dussen 1995). Europeans are, therefore, able to select a face of Europe and attach a particular meaning to it depending on the circumstances in which they find themselves.

The wealth of images of both Scotland and Europe has enabled the Scottish intelligentsia to articulate a new identity for the Scots which retains a sense of continuity and stability precisely because it is based on history. National identity, as with personal identity, is not static and has to adapt to changing circumstances. In order for it to function properly as an identity, however, it needs to provide a sense of continuity. In this, the Scots are fortunate in that they have a large depository of historical episodes which can provide all kinds of evidence in support of new ideas about themselves. The Scots are, therefore, well-placed to maintain their national identity successfully in this changing world and the pro-European stance of contemporary Scots can be understood as a demonstration of this.

Appendix

The 1979 and 1997 Referenda Results

(a) 1979 Referendum

Turnout: 62.9%	'Yes' vote	'No' vote
% of the vote cast	51.6	48.4
% of electorate	32.9	30.8

Source: James Mitchell (1996: 323).

(b) 1997 Referendum

Turnout: 60.4%	Scottish Parliament	Tax-raising powers
% of the vote cast	74.3	63.5
% of electorate	44.8	38.4

Source: The Economist, 20 September 1997.

References

Allan D 1993 Virtue, Learning and the Scottish Enlightenment. Edinburgh, Edinburgh University Press

Ascherson N 1993 Introduction. In: Prince G (ed) A Window on Europe: The Lothian European Lectures 1992. Edinburgh, Canongate, pp. xix – xxvii

Broadie A 1990 The Tradition of Scottish Philosophy. Edinburgh, Polygon

Clements A, et al 1996 Restless Nation. Edinburgh, Mainstream Publishing

Davie G 1961 The Democratic Intellect. Edinburgh, Edinburgh University Press

Davie G 1986 The Crisis of the Democratic Intellect. Edinburgh, Polygon

Delanty G 1995 Inventing Europe: Idea, Identity, Reality. Basingstoke, Macmillan

Finlay R J 1997 A Partnership for Good?: Scottish Politics and the Union since 1880. Edinburgh, John Donald Publishing

Ichijo A 1998 Scottish Nationalism and Identity in the Age of European Integration. Unpublished PhD thesis, University of London

Lenman B 1981 Integration, Enlightenment, and Industrialisation: Scotland 1746-1832. London, Edward Arnold

Lynch M 1992 Scotland: A New History. London, Pimlico

Massie A 1995 'Beautiful old union house is not beyond repair'. The Scotsman, 31 October 1995

Miller W 1981 The End of British Politics? Oxford, Clarendon Press

Mitchell J 1996 Strategies for Self-Government: The Campaign for a Scottish Parliament. Edinburgh, Polygon

Mitchell J, Bennie L 1995 Thatchersim and the Scottish Question. In: British Election and Politics Yearbook 1995. London, Frank Cass

Scott P 1992 Scotland in Europe: A Dialogue with a Sceptical Friend. Edinburgh, Cannogate

Scottish Constitutional Convention 1995 Scotland's Parliament, Scotland's Rights. Edinburgh, Scottish Constitutional Convention

Shoupe C A 1995 'Our kind of music': Accordion and Fiddle clubs and the Scottish dance tradition. Scotlands, Vol. 2, No. 2, pp. 8–104

Sillars J 1986 Scotland: The Case for Optimism. Edinburgh, Polygon

Smith A D 1991 National Identity. Harmondsworth, Essex, Penguin

Smout T C 1995 The culture of migration: Scots as Europeans 1500 - 1800. Paper presented at the 'Scottish Dimensions' Conference, at Ruskin College, Oxford, 24-6 March 1995

Walker A L 1994 The Revival of the Democratic Intellect. Edinburgh, Polygon

Wilson K, van der Dussen J (eds) 1995 The History of the Idea of Europe (Revised edition). Milton Keynes, Open University and London, Routledge

Section II

Introduction

Narratives of Nation and Identity

Mick Smith

Despite their different approaches and arguments, the four papers composing this section share a common concern with what might prosaically be termed 'storytelling'. The stories they attend to take different textual forms, as film, iconography or historiography, and make different truth claims, presenting themselves as 'fact' or 'fiction', or sometimes as something 'in between'. But all are retold and reviewed here because of what they have to say about Scotland's past, present and future as a nation and the elusive possibilities of Scottish identity.

In the first paper, Tim Edensor takes a controversial look at William Wallace's checkered career as an icon of Scottish popular culture, a career culminating in the recent hype of the Hollywood epic *Braveheart* and the rash of representations, exhibitions, and theatrical performances that followed in its wake. He rebuts the film's critics whom, he argues, try to set themselves up as guardians of Scottish culture and/or historical accuracy. Depending upon their political persuasion these critics have reviled *Braveheart* as either mere entertainment or as mass exploitation, as representing the dumbing-down and diminution of Scottish 'culture with a capital "C"', or producing a demeaning misrepresentation of 'genuine' folk culture. But these critics have, Edensor argues, missed the point. Where Wallace is concerned, the myth long ago replaced the man, and 'no amount of historical research can invalidate' his constantly shifting status in the popular imagination.

While Edensor's article focuses almost exclusively on William Wallace his defence of *Braveheart* is also a defence of the resilience and diversity of Scottish popular culture in general. Edensor is surely right about the impossibility and undesirability of fixing an essential and uncontestable reading of the past, a solitary truth that could somehow claim to provide the foundation of a unified

Scottish culture and identity. The imposition of such an exclusive vision would be indicative of a repressive and intolerant version of nationalism. A living culture with a constantly changing dynamic is inevitably marked by a diversity of interpretations that seek to resist cultural homogenisation through a 'dialogic environment where Scots negotiate with each other'.

As evidence of this dynamic, Edensor examines the myriad representations of Wallace in the 'Scotland's Liberator' exhibition held in Stirling's Smith Art Gallery during 1997. Here, amongst the pictures, souvenirs and ephemera of past generations he finds illustrations of the ways in which each age makes Wallace in its own image and in order to serve its own interests. This constant reworking of myth in everyday life is indicative of popular culture as a practice that, more than any other operates to constitute an imaginary community. *Braveheart* is only the latest, and certainly not the last attempt to alter and augment the Wallace myth, reinvigorating it by awarding it a contemporary relevance.

Edensor's paper raises some fascinating questions about the relationship between identity and popular culture, although it is inevitable, given his polemical purpose, and the limitations of a short article that some questions are left hanging. For example, Edensor only touches briefly on such topics as why the anti-English sentimentalism of *Braveheart*, its mixture of the mawkish and the macho, seems to have struck such a popular note in the 1990s. There is also the question of the degree to which contemporary popular culture actually expresses the experiences of the Scottish populace rather than reflecting the slick global commercialism of America's dream-factory.

Perhaps more importantly, Edensor's article also raises aesthetic and ethical questions, exemplified in his courageous defence of the (execrable) new statue at the bottom of Stirling's Wallace monument. The statue, holding a severed and dripping head in one hand, bears the unmistakable features of Mel Gibson, looking for all the world like a medieval Mad Max gone bad. It would take a braver man than me to argue that all objections to this 'representation' are really based on a 'desire to maintain purified images of Scottishness rather than the value of the work'. Edensor, however, carries his argument with panache. And it must be admitted that the recent vandalism of the statue, requiring the installation of metal railings for its protection, is more likely to attest to its ability to cause offence to intolerant nationalist sentiments than its upsetting the artistic integrity of Stirling's populace.

Leaving aesthetics aside, statue and film are not just accused of 'cultural mediocrity' but of 'cultural mendacity' and arguments about truth will, I think, prove to be central to the reception of Edensor's paper. While stories might be constantly remade, one might argue that the power of myths to move us still lies in their claim to encapsulate and express something essential and real about our origins as well as our current identities, a point brought home to me by a bouquet of flowers left at the foot of Wallace's/Gibson's new statue. This bore an inscription claiming that those who had placed it there were now ashamed to be English since, 'we had not realised how badly we had behaved until we saw the film'!

It is unlikely that the Scottish popular imagination would even recall, let alone lionise Wallace, had he not, in reality, defeated the English at Stirling Bridge. And, unless one accepts, as Edensor explicitly does not, that we now live in a state of Baudrillardian hyper-reality, then the question of who Wallace really was and what he actually did, ie of historical accuracy, surely remains a valid area of contention. One might argue that the role of myth, no less than history, is not just to create contemporary consanguinities and 'imagined communities' but to preserve a kind of 'truth' about what happened in other times and other places. Myth, too, entails an ethical relation to a past, recognising it as something 'beyond our power or remit to alter'. It preserves and sustains its particular truths even in the face of their unpalatable differences from our own age. This is a far cry from acquiring, appropriating and altering (his)stories wholesale, Hollywood style, for economic gain. In this sense, Edensor's paper opens up an entire field of debate about memory and forgetting, past and present, and the power and promise of Scottish popular culture. His paper undoubtedly represents only an initial skirmish in what promises to be a long battle.

The question of ethics emerges again in Eleanor Bell's article, this time in the setting of the contemporary Scottish novel. Like Edensor, she is motivated by a wish to combat those restrictive readings of nationhood and identity that seek to impose a false unity on a complex question. Ethics, for Bell, is understood in terms of a self-reflexive concern with estrangement and the processes that produce it. All too often nationhood can be formulated in a manner that seeks to define and circumscribe who belongs and who does not. It constructs inclusive boundaries that inevitably have the effect of excluding those now defined as 'other' from text, tradition and territory. Bell thus wants to distinguish between those authors who create a space for multiple interpretations of belonging and those that seek to pin down and fix the contours of a narrative's meaning. The former, ethical, relation is described in Homi Bhabha's terms, as one that sustains an 'incomplete signification' that, rather than imposing a specific textual taxonomy with which one is forced to identify, allows room for multiple identities to emerge and find themselves. In this way boundaries are transformed into 'in-between' places. Bell cleverly counter-poses the work of A L Kennedy and Alasdair Gray in order to elucidate her thesis with respect to Scotland's own boundaries and identities.

Kirsten Stirling's paper recuperates the debate over 'truth' and 'fiction' sparked by Edensor and Bell's discussion of the role of modern literature in 'writing the map of Scotland'. Maps are usually thought of as accurate scientific representations of geographic realities, determinate delineations of a region's topography, but they are also, inevitably, products of a contentious human history. The borders and territories they depict are, in this latter sense, arbitrary or 'fictional' constructs of symbolic and political, rather than 'scientific', importance. Stirling examines the spatial metaphorics employed by writers as varied as Hugh MacDiarmid, Alasdair Gray, and Iain Banks, claiming that their writings deliberately conflate the dichotomy between 'geographical reality' and 'imagined community', writing a kind of science/fiction. This is perhaps especially apposite in Iain (M) Banks' case, given his dual identities as a writer of both sci-fi and mainstream novels. However, Stirling argues that, despite their differences, all of these writers employ scientific rhetorics of one kind or another, whether cosmological, geological or evolutionary, in order to circumscribe their own or their characters' conceptions of Scottishness. She asks whether, given the recent political changes, these science/fictional maps of Scotland might be indicative of the 'shape of things to come'.

Kirsti Wishart continues this literary vein, examining the work of R B Cunninghame Graham, an unjustifiably neglected figure in the canon of Scottish writing. Graham might himself be considered to occupy an 'in-between' space, a liminal position that is, at least in part, the result of his self-imposed exile during his frequent travels. Graham was consistently critical of the colonial presuppositions of his contemporaries and equally uncompromising in his attacks on the sentimentalism of the popular kailyard tradition. In this way, his writings too seek to maintain an ethical relation to the cultures of both his Scottish homeland and his temporarily adopted residences abroad. He writes against all 'distorting image(s), the ways in which myth conceals reality and so creates a limited interpretation of the cultural life' of others. He resolutely refused to revile or reduce the cultures of others by comparing them unfavourably to his own, aware as he was of Scottish society's own faults. Through a judicious selection from his oeuvre and insightful commentary on key texts Wishart makes a compelling case for regarding Graham as an exemplar of 'the possibility of a form of nationalism that does not carry the negative connotations' of exclusion. In Graham's own words, 'to see things plainly, you have to cross a frontier'.

It seems then that the authors share more than a concern with story-telling since they all agree on the necessity to cross borders in order to fully understand Scotland's boundaries and identities. All agree that the present can only be understood in relation to stories told about the past and narratives of nation and identity need to be contextualised in terms of Scotland's wider geographic, political and cultural situation. But the other striking similarity between these papers is the authors' optimism about the future, an optimism based largely on the very diversity of interpretations, claims and counter-claims that they discover. All regard this variety of readings as indicative of a vibrant and pluralistic culture in debate with itself and others and willing to celebrate difference rather than impose a homogenous and exclusive kind of nationalism. In this sense, Scotland might be said to be a 'never ending story', told and retold by successive generations.

Scottish Popular Culture: Embarrassment or Asset? The Uses and Meanings of William Wallace

Tim Edensor

In this chapter I show how a popular, mythic icon, William Wallace, continues to be used in contesting and changing ways, in order to take issue with arguments which assert that Scottish popular culture is damned by embarrassing stereotypes. Fretting over Scottish television dramas and films, popular iconography and commodities, journalists and intellectuals, bolstered by their cultural capital, act as arbiters of taste in distinguishing between 'progressive' cultural products and practices, and those which stain Scotland's image and promote a 'sense of inferiority'. *Rab C. Nesbit*, tartan and tourist products are singled out to epitomise some deep-seated Scottish deficiency. It is argued that to achieve a 'mature' or 'modern' national identity, these dismal trappings of Scottishness – kitsch tartan souvenirs, hard men, romantic scenery and whimsical locals – need to be replaced by more 'contemporary' representations.

For instance, Tom Nairn laments the 'deformed' national identity evoked by an excessively kitsch Scottish popular culture. Summoning up militarism, Clydesideism, and romanticism, he reserves especial venom for the 'tartan monster', that 'prodigious array of kitsch symbols, slogans, ornaments, banners, war-cries, knick-knacks, music-hall heroes, icons, conventional sayings and sentiments...which have for so long resolutely defended the name of "Scotland" to the world' (1977, 162). In *Scotch Reels* (1982), Colin McArthur et al cry for more 'progressive versions' of Scottishness to be disseminated. McArthur argues that 'the melange of images, characters and motifs consuming tartanry and Kailyard' that feature in films about Scotland provide the frame-work within which Scots continue to imagine themselves, interpolating Scots with a sense of their own inferiority and stifling attempts to produce alternative images and stories (McArthur 1982:40). Cairns Craig asserts that these clichés 'need to acquire a new historical significance before they can be released into the onward flow of the present from the frozen worlds of their myths of historical irrelevance' (Craig 1982:15). And in 1994, McArthur was still moaning that Scotland seems destined to continually fulfil its role as 'the Romantic dream landscape par excellence' (McArthur 1994:104).

These arguments reveal a distrust of popular culture, which is captured by historian T C Smout:

> In popular culture, Scottish history appears as the stuff of heritage industry, colourful and episodic, but basically not serious. It is a poor foundation on which to identify a Scottish nation with a confident and empowered Scottish state (Smout 1994:109).

This disdain is akin to that expressed by Arnold, Leavis, Eliot and other cultural guardians, who claim they can distinguish between 'good' and 'bad' culture. Or perhaps given the leftist orientation of many Scottish intellectuals, such contempt reflects a Frankfurtian or Althusserian view of popular culture as antithetical to revolutionary ideals and aims. These various schools of thought believe that the academic is able to reveal which elements of Culture are 'authentic', nurturing and 'progressive'. Culture here is often high culture, culture with a capital 'C' or alternatively is nostalgically conceived as a form of 'authentic folk culture' as opposed to the kind of everyday creativity found in Scottish popular cultural forms and practices. Yet without denying the need for progressive critiques and historical scholarship to inform readings of texts and icons, as far as national identity is concerned, it is surely through popular culture that a sense of commonality is continually reproduced. Popular cultural symbols, everyday cultural practices and products are precisely what constitute an imagined community, tying people together in a collectivity through quotidian activities.

These anxieties have been rekindled by the realease of the film *Braveheart*, which has been both exceptionally popular in Scotland and at the same time subject to heated critique (Edensor 1997b). Commentators holding different political opinions castigate the film for its recursive stereotyping of Scotland and Scottishness, especially around issues of historical authenticity, anti-English sentiment and military triumphalism. Allegedly, these qualities ought not to be celebrated by a nation which presents itself as possessing a progressive and mature political culture, supposedly ready to attain independence/autonomy from the United Kingdom. Audrey Gillan argued that *Braveheart:*

> encouraged Scotland's lack of knowledge about itself. Greedy for confirmation as a romantically wild nation, our gluttony for feeding on myth and heathery legend reaches worrying proportions when it affects the entire socio-political consciousness of a nation (Audrey Gillan, *Scotland on Sunday,* 16/9/95).

Yet whatever the politics and poetics of the movie, however much experts declaim about historical inaccuracies, as Finlay asserts 'the continuing historical significance of Wallace lies not so much in the man but in the myth' (Finlay 1997:118). Whilst authenticity is one of the key themes by which value is attributed in popular culture as well as in the academic world, Wallace, along with Robert Burns, Mary Queen of Scots, Robert Bruce, Rob Roy, the debacle of Culloden, are 'complex icons of cultural, social and political belief' which no amount of historical research can invalidate (Finlay 1997:123).

Whilst they may articulate worthy sentiments against nationalistic banality and hysteria, these responses to *Braveheart* also indicate concerns about the 'dumbing down' imposed by 'Americanisation' or 'cultural imperialism'. It is true that Hollywood searches the globe for mythic figures and tales to repackage for a global market. According to German 'independent' film-maker Edgar Reitz, Hollywood has 'taken narrative possession of our past' (Morley and Robins 1995:93). Likewise, the selling of Scotland abroad to attract tourists tends to rely on representations which slip into 'the international image markets as tradable symbolic goods' (Caughie 1990:14). Womack has commented that:

> all Scots wear tartan, are devoted to bagpipe music, and are moved by the spirit of clanship... all these libels live on as items in the Scottish tourist package of the Twentieth century (Womack 1987:25).

Of course, the tourist industry does reproduce such signifiers, and it is not coincidental that *Braveheart* has been used to advertise the attractions of Stirling, yet the reception and use by Scots of symbolic material need not denote inferiority or false consciousness. For while Scotland may well be consumed abroad as a rather static and stereotypical set of signs, in Scotland itself, the reception of such global cultural forms occurs in a quite different cultural context. For the pre-existing traditions and the popularity of William Wallace ensure that they are repatriated, feeding into, complementing and adding allure to the diverse ways in which Wallace is used, rather than replacing these understandings with some standardised image. By implying that films, narratives and artefacts are encoded with dominant messages which are simply and consensually decoded, the cultural arbiters miss the contradiction and ambivalence in and across the discourses about Scotland and the diverse ways in which representations of myths and archetypes are reclaimed and recycled.

Such icons are complex and flexible resources. Heroes such as Wallace are typically incorporated into nationalist narratives to suggest continuity between past and present, and provide exemplary feats, characters and collectivities that can be summoned in appeals to future national achievement or self-determination. But they are shorthand metaphors or 'condensation symbols' (Cohen 1985:102), which are ceaselessly (re) appropriated by a wide range of contesting groups to express diverse meanings and points of identification.

Although he continues to argue for the replacement of recursive cultural forms with progressive versions, Colin McArthur does cautiously admit that 'images do not have intrinsic, essential, unchanging meanings' and draws upon Guilanotti's account of how Scottish fans in Italia '90 creatively used tartan to communicate varied meanings. (1993:104). The demands for 'representativeness' or 'progressiveness' place an unreasonable burden upon Scottish popular forms.

In order to highlight this complexity, I want to look at an exceptional and successful exhibition held in the Smith Art Gallery, Stirling, in 1997, *Scotland's Liberator*, to demonstrate how William Wallace has been variously used to enchant different kinds of politics and identities. I will focus on some of the representations of the figure and show how artefacts and symbols of Wallace have been utilised in a range of rituals and performances. These forms and practices reveal that the production of Wallace is everyday, contextual and ongoing.

Wallace provides a particularly apt example since many versions of his story feature many of the apparently negative themes through which Scotland is perceived, namely militarism, hyper-masculinity, tartan and kilts, elegiaism and loss. But Wallace is also an interesting icon because he has been used for a range of purposes, not only as a proto-nationalist, but also as the embodiment of bourgeois qualities of self-sacrifice, ability, civic duty and individualism; and as a socialist, a freedom fighter who sought to cast off feudal barons (Finlay 1997, Edensor 1997a).

Scotland's Liberator

In 1997, *Scotland's Liberator*, an exhibition at the Smith Art Gallery and Museum in Stirling, was organised to coincide with the 700th anniversary of the Battle of Stirling Bridge and capitalise on the upsurge of interest in Wallace raised by the movie *Braveheart*. The exhibition gathered various artefacts, works of art, texts, videos, and details of rituals and landscapes that have been inspired by Wallace, to convey his symbolic significance in Scottish art, literature and popular culture over the centuries. The exhibition attracted record numbers of visitors to the gallery.

Scotland's Liberator reveals the extraordinary proliferation of visual representations of Wallace, ranging from the medieval to the contemporary. Although generally informed by notions about how a masculine hero ought to look, there is no single image of Wallace that predominates. Instead there are many Wallaces – a rugged swordsman, an elegant statesman, a neo-classical figure in perfect proportion – differently garbed, some emphasising his body and his physicality, others paying attention to his humble clothing to conjure up a 'man of the people'. Stylistically and ideologically, these depictions epitomise the fluidity of Wallace as a meaningful character. Wallace has been painted in distinct metaphorical and allegorical ways to represent a range of causes and identities, in ancient and contemporary sculptures, paintings and engravings.

Besides these pictorial representations are photographs of some of the numerous statues dedicated to Wallace, in Scotland and beyond. Memoryscapes comprise 'archaeological metaphors' built into the landscape to provide a stage for organising a relationship with the past (Lowenthal 1985:xxiii). Attempts to delineate circumscribed forms of remembering are doomed by the vagaries of style which render earlier forms of symbolic transmission difficult to translate (Warner 1993).

In Stirling itself, there are several Wallaces, all very different in style. The familiar statue on the Athenaeum in Stirling, the figure at the Wallace Monument, and the form of the fierce, thickset warrior looming through the trees at Dryburgh in woodland adjacent to the River Tweed embody contrasting characteristics. And the muscle-bound Wallace in Aberdeen, the more classical model at Edinburgh Castle and those at Lanark and Brechin are all markedly different. The Wallace Monument testifies to the taste, values and priorities of mid-nineteenth century unionism (Edensor 1997a, Finlay 1997). The associated busts in the Hall of Heroes on the second floor of the memorial are men – there are no heroines – who were chosen to reflect the qualities of heroism which emerged out of nineteenth century romantic nationalism and bourgeois ideology. Their presence lends allure to the middle-class values of thrift, industry, religious devotion, enterprise and invention, qualities which were also imagined to be embodied in Wallace himself.

The recent unveiling of a 13 foot statue of Wallace at the foot of the Abbey Craig in Stirling, was controversially constructed in the likeness of Mel Gibson. A stonemason, Tom Church, inspired by the film, and convalescing after heart surgery, saw the rise of Wallace and the subsequent emergence of an independent Scotland as a metaphor for his own physical regeneration. The placing of the statue led to accusations of 'cultural mediocrity' and the diminution of a great figure by commercial and banal aesthetics. The *Stirling Observer* (September 10, 1997) opined that the memory of Wallace was being exploited, and a local SNP councillor declared that the statue would 'detract from the *true*, very important history which the monument stands for' (my italics). The statue has been defended by the marketing manager of the local tourist board on the grounds that it is this image of Mel Gibson that most people now associate with Wallace and it will attract tourists, and hence create jobs. Fears about the trivialisation of Scottishness are articulated in the notion that a filmic image is not conceived as a fitting form for an heroic piece of sculpture. Rather than interpreting the work as an interesting reworking and repatriation of a myth, critics seek recourse in the reified conventions of monumental sculpture, failing to acknowledge wider cultural processes and influences. For the sculpture is designed to appeal to contemporary popular responses to the film and the revalorisation of Wallace, rather than following some preconceived notion of commemorative art. But since there are so many other, more conventional, monumental representations of Wallace, it is curious that a threat is perceived. This statue seems to have crossed the boundaries between vernacular art and public sculpture, and the resulting consternation says more about the desire to maintain purified images of Scottishness than the value of the work.

In addition to these sculptural representations, images of Wallace are also found in objects of quotidian cultural production. The exhibition includes small figurines, models of the Battle of Stirling Bridge, and a marzipan piece of Wallace in combat with an English adversary. The inclusion of these popular creations signifies that Wallace is considered a suitable emblematic topic in the unheralded domestic art of thousands of model-makers, amateur artists, and embroiderers. As a popular motif in the 'grounded aesthetics' (Willis 1990) of everyday creativity, Wallace circulates through the artefacts of house-hold production, demonstrating that he is not merely passively consumed. Individual interpretations of Wallace are materialised, creators must reflect upon his significance and choose how to portray him.

The exhibition also includes samples of the vast range of ephemeral commercial products – souvenirs and trinkets that are part of the selling of tourist attractions and commemorative occasions. Commodities such as ash-trays, plates, plaques, postcards, chess pieces, badges, pens and a host of other items are embossed with Wallace's image. These souvenirs are again stamped by the aesthetic conventions of their age, but are so diverse in form that they lend an historical perspective to the material production of themed artefacts. The fluid process by which Wallace is represented is highlighted, even in what might be supposed to be a banal form of aesthetic manufacture. The recent trading of Wallace ephemera at tourist venues has received a fillip with the commercial success of *Braveheart* and a new series of tea-towels, T-shirts and mugs are being produced according to contemporary aesthetic and commercial criteria.

Some cultural commentators espouse a Baudrillardian hypothesis which assumes that we have reached some end point in the development of consumerism whereby the pure sign-value of things in a hyper-real present evaporates all meanings and contexts. However, I prefer to imagine that present day Wallace commodities – the images and objects produced out of *Braveheart* – will produce a similar glow of nostalgia and interest as the nineteenth century relics of Wallace mania displayed in the exhibition. Whilst the purchasing of souvenirs is frequently sneered at, the use and interpretation of such artefacts cannot be predicted. Stewart (1993:132–51) remarks that the collection of souvenirs involves the authentication of the tourist's visit, but also domesticates the spectacular, through taking home a representation which is 'appropriated within the privatised view of the individual subject', and rendered enclosable and thus possessed by the body (1993:138). This reinforces a relationship between collector and the symbolic subject of the souvenir, and furthermore, marks an event that is 'reportable', which, told as a biographical episode of identification, a souvenir of a visit or participation in an occasion can be situated within a larger narrative of belonging, melding individual and collective identity.

I do not want to discuss the politics of displaying artefacts in a museum although the selection of items featured in *Scotland's Liberator* is motivated by particular imperatives – as no doubt was the original decision not to feature Wallace-related material in the new National Museum of Scotland. Whilst the heritage industry undoubtedly attempts to 'fix history' (Crang 1994:341–2) in certain instances, and the emplacement of artefacts in a national exhibitionary complex conveys a particular kind of authoritative value, the use of symbolic sites, and the souvenirs which are purchased there are open to wide interpretative scope by tourists. The very fact that such things are exhibited in a museum indicates that their status as commodities does not stamp their character forever. As Appadurai (1986:13) has shown, a thing can 'move in and out of the commodity state'. As objects of interest in *Scotland's Liberator*, they feed back into the pool of resources that signify Wallace, contrasting with some and chiming with others in an intertextual circulation of signs and things.

In addition to these memorabilia, the name and image of Wallace is also used to lend allure to a variety of commercial interests. Wallace/*Braveheart* has recently been used to sell houses, a new shopping centre in Stirling and the Scottish National Party. Maclays, the sponsors of *Scotland's Liberator*, have relaunched their *Wallace Pale Ale* after a hiatus of several decades. In addition to these commercial uses, Wallace's likeness adds gravitas to official local documents, such as school certificates, situating the recipient in place by confirming the symbolic importance of Stirling.

A further level of representation is demonstrated by a map identifying numerous elements within the landscape; forests, trees, lakes, summits, cairns and caves, which are associated with Wallace. At a local level, it seems that over the centuries there have been attempts to translate enduring mythic episodes from the life of Wallace into local contexts so that stories remain remembered and materialised in the landscape. The profusion of Wallace's Crags and Wallace's Caves suggests that it is unlikely that a lowland Scot such as Wallace would have covered such a vast area of Scotland during his military campaigns. And yet as a national hero, Wallace has been represented and materialised by local geographical features, each testifying to a unique local myth.

This diversity of representations means that nowhere is there a fixing of the image of Wallace. It may be that Mel Gibson is the most conspicuous Wallace at the moment but he will surely be absorbed back into the mass of other representations, none of which will necessarily predominate. This proliferation prevents the reification of a single image which signifies the views of the powerful or freezes value. Instead, the various representations show that Wallace has been a figure upon whom diverse and contesting meanings and messages can be hung. His flexibility as myth is evinced in that distinct groups, from different eras, for various occasions and espousing divergent causes, have preserved Wallace's iconic importance but attributed miscellaneous cultural values to him. The fact that Wallace is used to charm diverse identities and objectives, means that the interpretation and consumption of these representations cannot be taken for granted. Furthermore, a confrontation with this proliferation of images thwarts a fixing upon any 'definitive' representation. As our eyes shift across the different portrayals, we confront a range of characteristics and qualities embodied in these different sculptures and paintings which make him elusive, and merge attributes to create temporary, imaginary aggregates of Wallace.

The notion of performance can be used to identify everyday rituals, commemorative occasions and activities such as visiting tourist centres, which are dramas performed at particular places by a range of actors (Edensor 1998). *Scotland's Liberator* also reveals that there are many performances shaped around Wallace, from commemorative occasions and political rituals to staged dramas. Wallace has been used in these performances to express and transmit meanings and feelings, reinforcing a link between participant, site and the figure celebrated. I have already alluded to the ways in which performances may be shaped around using and interpreting Wallace: through the granting of certificates and qualifications, through the purchase of tourist souvenirs, and also through the perusal of museum displays. In addition, the exhibition includes a theatrical area in which imaginative dramas can be enacted by visitors in the form of a wooden simulacra of Stirling Bridge. There is also a space for artwork and dressing-up in period costumes, so that visitors, usually children, can take on characters and act out medieval battles.

The exhibition highlights a number of current rituals associated with Wallace including the tourist pilgrimage to the Wallace Monument and the more emotionally charged, nationalist Wallace Day march at Elderslie. Also identified are particular ways in which Wallace has been the centre of various popular rituals through history. Celebrations and rituals may be typified by the incorporating ceremonies described by Connerton (1989) where prescribed movements and procedures discipline bodies to enact delineated performances (Edensor 1997a). In these cases, the attempts to fix meaning and inscribe the identity of the participants depends on the rehearsal and exact replication of a set of manoeuvres. A good example is the ritual enacted by the Free Colliers of Falkirk. The exhibition includes a video of the march and information about how Wallace is used to signify the struggle of the original colliers, who were in servitude in the eighteenth century, becoming a talismanic figurehead of their quest for freedom. An annual march takes place on the first Saturday in August when the colliers walk to a Wallace memorial they erected in 1810 to lay wreaths and make speeches. This use of artefacts both materialises the significance of the event and establishes a relationship between symbolic objects and those who use them. The use of music, through a pipe band, and a flag-waving display, produces an affective ceremony which ties participants together and expresses the emotive appeal of both the colliers' struggle, and by association, reinforces the significance of Wallace. This affective alliance is strengthened by the colliers marching with their pinkies interlinked.

However, performances may also be more carnivalesque occasions when bodily expression, drinking and conviviality predominate (Edensor 1997a). An example of the latter is the guising at hogmany, where typically, four or more guisers go from house to house, enacting a playlet called 'Galatians'. Formerly popular throughout Scotland but now confined to Biggar,

Lanarkshire, these short dramas always featured Wallace as the hero who, with supernatural strength, slays the villain of the piece. With Wallace at the centre of an ever-changing cast of characters, the performance of these short vernacular dramas attests to the dynamic ways in which various symbolic elements are creatively combined and recombined by participants, highlighting the flexibility of powerful myths which can be appropriated and adapted for various purposes. These performances are typified by a high degree of improvisation and the metaphorical role of Wallace is continually interpreted anew.

Besides these ceremonies, the exhibition also highlights staged dramatic productions. As part of the commemoration of the 700th anniversary of the Battle of Stirling Bridge, two recent dramas were staged in Stirling. A large-scale Battle of Stirling Bridge play was performed on the Castle esplanade in September 1997. Featuring a 200-strong cast, performing in front of an audience of 2000, the play ended with a singing of *Scots Wha Hae* and a fireworks display. Besides spectacular and highly choreographed battle scenes, there was much music and dance. This ambitious event was partly devised for a tourist audience but made few concessions to a 'balanced' view, presenting Wallace as an unadulterated hero. Nevertheless, the aesthetics of the play were commensurate with the imperative to produce an impressive spectacle. Another small ritual commemorated the Battle with 150 marchers walking from Dundee to Stirling, culminating in the planting of a special Wallace Oak tree by descendants of participants in the original battle.

A more challenging and politically engaged drama, *Wallace's Women*, was performed at Lanark and the Smith Gallery in October, 1997, by Castlegate Repertory Theatre, and featured in the 1998 Edinburgh Festival Fringe programme. The play confronts the gendered nature of national(ist) myths by exploring the role of the women alluded to in versions of the Wallace legend. The prominence of military cunning and derring-do in the story of Wallace is here supplemented by an attempt to conjure up aspects of the myth from women's perspective. The play, performed by an all-female cast, tells the story of Marion Bradefute, Wallace's lover, and other women mentioned in Blind Harry's *Acts and Deeds of William Wallace*, including his mother Lady Margaret Wallace, Queen Yolande, Marion's nurse Elspeth and her daughter, Bridget. The reinstating of these characters into the myth reverses the masculinised characteristics of the tale and imagines a medieval women's culture which blends Christian and Celtic belief in festivities, pagan cures and the influence of the environment. Although quite raw in parts, the drama was an ambitious attempt to critique the invisibilisation of women in the national story and restore a sense of their participation in great national events.

The play decentres the prominence of Christianity in most versions of the Wallace myth, and brings out a ribald and powerful femininity at variance to the stereotypical images of fey highland maidens. The women share a far from passive sexuality and are enthusiastic consumers of drink and drugs, which are used in the wild pagan celebrations in which they participate. *Wallace's Women* then, represents a struggle which takes place inside the popular myth of Wallace, which tries to deconstruct its gendered formation, and creatively uses the story to interrogate notions of Scottishness, masculinity and femininity, and the telling of history. The props for the play and the metaphors used allude to the symbols of pagan belief and ritual, with Wallace objectified as a disembodied dummy vested with magical significance in the ritual of Beltane.

This critical engagement with the myth is only the latest in a long line of political attempts to use Wallace in different metaphorical ways to lend credence to a cause, and movements have frequently engaged in dramatic performances and ceremonies which involve the icon, to spread their message. The exhibition highlights how the political campaigns of many nationalist movements abroad have dramatically used Wallace as a metaphor for national liberation and key figures in such crusades have been compared to him. Moreover, Chartists have marched under his banner, suffragettes have used his name, and socialists have claimed him as a common-born fighter for the rights of the oppressed. Even unionists have identified him as the originator of the United Kingdom (Finlay 1997).

As an example of popular cinema, *Braveheart* is only one of the many ways in which the story of William Wallace has been dramatised, whether in vernacular rituals, incorporating commemorations, political campaigns, and theatrical productions. The significant point is that these dramas utilise the mythical, metaphorical power of Wallace to enchant their own concerns. And all these performances are imprinted by the identities of the participants, their bodies, their passions and their beliefs.

Elspeth King makes the point that *Braveheart* is substantially drawn from Blind Harry's epic (King 1998: 8–9), itself woven together out of the local myths about Wallace that Harry collected during his journeys around Scotland. This work, the *Acts and Deeds of William Wallace,* is exemplary in that like all narratives about Wallace, it is constituted out of many strands. The recent development of a Wallace industry has seen the publication of a number of books that tell the story of his heroic deeds, varying from the scholarly to the popular, and yet all these tellers of the myth, whether poets, historians, novelists or film-makers, plunder from, and add to, the pool of cultural resources which surround Wallace. It becomes apparent that like the performances discussed above, such stories are important not only with regard to their claims to veracity but in terms of what they say about the teller and how they address contemporary fears and concerns. The profusion of Wallace dramas and narratives talk back to each other, are recycled and indicate the ongoing production of Wallace. And they are never static, are never performed in exactly the same manner, but are manipulated to gain the ear of the relevant audience and moulded to the circumstances in which they are told. Stories must shift to incorporate current considerations and morals, and even then they cannot anticipate how they will be received by listeners and viewers.

The continuous cultural production and consumption of Wallace should cause us to reflect again upon the significance of *Braveheart* and deflect the shrill panic of many commentators who were quick to detect embarrassing and stereotypical signs of Scottishness. In fact, *Braveheart* is merely a reworking of elements of the Wallace myth, albeit set in the more global form of cinema, using and supplementing existing narratives, dramatic portrayals and images.

Conclusion

Whilst it is wise to be wary of the dangers of cultural populism, I have shown, by using the cultural production and consumption of Wallace highlighted in the *Scotland's Liberator* exhibition, that Scottish popular culture is neither to be feared nor despised. I do not want to argue complacently that forms of capitalist production are not reproducing 'serial monotony'

(Harvey 1989: 295) in some instances, nor that critique of cultural forms is unnecessary, but it is important to consider the context in which cultural products are consumed and interpreted. For it is a feature of everyday cultural production that popular symbols and myths are reworked into contemporary concerns, and are ideologically 'chameleon', flexible discursive forms which enable wide scope for interpretation (Samuel and Thompson 1990: 3). The selection of mythic elements and their emplotment within larger narratives means that groups can transmit contrasting ideological messages by using the rallying power of particularly symbolic figures. Thus, the legend of Wallace is constantly reworked to provide antecedence and continuity to a diverse range of identities and political objectives (Tilly 1994: 247). And the fact that little is actually known about him expands the possibilities for his appropriation and extends the symbolic uses to which he can be put. Grounded, creative processes restlessly recreate Wallace in diverse subjective frames. Rather than highlighting a moribund and unconfident popular culture, this flexible appropriation of national symbols shows a dynamic, robust and open Scottish culture.

As I have indicated above, the message conveyed by many cultural commentators and some academics is that Scottish popular culture is embarrassing at best, and dangerous at worst. Yet this view from on high misrepresents and misunderstands the dynamism of popular culture, for as Alexandra Howson has argued, national identities are constituted around discursive practices and cultural resources which emerge from a diversity of sources, but these are dynamic rather than static. Within these discourses alternative versions are proffered and counter-narratives are formulated (Howson 1993: 38). It is difficult to fix meaning in a globalising world where a proliferation of informational and image flows cross and penetrate national space (Appadurai 1990). The old myths are being decentred or disembedded by these flows but simultaneously are apt to be revived to sustain reified notions of identity in the face of this onslaught.

Yet despite these defensive responses, there is no essential Scotland, but rather a fluid entity which is increasingly incorporating difference, denying the conditions within which exclusive nationalisms thrive. The diverse visual representations, dramas and artefacts revealed in *Scotland's Liberator* bring into focus the diversity of contemporary Scotland and show that any essentialist, exclusive notion of national identity is a fantasy. Instead, Scotland is displayed as a variegated, complex place in which a range of identities merge, squabble and ignore each other, but rarely form into large groups of crude nationalists. It seems that what characterises contemporary Scottish popular culture is not so much any negative commonalities or homogenising features but rather a shared set of cultural resources and themes which are interpreted and used in often contesting ways. The use of Wallace before and after *Braveheart*, even in *Braveheart*, is marked more by interpretations which are shaped as much by gender, class, religion and region as a crude, recursive national identity. These expressions of art, drama and creativity and use of symbolic objects cut across a sense of nationhood in the ways in which they talk back to history and evoke identity. What this proliferation enables, rather than the serial reproduction of negative stereotypes, is a dialogic environment where Scots negotiate with each other, certainly reproducing and reinterpreting old notions, but also producing new meanings, forms and practices.

References

Appadurai A 1986 'Introduction: commodities and the politics of value'. In: Appadurai A (ed) The Social Life of Things: Commodities in Cultural Perspective. Cambridge, Cambridge University Press, pp 3-63

Appadurai A 1990 'Disjuncture and difference in the global cultural economy'. In: Featherstone M (ed) Global Culture. London, Sage

Caughie J 1990 'Representing Scotland: new questions for Scottish cinema'. In: Dick E (ed) From Limelight to Satellite. London, BFI

Cohen A 1985 The Symbolic Construction of Community. London, Tavistock

Connerton P 1989 How Societies Remember. Cambridge, Cambridge University Press

Craig C 1982 'Myths after history: tartanry and kailyard in 19th century Scottish literature'. In: McArthur C (ed) Scotch Reels: Scotland in Cinema and Television. London, BFI, pp 7-15

Crang M 1994 'On the heritage trail: maps of and journeys to olde England'. In: Environment and Planning D: Society and Space, 12, pp 341-55

Edensor T 1997a 'National identity and the politics of memory: remembering Bruce and Wallace in symbolic space'. In: Environment and Planning D: Society and Space

Edensor T 1997b 'Reading Braveheart: Representing and Contesting Scottish Identity'. In: Scottish Affairs, October

Edensor T 1998 Tourists at the Taj. London, Routledge

Finlay I 1997 'Heroes, myths and anniversaries in modern Scotland'. In: Scottish Affairs 18, Winter, pp 108-25

Gillan A 1995 'Brave hearts, forgetful of a troubled past, play the patriot game again', *Scotland on Sunday*, 10 September, p16

Hall S 1980 'Encoding/decoding'. In: Hall S, Hobson D, Lowe A and Willis P (eds) Culture, Media, Language. London, Hutchinson

Harvey D 1989 The Condition of Postmodernity. Oxford, Blackwell

Howson A 1993 'No gods and precious few women: gender and cultural identity in Scotland'. In: Scottish Affairs, 2, Winter, pp 37-49

King E 1998 'Blind Harry's Wallace'. In: Scottish Book Collector, 5, Spring, pp 8-9

Lowenthal D 1985 The Past is a Foreign Country. Cambridge, Cambridge University Press

McArthur C (ed) 1982 Scotch Reels: Scotland in Cinema and Television. London, BFI

McArthur C 1993 'Scottish culture: a reply to David McCrone'. In: Scottish Affairs, 4, Summer, pp 95-106

McArthur C 1994 'Culloden: a pre-emptive strike'. In: Scottish Affairs, 3, no. 9, pp 97-126

McCrone D 1992 Understanding Scotland: The Sociology of a Stateless Nation. London, Routledge

Morley D, Robins K 1995 Spaces of Identity. London, Routledge

Nairn T 1977 The Break-up of Britain. London, Verso

O'Shea A 1996 'Modernity, cinema and the popular imagination in the late twentieth century'. In: Nava M, O'Shea A (eds) Modern Times: Reflections on a Century of English Modernity. London, Routledge, pp 239-68

Rojek C 1993 Ways of Escape. London, Macmillan

Samuel R, Thompson P (eds) 1990 The Myths We Live By. London, Routledge

Smout TC 1994 'Perspectives on the Scottish identity'. In: *Scottish Affairs* 6, Winter, 101-113

Stewart S 1993 On Longing: Narratives of the Miniature, the Gigantic, the Souvenir, the Collection. London, Duke University Press

Tilly C 1994 'Afterword: political memories in space and time'. In: Boyarin J (ed) Remapping Memory: The Politics of Time Space. Minneapolis, University of Minnesota Press

Warner M 1993 Monuments and Maidens. London, Verso

Willis P 1990 Common Culture. Milton Keynes, Open University Press

Wilson F 1997 'A bunch of Wallies?' Lead article, *Stirling Observer*, September 10

Womack P 1987 Improvement and Romance: Constructing the Myth of the Highlands. London, Macmillan

Postmodernity, Ethics and Nationhood in the Contemporary Scottish Novel

Eleanor Bell

In *Nation and Narration*, Homi Bhabha states that 'there is a tendency to read the Nation rather restrictively'(1990:3). In order to combat such restrictive readings, Bhabha proposes a form of 'incomplete signification', which allows representations of nationhood to remain open to meaning and potential, rather than be captured in any holistic or totalising way. Bhabha states:

> What emerges as an effect of such 'incomplete signification' is a turning of boundaries and limits into the in-between spaces through which the meanings of cultural and political authority are negotiated (1990:4).

It is this importance of 'in-between' spaces with which I will be concerned here. In particular, I will be looking at the work of A L Kennedy and Alasdair Gray, suggesting that rather than encapsulating the nation, these novels are, alternatively, more concerned with the political and the ethical dimensions of their respective environments. The novels which will be discussed, namely *So I am Glad* and *1982 Janine*, are both clearly political. However, I will be suggesting that it is precisely in the more ambiguous in-between spaces, as suggested by Bhabha above, that the ethical has an increased potential to emerge. In these texts, ethical spaces are created through self-consciously highlighting the processes of construction implicit to formulations of national identity, rather than to any simple readings or standard assumptions. Therefore, intrinsic to both texts is a form of questioning as to what being Scottish means, or potentially could mean, and there is an open-ended approach to nationhood at work here.

In considering the ethical and Bhabha's notion of the in-between, I will also be reflecting on Julia Kristeva's notion that postmodern texts can serve an ethical function. Kristeva has written that postmodern novels are often challenging in their mode of representation, in the layers of possibility that they offer, and it is this form of intertextuality which, I will argue, particularly points to manifestations of the ethical in these novels.

In his 1994 book, *Ethics, Theory and the Novel*, David Parker discusses the need for what he terms 'ethical articulateness' as a means of dissociating and deciphering the seemingly endless political subject positions available in literary study. For Parker, it is necessary to develop an ethical vocabulary in order to escape what he describes as the 'intellectually stifling atmosphere of judgmental self-righteousness,' and he writes:

> An ethical vocabulary is needed in which to articulate the humanly destructive impulsions that can lurk precisely in the thirst for righteousness, including political righteousness (1994:196).

The ethical in this respect cannot be as easily categorised as the political, for it always escapes final definition, and it is precisely in this respect that it remains ethical; always having more work to do. In this way the ethical has a special function and role to play within Scotland, for it both helps to map out the political, yet also transcend it, pointing out the necessary directions which perhaps future politics might take, but doing so in especially subtle and discreet ways. The ethical has a notable relevance in its ability to draw attention to the in-between spaces of margin and centre, between political perspectives and political possibilities; and this is something explored in each novel in their obvious concerns with marginal characters in a late twentieth century, postmodern Scotland.

J Hillis Miller has also focused on this break between the ethical and the political in his 1987 book *The Ethics of Reading*. For Miller, it is necessary to distinguish between the two precisely because they are so inevitably interconnected. Miller, in his study of the ethics of reading, suggests that the ethical is often a form of narration that must by necessity be distinguished from the political:

> No doubt the political and the ethical are always intimately intertwined, but an ethical act that is fully determined by political consideration or responsibilities is no longer ethical. It could even in a certain sense be said to be amoral (1987:4).

A key feature that unites *So I am Glad* and *1982 Janine*, and which might be potentially useful in discussing this split between the ethical and the political is that of estrangement. Each of the central characters could be described as fundamentally estranged, both at a psychological level and with regard to their Scottish surroundings, which are often oppressive and alienating. In this limited space it is only possible to point out potential, provisional differences between the political and the ethical, yet the theme of estrangement seems to provide a particularly relevant example. Estrangement is central to each text in highlighting political factors, marginality and oppression, yet it can also be viewed from an ethical standpoint, precisely because it is concerned with exploring the processes of 'incomplete signification'; rather than encapsulating or finally determining them. From an ethical perspective, estrangement, like the political, cannot be reduced to the nation itself in any reductive way, yet it can however point out some of the processes at work 'in-between' politics and the nation.

The character of Jennifer Wilson in *So I am Glad* defines herself as incredibly calm; a calmness she has cultivated throughout her life as a means of controlling her emotions, and sustaining her detachment from a world that she often perceives as incomprehensible anyway. She states:

> But I am quite happy to tell you that what appears to be peace and calmness is, in fact, empty space – or, to be more exact, a pause. I am not calm, I am spontaneous, When something happens to me, I don't know how to feel (Kennedy 1996:5).

This emptiness seems to be recurrent for Jennifer, and it both signifies and is symbolic of the estrangement she feels with respect to her environment. The world that Jennifer inhabits appears inadequate, and this has consequently resulted in her development of depression and reclusiveness. In her partial removal from her world, she is therefore able to make her conscious experience of it more liveable.

Jennifer is clearly concerned with the role of politics in Scotland. Yet the country with which she associates her political disillusionment is Britain, rather than Scotland particularly. Scotland, in its apparent colonialised and repressed state, does not even merit a suitable position in the hierarchies of power, for the dominance of a few powerful countries have left many others silent, Scotland notably included. This is a sentiment found throughout the novel, and is particularly evident when Peter returns home from Romania, and discusses experiences of his life there and states:

Do you know how bad this country looks, smells? For what we're supposed to be?
For what we think we are? You wouldn't believe the crappy little dribbles of money we
send out to anyone who actually needs it over there. Oh, we get it right sometimes,
but, shit, the fuck ups. They think we're crazy. Nothing personal, they're sorry for
you when you're there – they like the Scots but they're sorry for us. And they have...
their opinion of Britain is... interesting, Do you think the Empire was like that?
Have we always gone abroad to majorly screw up? Is that what we're for? (Kennedy
1996:146).

Scotland, to a large extent, has been masqueraded under the shadow of a larger
power and this has resulted in many detrimental results both for the Scots and
for many other postcolonial cultures outside of Britain. Jennifer explains this
further towards the end of the novel, when she states:

...I live in an intensely arrogant and racist island. Those leaving are scrutinised far
less than those unfortunate foreign souls arriving on our blessed shores, those who
have white skins may be almost ignored while this is not at all the case with those
who do not, and those who have British passports of the old, blue variety are
generally regarded as the happiest, whitest, most innocent voyagers on earth
(Kennedy 1996:257).

Yet despite such blatant and numerous political comments made throughout
the novel, we are left wondering about the role of Scotland itself. The novel
certainly aims to represent, and is clearly concerned with Scotland, Glasgow
in particular, yet the relationship with the country is not resolved in any way
at the end of the novel. There are no simple solutions to Jennifer's feelings of
dissatisfaction with her country, and instead we are left with an impression
that many things could be better within it, if only it had the power to change
itself, or be changed from the outside, in some desirable, beneficial way.
However, there are no 'restrictive readings' placed upon the country here, and
it is not finally reduced to a political level. It is important to remember that the
novel is fundamentally a love story – love perhaps being a metaphor for the
possibility of change: for the existence of ethical possibilities rather than
political definitions. In this novel, Scotland is very much regarded as existing in
an in-between stage – that is, having the potential to be something much better,
yet also, perhaps temporarily, caught in a form of political and intellectual stasis.

It is only in the conclusion of the novel that the allegorical possibility of optimism emerges, and even then it remains tangential and provisional.

In *So I am Glad*, there exists an underlying tension between the forms of representation adopted. There are two contrasting worlds here: one of Glaswegian realism and another of fantasy, brought about by the intervention of Savinien Cyrano de Bergerac, returned to life after several hundred years absence. It is when Jennifer begins to accept that Savinien potentially could be whom he states himself to be that she also becomes liberated from her prior feelings of entrapment and estrangement. Savinien in this sense represents a break from her everyday culture, for he signifies freedom and a break from her previous, dull world. As a famous historical figure who has suddenly returned to life, and of all places in Glasgow, he offers Jennifer new perspectives and insights into her world; allowing her consequently to challenge the kinds of estrangement she had previously endured.

Jennifer, it seems, writes this novel in order to tell the story of Cyrano de Bergerac, to relay their love story as well as to shock her audience, and in doing so the novel becomes increasingly complex. For it is only when we begin to identify with the realism implicit within the novel that the fantasy is then interwoven, in suitably postmodern ways, seemingly incorporated in order to destabilise and undermine any comfortable assumptions of only realistic devices being at work here. Despite Jennifer's obvious concerns with the political nature of her country, we are nevertheless frequently reminded that there are many other ideas working alongside the political aspects. It is in this process that ethical space is to be found.

For Kristeva, postmodern fiction, and its experimental, intertextual nature, has specifically allowed for ideas to be generated and presented in new ways. Kristeva suggests that this in turn has produced interesting ethical reverberations and spaces, whether at conscious or unconscious levels of the text:

> Let us say that Postmodernism is that Literature which writes itself with the more or less conscious intention of expanding the signifiable and thus human realm (Brooker 1994:199).

Similar thoughts are echoed in *Revolution in Poetic Language*, where Kristeva calls for the need to 'carry out an ethical imperative', and as one critic has written of this notion:

To 'carry out the ethical imperative' is thus to make visible the processes underlying the production and dissolution of meaning and identity, the processes that constitute the subject itself. Practices and tests which bring these processes to light are those that lead to ethical awareness (Kelly 1990:35).

So I am Glad, it seems, closely identifies with these statements, for it corresponds both with the postmodern elements described by Kristeva, in its historical playfulness and parodic tone; and it is also self-conscious about the role and processes of national identity at a more unconscious level of the text. Such postmodern forms and concerns with the process of national identity are also a fundamental aspect of Alasdair Gray's *1982 Janine*. Similar to *So I am Glad*, the text is concerned with a self-conscious position with regard to a Scottish cultural identity, where national identity always remains fluid rather than fixed. Therefore the character of Jock McLeish in *1982 Janine* reflects upon the West of Scotland, to which he belongs, and seems depressed with his very connection to the land. For Jock has reached the point where he, like Jennifer Wilson, has become completely disillusioned with his culture as a result of its political climate and with the consequences of this upon his life.

In his reasons for writing *1982 Janine*, Gray has stated that he wanted:

...to show a sort of man everyone recognises and most can respect; not an artist, not an egoist, not even a radical; a highly skilled workman and technician, dependable, honest, and conservative, who should be one of the kings of his age, but who does not know it, because he has been trained to do what he is told. So he is a plague and a pest to himself, and is going mad, quietly, inside (Gifford 1988: 113).

The estranged character of Jock is therefore one that quite simply could be anyone; for estrangement, according to Gray, is a symptom of the age. This is perhaps why Jock for the most part has such a low opinion of himself when he says things such as 'I am not a man, I am an instrument' (Gray 1984:105) and 'I am shit' (129). Therefore, like Thaw in *Lanark*, Jock retreats into his own imaginative world in order to escape from his claustrophobic Scottish environment. Where in *So I am Glad* there is a tendency to blame Britain for the colonialism of Scotland, in Gray's novel Jock is willing to accept the kinds of cultural inferiorism as discussed by Beveridge and Turnbull in *The Eclipse of Scottish Culture*, where they state that a sense of inferiorism works hand in hand with colonialism. Jock therefore begins to hope for a third world war; one which would devastate Scotland in particular. Paradoxically, he is willing to let Edinburgh emerge untouched due to its large influx of tourists, and therefore its 'non-Scottish' elements. He states:

> It's a pity about Edinburgh. It has almost nothing to do with Glasgow but stands too near to go unscathed. Let's hope that only the people die and the buildings and monuments are undamaged, then in a few years the Festival can resume as merrily as ever. It is mostly the work of foreigners anyway (Gray 1984:136).

The impact of Jock's statements here lie in what he does not say about Scotland. What he omits is how Scotland could improve; the ways in which it could be rejuvenated: Jock, it seems, has been too submerged by the indoctrination of Thatcherism. He recognises that his views represent '...a natural Falstaffian approach to life', but this is because, on the whole, 'Britain has become very Falstaffian' (137). Jock's views, however, are not the only ones represented in the novel. Towards the end, Gray himself seems to appear in order to contradict the pessimism of his central character. Gray complicates any simple assumptions of a pessimistic landscape by then disagreeing with his central character, putting him in his place with respect to Scottish politics. He states:

> Though Jock McLeish is an invention of mine I disagree with him. In Chapter 4, for example, he says of Scotland, 'We are a poor little country, always will be.' In fact Scotland's natural resources are as variedly rich as those of any other land. Her ground area is greater than that of Denmark, Norway or Finland. Our present ignorance and bad social organisation make most Scots poorer than most other north Europeans, but even bad human states are not everlasting (345).

Gray self-reflexively intervenes here, in the style of much postmodern fiction, in order to disrupt any singular meanings of what Scotland either is, or could be. He steps in to remind his audience that estrangement is not the only condition of the Scot; and indeed this itself appears to be one of the most important aspects of the novel. Here he adopts postmodern techniques in order to open out the processes of meaning as they pertain to Scotland, rather than simplifying any particular viewpoint. It is easy to sympathise with Jock, and understand his position: yet Gray also sounds convincing and optimistic. In providing such dissimilar perspectives, the text also shows similarities with Kristeva's viewpoint that postmodernism is able to 'expand the signifiable'. It is in such postmodern processes of questioning and highlighting contrasting viewpoints that ethical perspectives have the space to manifest, for they aim to complicate the methods of representation, and therefore any singularity of meaning. The ethical, therefore, lies in the 'in-between' space of the conscious and unconscious of the text itself; escaping any simple reductions.

In both texts there appear to be shared ethical concerns with Scotland, whether these are expressed consciously or unconsciously. What emerges from these ethical concerns is that 'Scottishness' can really only exist in the in-between spaces as defined by Bhabha (1990). There is a further parallel with the work of Frantz Fanon, and this need for 'incomplete signification', when he states that 'culture abhors simplification' (Bhabha 1990:303). Any kind of 'nature' or 'essence' of Scotland is therefore complicated by these novelists in their use of self-reflexiveness and historiographical devices respectively. The texts discussed contain obvious political commentaries concerning their respective environments; yet ethical spaces have their potential in precisely what is not said about Scotland and 'Scottishness'.

References

Beveridge C, Turnbull R 1969 The Eclipse of Scottish Culture: Inferiorism and the Intellectuals. Polygon

Bhabha H K 1990 Nation and Narration. London, Routledge

Brooker P (ed) 1994 Modernism/Postmodernism. London, Longman

Gifford D 1988 Private Confession and Public Satire in the Fiction of Alasdair Gray. In: Chapman 50/51

Gray, A 1984 *1982 Janine*. London, Penguin

Kennedy, A L 1996 *So I am Glad*. London, Vintage

Kristeva J 1984 Revolution in Poetic Language. Trans Margaret Walker. New York, Columbia Press

Miller J H 1987 The Ethics of Reading. New York, Columbia University Press

Oliver K (ed) 1990 Ethics, Politics and Difference in Julia Kristeva's Writing. London, Routledge

Parker D 1994 Ethics, Theory and the Novel. Oxford, Oxford University Press

The Shape of Things to Come:
Writing the Map of Scotland

Kirsten Stirling

In November 1997 the front page of the *Scotsman* carried a satellite picture of Scotland. On the inside pages there were close-ups of various towns, but the front-page carried the far more striking image of the whole country. The image has since been made into postcards and pictures and is selling well. The image started me thinking about what it was about this image of Scotland that prompted an emotional response in me, a mixture of familiarity and distance.

The vantage point of the satellite allows us the distance necessary to see Scotland as a whole. The recognition of the shape of Scotland triggers an emotional response, but it is based on our knowledge of the shape of Scotland which comes from the maps of Scotland we have seen. The picture we are seeing now is 'real', but it is a reality which is produced, first, by the technology we know to be involved in the taking of a photograph from space, and validated by the knowledge of the shape of Scotland inscribed in maps, which are equally a product of science.

Our appreciation of this photograph then is part of a complex web of looking, of knowledge, power and possession, of the interaction of aesthetics and science. The map of Scotland exists on the level of a scientific text, with all the claim to objectivity and rationality that implies, but then the knowledge inscribed in this sort of map leads to the iconisation of the map of Scotland.

The process of mapping implies scientific objectivity. A map claims to be an accurate representation of real territory. It claims to show everything. The distance of the observing 'eye' from the map boosts the implication of objectivity – we are at a remove from what we see, we are no longer implicated in the details. This is not the case, of course, and a spate of human geography books have begun decconstructing the map's pretension to scientific objectivity. Mark Monmonier's *How to Lie With Maps* (1991) and *Drawing the Line: Tales of Maps and Cartocontroversies* (1995) engage with just this process of challenging the scientific transparency of maps and the values written into maps, treating maps as authored texts. Just as spatial metaphors, metaphors of mapping, recur in contemporary criticism and theory so the analogy of reading and the text-metaphor has been commonly used in modern geography. Modern literary theory has been applied. A map is a cultural text, a collection of codes, and may be deconstructed.

A map, then, is necessarily subjective, and at the same time subject positions are mapped. We locate ourselves on the map of Scotland. The familiarity of the map in fact allows us awareness of our subject positions on it, and awareness of our relationship to territory. So the shape of the map begins to function as a cultural icon, as a result of this combination of scientific objectivity and territorial subjectivity. The shape of the map has been presented and represented to us in a variety of forms, two obvious examples being the stylised map which whirls at the beginning of the news programme *Reporting Scotland,* and the new Scotrail logo, in which the map morphs into the speedlines of the Scotrail logo. The familiar shape of the map of Scotland allows the subject recognition of location.

Roderick Watson's article 'Maps of Desire' builds a tour of Scottish literature in the twentieth century round the idea of mapping literature (Devine and Finlay 1996). He refers to his own quotation from *The Poetry of Scotland*: 'the main state left to a stateless nation may well be its state of mind, and in that territory it is literature which maps the land'. He proceeds to write a cultural map of Scotland by surveying the literature of Scotland. In the field of Scottish studies and particularly that of Scottish literature, the conceit of the map functions, as with *Reporting Scotland* and Scotrail, to tie the field of study more closely to a sense of national identity. A visual image of this appears on the front cover of the distance-taught MPhil run by the Department of Scottish Literature at the University of Glasgow: a map of Scotland is made up of words: those of Burns in Ayrshire, Stevenson's words in Edinburgh. This recalls the dustjacket of the first edition of *Scottish Scene*, edited by Lewis Grassic Gibbon and Hugh MacDiarmid, which shows the figures of writers standing on the Scottish map, with MacDiarmid himself at the top, surveying the lay of the land from the vantage point of Shetland (Grassic Gibbon and MacDiarmid 1934).

The shape of the map functions as an emblem of national territory, a symbol of the 'imagined community'. But the scientific status of maps (as of satellite photos) means that there is a tension between the discourse of nation as a cultural construction and the growing number of narratives of scientific validation of Scotland as a nation, which I shall be considering here. The interaction of the discourses of science and fiction allows us to question the assumed factuality and objectivity of scientific discourse and also the assumptions inherent in the representations of Scotland presented to us in the fictional texts we read. In what ways do we 'see Scotland whole'?

The phrase to 'see Scotland whole' is from Hugh MacDiarmid, who demonstrates a universal perspective from his earliest poems in Scots; his short poem 'The Bonnie Broukit Bairn' represents the planets including the earth from a vantage point which must be in space. This, in a poem which predates space travel, is quite remarkable. MacDiarmid is very much concerned, in his autobiography *Lucky Poet* and elsewhere, with the idea of 'seeing Scotland whole'. He uses this phrase 'to see Scotland whole' in a partially geographical sense, emphasising the importance of vantage points from which to appreciate Scotland, and advocates several of the 'best views in Scotland' as suitable points for contemplation, both visual and philosophical. This geographical vision of Scotland implies an appreciation of Scotland in all ways: literary, historical and natural. There are two implications in this phrase: one inclusive and one exclusive. 'Seeing Scotland whole' can mean apprehending the whole of Scotland at once. The emphasis on vantage points implies a certain distance on the part of the observer. The vantage points cited by MacDiarmid are imperfect: to really see Scotland whole we must share the vantage point of the satellite, be totally outside Scotland, outside the earth's atmosphere: or we must reduce Scotland to fit within our sight, reduce it to a logo which signifies 'Scotland' to us but which itself does not show the plurality Scotland entails.

But 'to see Scotland whole' also implies to see Scotland as a whole, not as a part of something else, and this is implicit in MacDiarmid's use of the phrase. We can see this tendency continuing in present-day representations and logo-isations of the map of Scotland. More often than not Scotland is represented as apparently unattached to anything – to, for example, England – Scotland appears to be floating on its own in a sea. Cultural representations of the map of Scotland do reproduce these aspects of MacDiarmid's phrase: a desire both to homogenise Scotland and to distinguish it, if not physically separate it, from England.

In her book *Tendencies*, Eve Kosofsky Sedgwick (1993) discusses the role of maps in the construction of 'nation-ness'. She compares the weather-maps of America and Canada, noting that the map of America totally excludes Canada: the map ends abruptly at the top of America. Participation in shared weather is a national experience, is the message given by these maps. The Canadian weather-map, however, extends southwards to the Mason–Dixon line. Sedgwick suggests that due to its different history Canada may have a structure which makes a single definition of 'nation-ness' impossible. America is a dominant and exclusive nationality which has no need to think north to Canada. Canada, on the other hand, cannot but be aware of its larger neighbour (Kosofsky Sedgwick 1993: 149).

There is a different dynamic, however, between Scotland and England. Maps of England do, on the whole, tend to include Scotland. It is a form of inclusiveness. The image of the map of Britain seems to be important to a sense of English identity. Maps of Scotland, on the other hand, are far more conscious of their boundaries. Occasionally, the line of the English coast continues down, a bleak line drawing protruding from the mass of detail which is Scotland. The geographical fact that (mainland) Scotland and England are parts of the same island is indisputable. But we are constantly presented with images of the map of Scotland which ignore England completely, and I would like now to consider several ways in which different authors have used this image to represent, in their own ways 'Scotland as a whole'.

Both Iain Banks and Alasdair Gray play with the idea of Scotland as geologically defined by landscape. In Iain Banks' *The Crow Road*. Kenneth (the father of the narrator) tells his children a story which has the same intrinsic message as Gray's statement:

> It was a well-travelled country, dad told us. Within the oceanic depths of time that lay beneath the surface of the present, there had been an age when, appropriately, an entire ocean had separated the rocks that would one day be called Scotland from the rocks that would one day be called England and Wales. That first union came half a billion years ago. Compressed and folded, the rocks that would be Scotland – by then part of the continent of Euramerica – held within their crumpled, tortuously layered cores the future shape of the land (Banks 1992: 306).

This story is obviously fictional: Kenneth also tells the children about the mythosaurs, large reptiles who roamed the country eating rocks. But the very fictionality of the description is important. It seems there is a need to tell stories about the origins of Scotland – an imagined community – but a community imagined in terms of scientific validity. This story tells us that the existence of Scotland the nation is geologically determined. We must validate the shape of the map of Scotland to ourselves, justify it by narrating its geographical and geological difference from England. The shape of Scotland is located in the scientific context of the theory of continental drift, incidentally another of Mark Monmonier's 'cartocontroversies' (1995: 148–88). It is perhaps ironic that an image of a unified globe contains the essentialism inherent in the phrase 'the rocks that would one day be Scotland'. The existence of Scotland must thus be predetermined, and as the passage says, the shape of Scotland, the familiar visual icon which allows us to situate ourselves, exists as a concept before it becomes a physical form. There is a certain essentialism in 'the rocks that would one day be called Scotland' – the existence of Scotland is predetermined.

If the nation can be defined scientifically – if, that is, a limit can be drawn defining 'Scotland' as a bounded space, then does nationality stem from this scientifically defined nation? In the 1997 edition of *Why Scots Should Rule Scotland*, Alasdair Gray states: 'landscape is what defines most lasting nations' (1997: 1). Such a statement immediately sets up the ideological presumption that nations are geologically created rather than being 'imagined communities'. He goes on to define 'Scots', for the purposes of his book, as 'everyone in Scotland who is able to vote'. He acknowledges that this definition is imperfect, as it excludes those of Scottish birth under the age of eighteen or in jail, while including English landowners in Scotland, but this sleight of hand allows him to escape any charge of racism or ethnocentricity. If, then, Scottishness is defined by living in Scotland and being able to vote, and it is not dependent on birth, Scottishness must therefore be an acquired trait, a construction. His nation is defined by land, rather than by people.

His definition of what constitutes the land that is Scotland allows us no space for doubt. Describing the processes of immigration and emigration throughout history, during which people 'become' Scottish, he says: '... like every other European land a great mixture of folk has poured into this irregularly shaped national container ...' (1997: 4). While the Scottishness of any individual Scot apparently fluctuates depending on his or her spatial location, Scotland itself has permanent fixed boundaries which themselves determine its existence. The word 'container' implies rigid, inflexible boundaries, and also a sense of interiority: everything outwith its boundaries is extraneous. Our attention is also drawn, again, to the shape of the map, which Gray describes elsewhere as resembling 'a fat messy woman with a surprisingly slim waist' (Gray 1984). 'This irregularly shaped national container' triggers the shape of the map in our heads. According to MacDiarmid, the irregular shape of the map is connected to our national psyche: the asymmetry of Scotland's map and landscape apparently governs the Scottish ability to hold contradictory ideas (MacDiarmid 1943).

Edwin Morgan goes even further in his visual separation of Scotland from England. In two of his *Sonnets from Scotland* (1984) Scotland becomes physically detached from England. In 'Outward Bound' it becomes an island, floats off into the Atlantic, past Greenland, Key West, Lanzarote: it is powered by Amazing Grace –'it moved on pure sound': 'there was no ground/of being, only being, sweetest and best.' Geographical location is no longer important – again, as with the container motif, Scotland is self-sufficient. Being is enough in itself. In the next poem in the series, 'On Jupiter' the physical detachment of Scotland is even more pronounced: Scotland is found on Jupiter. Both poems make use of shifting imagery based on the shape of the nation. Both use the image of a dog shaking itself dry, and 'Outward Bound' represents Scotland as a series of images – Scotland is an island, a sea-monster, a log, a dog. In this poem Scotland 'Like a sea-washed log/ ... loved to tempt earnest geographers/duck down and dub them drunk hydrographers' Scotland becomes removed from the fixity of the map – the 'earnest geographers' can no longer control the mapping of Scotland because impossibility cannot be mapped.

This manipulation of space representation, the visual separation of Scotland from England, can be read simply as textual wishful thinking. And certainly, while an assertion of Scotland's distinct cultural identity is part of it, a statement of the desirability of a distinct political identity for Scotland is perhaps the most important message being given. As a result of the increasingly unpopular political connection there seems to be a need to disassociate Scotland from England geographically. But by representing Scotland visually as a separate and distinct entity, there is a sense in which the political situation of Scotland is ignored. It elides discussion of Scotland's political existence as part of Britain and geographical existence as part of a larger island. If the image of Scotland separated from England is in part a reaction against Scotland's political situation, it will be interesting to chart developments in representations of the map in post-devolution Scotland; or even an independent Scotland. Might Scotland's obsession with fictional, representational boundaries diminish if actual political boundaries were in place?

References

Banks I 1992 The Crow Road. London and Sydney, Scribners

Grassic Gibbon L, MacDiarmid H (eds) 1934 Scottish Scene. London, Jarrolds

Gray A 1984 1982 Janine. London, Cape

Gray A 1997 Why Scots Should Rule Scotland. Edinburgh, Canongate

Kosofsky Sedgwick E 1993 Tendencies. Durham NC, Duke University Press

MacDiarmid H 1943 Lucky Poet. London, Methuen

Monmonier M 1991 How to Lie with Maps. Chicago and London, University of Chicago Press

Monmonier M 1995 Drawing the Line: Tale of Maps and Cartocontroversies. New York, Henry Holt

Morgan E 1984 Sonnets from Scotland. Glasgow, Mariscat

Watson R 1996 Maps of Desire. In: Devine T M, Finlay R J (eds) Scotland in the Twentieth Century. Edinburgh, Edinburgh University Press

R B Cunninghame Graham:
Between the Kailyard and the Empire*

Kirsti Wishart

It was only with the arrival of Cedric Watts and Laurence Davies' 1979 biography that the writing of R B Cunninghame Graham (1852–1936), laird, first socialist MP in the Houses of Parliament and first President of the National Party of Scotland, received serious critical attention (Watts and Davies 1979). Nevertheless, academics have been slow indeed in recognising the rich pickings to be gleaned from Graham's literary output. If he is mentioned at all it is as one of the few writers to challenge the cosy sentimentality of the Kailyard writers (Bold 1983). A reader coming across his best known story 'Beattock for Moffat', in which a dying Scot travels back to his home town from London accompanied by his gruff yet loyal fellow countryman and a pathetically weeping Cockney wife, however, will have difficulty in marking out the characteristics that should liberate him from Kailyard confines. His only sustained piece of writing on Scottish subject matter is his guidebook to the district of Menteith. Other works include histories of the Jesuits in South America and the Spanish conquest, and a biography of his ancestor Charles Doughty (1901, 1922, 1925). The work for which he is perhaps best known is *Mogreb-el-Acksa* (1898), an account of his travels in Morocco. He produced fourteen collections of sketches, a hybrid literary form blending fact and fiction. Despite ancestral ties to the family homes of Gartmore and Ardoch he spent much time in London and frequently travelled abroad in his later years to escape the harsh climate of Scotland. This lack of cohesion makes it very difficult to place him within a literary context, while his absence from Scotland in terms both of subject matter and geographical location raises the question how far he can be regarded as a Scottish writer. The problem of 'placing' Graham in both a critical and geographical sense

* This paper was published in *Scotlands* 5.1, ed Christopher MacLachlan, 1998 Edinburgh, Edinburgh University Press and is reproduced with permission.

should lead not to his neglect but to a re-evaluation of the limitations imposed by the current critical paradigms that exist in relation to the 'exiled Scot'.

Only in recent years has serious research been undertaken to ascertain the true complexity of Scotland's relationship with the British Empire (Finlay 1997, MacKenzie 1993). In studies of late ninteenth and early twentieth century Scottish literature the nature of that involvement remains unexplored. While post-colonial theorists explore the complexities of the colonial relationship, Scottish commentators prefer to view the experience of imperial Scots in terms of binary opposition. Scots either became the colonised or the colonisers. The opportunities created overseas resulted in a drain of talent, the deformities of the Kailyard and the lack of a coherent form of political nationalism. For the most influential inferiorist readings of the supposedly uniformly detrimental results of Scotland's contribution to the British Empire see Craig (1961), Nairn (1981), Harvie (1977) and MacGillivray (1987). MacGillivray provides an important re-evaluation of the literary contribution of imperial Scots but claims such writers effectively relinquished their Scottishness for the imperial endeavour. It should come as no surprise that such a nation should produce a writer who, with Jekyll and Hyde, created one of the defining myths of the colonial experience (Thornton 1968). Alan Riach, in his Introduction to Hugh MacDiarmid's *Contemporary Scottish Studies* (1995: vii) reiterates this view and does so clearly with the Caledonian antisyzygy in mind, emphasising the supposedly unstable, repressive nature of Scotland's imperial past. The nation both 'became invisible and ... internationally recognisable in stereotypes and caricatures' due to members of its artistic community becoming 'exiled from their own national identity.' They 'became bulwarks of the British establishment while an incalculable number of Scots became both the victims and the perpetrators of the Empire itself.' Gone is the pride expressed in the achievements of Mungo Park, Mary Slessor and David Livingstone. Instead there is shame at the complicity of Scots in the exploitation of other peoples, despite the Highlands having suffered an equivalent fate, and the failure to sustain its native population. Repeatedly, the possibility of a dialectic and the fact that no nation can exist in and of itself but rather defines itself, in relation to other cultures, is ignored. As Said states, 'imperialism consolidated the mixture of cultures and identities on a global scale,' and so 'no one today is purely one thing.'(Said 1994: 407). Cairns Craig's *Out of History* (1996) does offer a means of re-interpreting the inferiorist image of the 'Wandering' or 'red' Scot as defined by Christopher Harvie (1977: 17). *Out of History* concentrates mainly on the nature of the dialogue between Scotland and England, but the quotation below should lead us to look further afield to the wider horizon of the Empire:

> ... all cultures, at all times, exist in a dialectic with other cultures, exist in the dialectic of spatial production. The peripheral culture is, in its fragmentation, just as much a culture as the core culture in its unity. The culture of the core is equally shaped – deformed – by the dialectic with its peripheries (Craig 1996:117).

In the light of recent post-colonial theory that attempts to do away with a Manichean division between coloniser and colonised but explores the meeting points between cultures (the 'Third Space' as identified by Homi Bhabha or in a more literal sense the 'contact zone' as defined by Mary Louise Pratt) the same technique should be adopted in relation to those writers considered 'lost exiles' (Pratt 1992, Bhabha 1994).

MacDiarmid uses the criticism of G. Gregory Smith in his discussion of Graham in the *Contemporary Scottish Studies* series:

> ... in Scots the zest for handling a multitude of details rather than for seeking broad effects by suggestion is very persistent. An exhaustive survey would show that the completed effect of a piling up of details is one of movement, suggesting the action of a concerted dance. The whole is not always lost in the parts; it is not a compilation impressive only because it is greater than any of its contributing elements, but often single in result (MacDiarmid 1995: 38).

In his Centenary appreciation, MacDiarmid fails to apply the sentiment of Smith's writing to the example of Graham. He is presented as if caught between two seemingly irreconcilable states. On the one hand he 'incarnated again the tradition of the Wandering Scot and of the best features of Scottish Internationalism'(MacDiarmid 1952: 33). On the other, his example becomes propaganda for MacDiarmid's desire to ensure a Scotland that would have the ability to sustain its own talent. Had Graham chosen to write more often about Scotland then his reputation as 'the greatest Scotsman of his generation' would have been sealed. Instead, alongside Carlyle, Stevenson and Geddes he becomes one of the many Scots who feel:

... the need to escape from the intolerable anti-cultural, anti-intellectual atmosphere of their native country and go where they could find and fraternise with people of their own kind and enjoy the clash of like minds and the active co-operation and competition of men and women with similar creative abilities (MacDiarmid 1995: 17).

Although Professor John Walker's collections have served to draw some attention to his output the fact that the sketches are grouped together by place does a disservice to one of the great assets of Graham's work (Walker 1978, 1982, 1985). Drawing on his travel experiences in North Africa, South America, North America and Spain the scene shifts from sketch to sketch. One moment we are following the crowds of the working classes of Glasgow, part of the funeral cortege for Kier Hardie, the next we are with the Arabs in North Africa. As Cairns Craig (1996: 116) states, 'if postmodernism really is a major shift in the underlying epistemology of western culture, it may be because the most structurally valuable attributes are now diversity and openness to cultural change rather than the stabilities of unity and coherence.' It may be that it is only now as the anxieties surrounding the attainment of an 'authentic' Scottish identity, whatever that may be, have been assuaged that we have the critical apparatus to fully appreciate the vision of the world Graham has to offer. His writing, with its instability, its shifts in tone and scene, draws together the peripheral and the core, marking the points where one infiltrates and informs the other. The boundaries between the supposedly binary oppositions of the 'stay-at-home' and the 'wandering' Scot become blurred.

Along with his good friend Joseph Conrad, Graham can be described, to adopt Mary Louise Pratt's term, as a 'hyphenated white man'. Pratt (1992: 213) writes in relation to Henry Stanley, Roger Casement and Joseph Conrad: 'Each was a white man whose national and civic identifications were multiple and often conflicted; each had lived out in deep personal and social histories the raw realities of Euroexpansionism'. Able to trace his ancestors back to Robert II and yet with a Spanish grandmother, Graham enjoyed an upbringing that enabled him to view the world 'synoptically' or according to Edward Said's term 'contrapuntally' in both spatial and temporal terms. While both his brothers entered careers that firmly upheld the British Empire he, by maintaining an interest in his Spanish heritage, identified himself as standing in opposition to the British imperial ethos. Spain was regarded as an empire past its prime, its failings due to its religious and racial difference from Britain's Anglo-Saxon, Protestant imperialism. Although never declaring himself firmly committed to any Church, Graham does display an interest in Catholicism at a time when it was clearly identified as 'Other'. His first collection of sketches entitled *Father Archangel of Scotland* (1896) which he produced with his wife Gabrielle begins with an account of George Leslie, born in Aberdeen, who converted to Catholicism after travels on the Continent in the early 1600s and undertook a missionary expedition in Scotland. Graham says, 'the attempt to preach Catholicism in Scotland ... always seemed to me one of the most desperate of ... theological filibustering expeditions.'(1896: 3–4). By neatly subverting the missionary ethos associated with Scottish Protestantism he displays his attempt to invert the strict divisions required to maintain faith in Empire between 'here' and 'there', the 'civilised' and 'uncivilised'. Graham's Scottishness, as we shall see, was of great importance in formulating his criticism of the inequities of the Empire but his 'otherness' within his ancestral homeland allowed him a critical perspective on the doings of the Imperial Scot.

Graham's interest in areas of overlap, where cultures meet and interchange, was a view informed by the district of Mentieth where he grew up and where he spent his later years. On the borders between the Highlands and the Lowlands his estate in Stirlingshire can be regarded as his first 'contact zone'. Pratt (1992: 7) uses the term 'contact zone' to 'invoke the spatial and temporal copresence of subjects previously separated by geographic and historical disjunctures, and whose trajectories now intersect'. Before we even begin his guide-book *Notes on the District of Mentieth* (1895) Graham places this most regional of works within an international context with the statement 'All rights reserved, except in the Republic of Paraguay', drawing together and confusing the separation between the parochial and the exotic. This interchange is maintained throughout the book which is studded with references to Graham's experiences in North and South America and his knowledge of current events in the colonies and the history of Spanish colonialism. Although there is a slightly boastful edge to this display of the author's peripatetic lifestyle it is crucial to his interpretation of the area. When writing about the Highlands it is clear that Graham regards them as distinct in both geographical and temporal terms and so appears to be placing them 'out of time'. His description of the

Highlander clad in 'deerskin moccasins' refers to the image of the noble savage created by Scott, and is also indicative of the blend present in tour guides of the time of fiction and geographical fact. However, when referring to internecine conflict he cites it as analogous to the repression of the French in Algeria or the British of the Zulus. In *Notes*, Graham writes:

> Graham of Buchnay relates how Lord Glencairn's expedition lay seige to the Laird of Lethen's house and lost 5 men. "We departed and burnt all Lethen's land." A military incident told in a military fashion for soldiers, quite in the manner of the French in Algeria or the English in Zululand (60).

Graham politicises the clan warfare, instead of 'framing' it as an event that occurred 'out of time'. Rather he locates it within the historical narrative of imperialism. Working dialogically, it serves to challenge the notion of imperialists, as based on the Enlightenment belief in progress, that the Empire was a new chapter in ensuring the progress of all peoples. Instead, Graham sees the Empire as retrogressive, re-enacting the atrocities of several centuries past.

Graham's collection of sketches *The Ipané* (1899) was the first in the series produced by the publisher Edward Garnett entitled 'The Overseas Library'. Garnett's intention behind the series was to upset the distinction between the imperial centre and the colonies by relating the experience of those working within the Empire. In his mission statement he writes: 'In the case of the English in India, ten years ago, while the literature of information was plentiful, the artist was absent; Mr Kipling arrived and discovered modern India to the English imagination.' Graham voices some discomfort with the idea that writers can 'reveal' the truth about a certain area, that a Western eye is required to document a region before it can truly be said to exist. Indeed, several of the sketches in *The Ipané* serve to challenge or deconstruct the ways in which the image of an area is generated.

Although operating within the market associated with the Kailyard writers, Graham's intentions were clearly to break what he felt to be the émigré view of Scotland. In the preface he writes 'None of the following sketches and stories have the least connection with one another, or with each other.' Here there are echoes of his Kiplingesque assertion at the beginning of *Mogreb-el-Acksa* (1898) that it is not his intention to blend East and West as he believes the two are as oil and vinegar. However, by setting descriptions of Scottish life within an international context, inevitably he undermines the moral authority of Scottish imperialism, one connected with the 'exportation of Calvinist morality and Anglo-Scottish education'(Malzahn 1996). The cultural relativism destroys the sense of hierarchy, of one culture assuming superiority over another. In 'Salvagia', a Scottish town where the inhabitants have pictures of 'Bunyan on the wall', men are 'not quite civilised, nor yet quite savages, a set of demi-brutes, exclaiming if a woman in a decent gown goes past, "There goes a bitch."' (1899:192).

'A Survival', a sketch in the same collection, begins with an attack on the concept of the Kailyard but in doing so identifies the dialectic that brought this about. Blame does not lie at the door of the Scots or the English, but rather on the interplay between the two, one responding and benefiting from the demands of the other. In his objections to the writers associated with the Kailyard, what was regarded as the misrepresentation of Scots, there is a heightened awareness of the way in which the Scot became the 'Other', thereby limiting the possibilites of what it is to be Scottish. The Scot becomes 'weighed down with the responsibility of being Scotch' (162). As is demonstrated in the scathing passage below, Graham is fighting a distorting image, the ways in which myth conceals reality and so creates a limited interpretation of the cultural life of nations other than Anglo-Saxon England:

> ... for the idiots, the precentors, elders of churches, the "select men," and those
> land-ward folk who have been dragged of late into publicity, I compassionate
> them, knowing their language has been so distorted, and they themselves have
> been rendered such abject snivellers, that not a henwife, shepherd, ploughman, or
> any one who thinks in "guid braid Scots," would recognise himself dressed in the
> motley which it has been the pride of kailyard writers to bestow (1899: 157-8)

Writing in 1899, a year after the term Kailyard was coined, Graham displays an acute sensitivity to literary representations of Scotland, informed by his sympathy towards peoples of other lands who suffered the same form of misrepresentation.

For all his criticism of the Kailyard, however, Graham does not ultimately suggest that we should do away entirely with the myth of the nation. *Notes on the District of Menteith* ends with the possibility that past, present and future may combine alongside the brute reality of the modern world and the supernatural, mythic element. Writing about a local hill that is held to be a gathering place for fairies, he comments:

All in good time the fairies will get accustomed to changed conditions, and dance as merrily upon the girders of a railway bridge as formerly upon the grass and tussocks. The motley elements which went to make the history of Mentieth are gone and buried, but their shadows still remain. The Earls of Mentieth, from Gillechrist to the Beggar Earl, the fairies, the Reverend Mr Kirk, Rob Roy, the monks of Inchmahome, the Romans, Peghts, the Caledonian cattle, with the wolves, John Graham of Claverhouse and Mary Queen of Scots, have left Mentieth for ever, but the shadow of their passage still remains; at least I see it (1895: 85).

What we can see in Graham's writing is an attempt to open out the definitions of what it might mean to be Scottish, an aim that is bound inextricably with his experience of life on the colonial frontier, but one which also allows for the possibility of retaining the popular 'inauthentic' image of Scotland. The region's history, fauna and 'Peghts' (picts or fairies) can co-exist; the idea of there being one image or factor that sums up a region is negated. In combining the hard-bitten reality of the grim life of a Scottish town 'In Salvagia', while retaining an attachment to a mythic, romantic image of Scotland, he challenges the continued assumptions that continue to limit the paradigms of Scottish literary criticism: the Manichean division between the 'false' Kailyard and the 'truth of realism' for example. As Robert Crawford writes of J G Frazer: 'Frazer, like Stevenson, looks backwards. But Frazer, like Stevenson, also points forwards ... A Janus-figure, Frazer is crucial to the connections between the Scottish tradition and international modernism.' (Fraser 1990: 35). The same holds true for Cunninghame Graham, a figure who marks an intersection, retaining an attachment to a romantic mythic past but, as evinced by his political career, acutely aware of the dangers of nostalgia in concealing the needs of modern Scotland.

The literary use of dialect as a means of reducing cultural or racial difference to stereotype appears in a later sketch, 'At the Ward Toll'. At the beginning of his literary life Graham was highly suspicious of the use of dialect in literature as is evident from an extract from *Father Archangel of Scotland*:

neither of them can command a dialect in which to wrap their platitudes, so that they must go forth to a hard world, unveiled in Irish, Welsh, Manx, Somerset, or even in that all-sufficient cloak of kailyard Scotch spoken by no one under heaven, which of late has plagued us (1896: ix).

Although his view softens later in his career, 'At the Ward Toll' in his collection
Faith (1909) demonstrates the way in which literary representation can belittle
one from another culture. While riding through the mist veiled landscape of
Mentieth, Graham happens across a Spanish traveller who, to a modern-day
reader, brings to mind Manuel of *Fawlty Towers*. He 'knew a "litel Inglis",
which he would spika so that I might hear.' On learning that Graham speaks
Spanish Ildefonso López thanks him in his own language for some cigarettes
declaring they 'were better far than bread when the heart is empty and the feet
sore, and that the scent of them was sweeter than the orange flower or than
the incense in a church' (p.114). The lyrical nature of his reply counteracts any
superiority the reader may have felt towards a non-native speaker.

Once the traveller has left Graham rides on to discover:

> All was as lonely and as northern as before but the spell had been broken by
> Ildefonso López in his brief apparition out of the mist and gloom of the October
> evening, and though I knew I rode along the road towards the Kelty bridge, and marked
> unconciously the junipers that grow just by the iron gate that opens on the path
> towards the Carse, it seemed somehow that I was entering Vigo, by the north channel
> between the Cies and the high land on which a clump of pine trees overhangs the
> sea (p 115).

The cold and misty Protestant northern climate becomes layered with the
warm climes of Catholic Spain, the present and memory infecting one another.
The constant references made to the mists or snows of Mentieth suggest
Graham embracing the ill-defined, preferring areas without clear markers a
time when as he remarks in a sketch entitled 'Mist in Menteith', 'nothing is
stable'. This process of decentring is, in the work of some modernist writers,
perceived as a threat, most notably in the case of Conrad. Uncertainty of place
results in uncertainty of the self. In contrast, Graham regards the indeterminate
nature of the landscape as the opportunity for a fruitful opposition to be
brought about. A palimpsest is created where past and present co-exist and
inform one another.

Graham is an important transitional figure between the ideas of those
associated with the Celtic Twilight and in creating a brand of Scottish modernism,
one that combined the provincial with the international and in doing so sought
to create an anti-imperialist identity for Scotland. MacDiarmid draws attention

to this lineage when he highlights the similarities between a piece by Graham and the work of Annie S. Swan (1995: 38). The sketch 'Tobar Na Réil' ('The Well of the Star') may at first appear a slice of Celtic whimsy, but it displays Graham's knowledge concerning the means by which language may be used as a means of control. A drink from the well allows the drinker to understand the language of the trees and animals, the location being:

> a borderland of races in the past, a frontier where the Lowland hob and Highland pixie met on neutral ground, to dance upon the green, seemed to invite experiment, and call for its Columbus to explore a newer world than he saw in Guanahani from his Caravel (Walker 1982: 45–6).

A naively idealistic view of a colonial encounter is conveyed, the meeting an opportunity for exchange and experiment. The author's knowledge of the unlikely nature of such an event is conveyed in the following paragraph, which carries the suggestion of the imbalance in power that threatens to negate the possibilities offered by the colonial encounter. Instead of bringing about a fruitful exchange language becomes a means of subjugation:

> A gentle world in which no hatred reigns; where envy and all malice are unknown, where each one tells his secret to his friend unwittingly, because the speech they use is universal and without volition, and not as ours, confined to persons and articulate. The speech that lives in the clear water of the well, at the conjuncture of the star, has no vocabulary, no rules, no difficulties, but he who has it speaks as does the wind, and saying nothing in particular, is understood of all. Thus it can never lie, or lead astray, and so is valueless to us, as valueless as gold upon a desert island, with *no one to enslave* (p 46).

During the 1890s, when Graham's sketches began to appear in collected form, Britain had achieved the heights of the imperial endeavour. Travel, scientific journals and fiction overlap and inform one another thereby creating a discourse by which the West viewed the Rest. Rarely do Graham's sketches attain the 'pure' form of fiction, as the author, who began his writing career with politically slanted journalism appears incapable of subsuming his own personality for the sake of the story. While this may appear amateur to the reader, the form of his work is best understood as a complement to its political message that sets out to undermine the authority of the imperial discourse. He displays an acute

154

sensitivity to the means by which this discourse was maintained 'The Gualichú Tree' is an account of a tree worshipped on the plains of Argentina. As in other examples of his work, Graham is recording certain customs that are being slowly eroded by the work of Western imperialists. Where the piece differs from a purely anthropological account is the way he makes explicit how such studies acted as a front-runner for the continued destruction of indigenous traditions. As Said writes in relation to Conrad, Graham in his 1902 sketch 'The Gualichú Tree' enables us to see 'imperialism as a system' (Said 1994: 407):

> The earliest travellers in the southern plains describe the tree as it still stood but twenty years ago; it seemed to strike them but as an evidence of the lowness of the Indians in the human scale. Whether it was so, or if a tree which rears its head alone in a vast stony plain, the only upright object in the horizon for leagues on every side, is not a fitting thing to worship, or to imagine that a powerful spirit has his habitation in it, I leave to missionaries, to "scientists", and to all those who, knowing little, are sure that savages know nothing, and view their faith as of a different nature from their own (p 14).

Here Graham succeeds in combining an ethnographic travel account with an implicit criticism of the way a subjective account could become scientific fact and later be used for colonial purposes. J G Frazer himself 'argued that colonial officials could not control their subjects without anthropological training' (Kuklick 1991: 185). The 'field work' of travellers could be used as 'evidence of the lowness of the Indians in the human scale'. Anthropology combined with a misreading of Darwin encouraged the belief that certain peoples were destined to die out due to the weakness of their race. This effectively absolved the imperialist nations of their responsibilities towards so-called weaker races. Graham mentions the tree in the prologue to Robert Kirk's *The Secret Commonwealth of Elves, Fauns and Fairies*, (1933) which contains a lengthy introduction by Andrew Lang. Gradual decline in the knowldege of Scottish folk-ways is linked explicitly with the processes of modernisation taking place in the 'less-civilised' regions of the world. Andrew Lang's own collections of folk tales from around the world disallows the possibility of an unsettling cultural relativism by claiming the study of 'savage' cultures allowed Western civilisation to learn its own primitive beginnings. 'Primitive' cultures are thereby sealed off as museum pieces to be studied. By making clear his anti-imperialist sentiment, Graham cannot be accused, as has been the case with the Modernists, of simply carrying on the plunder of other peoples, this time in an intellectual as opposed to material sense. He does not include examples of native life simply in order to reinvigorate a moribund Western artistic tradition but rather does so to highlight the complicity of self-designated impartial observers in the decimation of indigenous cultures. His identity as both insider and outsider places him as a precursor to the identity of such 'provincials' or 'barbarians' of the Modernist movement as Pound, Eliot, Lewis and Lawrence as identified by Robert Crawford (1992: 216-271).

As in his relationship to the literary representation of Scotland, Graham can at times present a contradictory attitude towards aspects of colonialism. D H Lawrence's criticism of *Pedro Valdivia* (1926), that he failed to fully convey the full horror of the brutalities committed by the conquistadores against the natives of Chile:

> Valdivia was not usually cruel, it appears. But he cut off the hands and noses of two hundred 'rebels', Indians who were fighting for their own freedom, and he feels very pleased about it. It served to cow the others. But imagine deliberately chopping off one slender brown Indian hand after another! (Watts and Davies 1979: 213)

Certainly Graham's accounts of the Spanish conquest of South America can appear surprisingly lenient considering the frequently coruscating nature of his attacks against Western imperialism. As the title *A Vanished Arcadia,* his history of the Jesuits in Paraguay from 1607 to 1767, would suggest, he conveys an admiration of the brand of paternalistic colonial rule and can fail to apply his usual rigour to the assumption of Western superiority even the most benevolent form of imperialism maintains. Yet his histories can also be read as a critique of British imperialism and the Protestant ethos that regarded Spain as an empire past its prime, its failings due to its religious and racial difference from Britain's Anglo-Saxon Protestant imperialism. Graham's historical battle was the undoing of 'Anglo-Saxon complacency in criticizing the Spanish Conquest of America' (GoWilt 1995: 218). His histories served to remind readers of the fleeting nature of Empires that those considered great in their day may fail to meet the demands of history. As demonstrated in his account of *The Conquest of the*

River Plate (1924) they draw comparisons between imperialism past and present, and in doing so reveal the fundamental acquisitiveness that lies beneath high-minded ideals down through the ages:

> After the fashion of all conquering peoples, they believed they had a mission to civilize and to bring light into the waste places of the earth. Others have had the same belief, and with the same results. It is a creed that makes men merciless; the Spaniards suffered from it, and so have we ourselves (p 10).

Watts and Davies comment on Graham's neglect that there is 'no dog-show for mongrels, and little critical acclaim now for writing as heterogeneous'(1979: 154). Commenting on *The Satanic Verses* Salman Rushdie celebrates the fact of :

> hybridity, impurity, intermingling, the transformation that comes of new and unexpected combinations of human beings, cultures, ideas, politics ... *Mélange*, hotchpotch, a bit of this and that is how *newness enters the world*. It is the great possibility that mass migration gives the world, and I have tried to embrace it. *The Satanic Verses* is for change-by-fusion, change-by-conjoining. It is a love song to our mongrel selves (1992: 394).

Rushdie also states 'To be a migrant is, perhaps, to be the only species of human being free of the shackles of nationalism (to say nothing of its ugly sister patriotism) ... To see things plainly, you have to cross a frontier' (1992: 124-23). It is this process that Graham's writing enacts. Graham was an important figure to have on the platform of the National Party of Scotland which he joined at its inception in 1928. Concerned by the homogenising force of modernisation he had witnessed both on the colonial frontier and in his home district of Menteith and the difficulty in securing rights for the Scottish working class, he felt that a form of political nationhood was required if Scotland was to retain both its cultural and economic independence:

> We must have a sentiment that shows us that the slums of Glasgow are a slur not only upon the world, but upon every individual one of us, that shows us that the Highlands of Scotland are not only a crying scandal to Scotland and to the Empire, but that they call aloud to us as a scandal against humanity (Watts 1981: 91).

In the same speech, Graham points to both Ghandi and Mussolini as exemplars of the benefits of nationalism, suggesting his own brand of cosmoplitan patriotism may have caused him to ignore the potentially dangerous aspects of political nationalism. That his knowledge and sympathy for other cultures may not have been shared by others is evident in his attempt to combat any anti-Irish feeling latent within the Party:

> Nothing is further from my mind, nothing is more repugugnant to my nature, than to exclude men from any country on account of their religion. Most of my own life has passed amongst Roman Catholics. My wife, long dead, was a Roman Catholic. I find that I have had as much liberty and courtesy and as much humanity shown to me in Catholic countries as I have here at home in Scotland and in England (National Library of Scotland, MSS. Acc. 3466, p 8).

To challenge Rushdie's argument, Graham acts as an example of the way in which a close attachment and appreciation of one's homeland, may result in an acute appreciation of the similarities, the sympathies that can exist with other countries and other peoples. In turn, this can develop into a form of nationalism that in promoting the values of Scotland does not seek to limit the sense of what it might mean to be Scottish, to exclude others or to impose those views on those who lie beyond the border between ourselves and the rest of the world. In today's pluralist Scotland it is time to recognise the achievement of a man who felt that nationalism could only truly exist with a keen awareness of the benefits of internationalism.

References

Bahbha H 1994 The Location of Culture. London, Routledge

Bold A 1983 Modern Scottish Literature. London, Longman

Craig C 1996 Out of History: Narrative Paradigms in Scottish and British Culture. Edinburgh, Polygon

Craig D 1961 Scottish Literature and the Scottish People 1680-1830. Chatto and Windus, London, pp 273–93

Crawford R 1990 'Frazer and Scottish Romanticism: Scott, Stevenson and *The Golden Bough*'. In: Fraser R (ed) Sir James Frazer and the Literary Imagination: Essays in Affinity and Influence. MacMillan, pp 18–37

Crawford R 1992 Devolving English Literature. Oxford, Clarendon Press

Finlay R 1997 A Partnership for Good? Scottish Politics and the Union since 1880. Edinburgh, John Donald

GoWilt C 1995 The Invention of the West: Joseph Conrad and the Double Mapping of Europe and Empire. California, Stanford University Press

Graham G, Graham RBC 1896 Father Archangel of Scotland. London, Black, pp 3–4

Graham RBC 1895 Notes on the District of Menteith, for Tourists and Others. Edinburgh, Black

Graham RBC 1898 Mogreb-al-Acksa. London, Heinemann

Graham RBC 1899 The Ipané. London, Fisher Unwin

Graham RBC 1901 A Vanished Arcadia: Being Some Account of the Jesuits in Paraguay, 1607 to 1767. London, Heinemann

Graham RBC 1902 Success. London, Duckworth

Graham RBC 1909 Faith. London, Duckwort

Graham RBC 1913 A Hatchment. London, Duckworth

Graham RBC 1924 The Conquest of the River Plate. London, Heinemann

Graham RBC Doughty Deeds: An Account of the Life of Robert Graham of Gartmore. London, Heinemann

Harvie C 1977 Scotland and Nationalism: Scottish Society and Politics, 1707-1977. London, George Allen and Unwin

Kirk R 1933 The Secret Commonwealth of Elves, Fauns and Fairies. Eneas Mackay, Stirling

Kuklick H 1991 The Savage Within: The Social History of British Anthropology. Cambridge, Cambridge University Press

MacDiarmid H 1952 Cunninghame Graham: A Centenary Study. Glasgow, Kegan Paul

MacDiarmid H 1995 In: Riach A (ed) Contemporary Scottish Studies. Manchester, Carcanet

MacGillivray A 1987 'Exile and Empire". In: The History of Scottish Literature, Volume 4. Aberdeen, Aberdeen University Press, pp 411–427

MacKenzie J 1993 'Essay and Reflection: On Scotland and the Empire'. In: The International History Review, XV, 4, November, pp 661–880

Malzahn M 1996 'Between the Kailyard: Configurations of Scottish Culture'. In : Scottish Literary Journal, Vol 23, Nov., 1996, pp 54–68

Pratt ML 1992 Imperial Eyes: Travel Writing and Transculturation. London, Routledge

Rushdie S 1992 Imaginary Homelands. London, Granta

Said E 1994 Culture and Imperialism. London, Verso

Thornton AP 1968 For the File on Empire. London, Macmillan

Walker J 1978 The South American Sketches of RB Cunninghame Graham. Edinburgh, Scottish Academic Press

Walker J 1982 The Scottish Sketches of RB Cunninghame Graham. Edinburgh, Scottish Academic Press

Walker J 1985 The North American Sketches of RB Cunninghame Graham. Edinburgh, Scottish Academic Press

Watts C (ed) 1981 Selected Writings of Cunninghame Graham. London & Toronto, Associated University Presses

Watts C, Davies L 1979 Cunninghame Graham: A Critical Biography. Cambridge, Cambridge University Press

Section III

Introduction

Tourism, Heritage and Community

Jonathan Skinner

Brought together here are four chapters which consider the positioning of Scotland and her inhabitants as we enter the new millennium. Recent political changes in Scotland (see other sections in this volume) have heightened discussion and investigation into the changing faces, fashions and tongues of Scottish identity. As a whole, these pieces reveal just some of the rich diversity in representations of Scotland and Scottishness; they show that Scotland the Brand's worn tartan stereotype (McCrone et al 1995) is not blandly seared into the Scottish consciousness. Central to these papers are the issues of tourism, heritage and community: a key question being how community is fostered and represented, not only to tourists, but also to the indigenous. This question is considered through examinations of state versus civil society divisions in rural and urban environs (Morton and Morris), the re-imaging of a Scottish city such as Dundee – 'City of Discovery' (Di Domenico), a comparison of national museums in Scotland and Bavaria (Grabmann), and an assessment of the state of farm tourism in Scotland (Morris and Gladstone).

With selective historical hindsight, *Zeitgeist* Scottish nationalist popular culture has collapsed the last three hundred years – from loss of independence with the Act of Union (1707) to the recent establishment of the Scottish Parliament (1999) – into a narrative of struggle not just for political survival, but also economic survival with the heinous clearances in the Highlands, and cultural survival following the oppression of Highland costume by the English (see Trevor-Roper 1992:24, McCrone 1992:18, 181). Certainly, *Braveheart* followers might see these years as Scotland's age of evolution to devolution, rather than Britain's Golden Enlightenment Age. In trying to assess this period, Scottish sociologist David McCrone notes that Scotland survived as a 'stateless nation', as a separate 'civil society' (1992:3) with a strong sense of identity and difference from the rest of Britain. His reference to Scotland as a civil society pays heed to Scottish thinkers of old such as soldier, theologian and writer on politics Adam Ferguson (1723–1816) and ethnographer, theologian and encyclopaedist William Robertson-Smith (1846–1894) who articulated an implicit concern for the position of Scotland in their histories of 'civilised' society (Ferguson's *An Essay on the History of Civil Society*) and 'uncivilised' society (Robertson-Smith's *The Religion of the Semites*)(see Skinner 1995). Both works and authors subsequently went on to influence the course of sociological and anthropological thought in Britain, amongst other disciplines: Ferguson with his press for the inclusion of civic and communal values in the emerging modern commercial society, Robertson-Smith with his ethnographic exploration into the social nature of religion, namely the connection between ritual *actions* which come before mythic *beliefs* (Boskovik 1995:304). Ferguson's influence, in particular, can be found in several of the chapters in this section such as 'Civil Society, Civic Community: breaking the rural-urban continuum in the global age?' for example.

In this first chapter, Morton and Morris argue that the governance of Scotland has emanated from the modern period, namely from 1707. Civil society, according to the authors, emerges from a local community level, with boundaries defined by local government (the local state). These boundaries are both symbolic and administrative and can be found in both urban and rural locations from Edinburgh to the Orkneys: property franchises with residential rights and privileges in Edinburgh marked the limits of the city as it grew in the nineteenth century for example; and on the 70 Orkney islands, the local Council's new Structure Plan (1993) repeats such boundary marking by encouraging specific nucleated settlements rather than ribbon developments to boost existing settlements to encourage young families to stay, and to foster regional diversity between the 20 inhabited islands so that tourists will keep returning to sample the region. It is worth observing here – after Anthony Cohen (1987) – that boundaries are symbolically constructed, and that – after Fredrik Barth – it is the boundary which defines the group and not its content (1969:15). It is no surprise then, in this Scottish example of boundary and group maintenance by legislation, that Morton and Morris conclude that, in this increasingly globalised world, a sense of Scottish regionalism and Scottish civic identity has not been abraded away. It has, rather, as *Reimagining Culture* (Macdonald 1997) – a recent study of community in the Hebrides – demonstrates, resulted in a contemporary linguistic and cultural 'Gaelic Renaissance' from the bottom-up.

'Other Voices, Other Worlds' is how the Orkneys advertises itself to its international tourist audience in an increasingly competitive market. Glasgow – 'City of Culture', or 'Glasgow's Miles Better' are other recent slogans attempting to regenerate interest in an industrial Scottish city in a post-industrial age where there is an apparent absence or rejection of any particular metropolitan sense of community (see Charsley 1986). Dundee – 'City of Discovery' in Angus, 'Land of Adventure' – is another city with rebranding slogans, or 're-imaging of place' according to Maria Di Domenico in the next chapter in this section. This old industrial city of jam, jute and journalism has recently undergone great urban regeneration on a par with Glasgow. In this second chapter Di Domenico shows us that Dundee's regeneration has taken the form of industrial heritage re-development for tourism. Heritage, in the sense of 'industrial heritage tourism' – the old docks, mills, warehouses and machinery, for instance – relates less to an accurate historical representation of the past than to a modern-day invention of the past, past traditions and past communities; a reflection of the present framed as the past, or even 'the past and the present in the present' (Bloch 1977).

Di Domenico presents a detailed account of the work of the Dundee Heritage Trust, an initiative and a business which has boosted tourism to Dundee by creating and marketing new tourism sites such as the Discovery Point (Captain Scott's Antarctic ship) and Verdant Works (a renovated jute processing factory). This heritage discovery in Dundee is appreciated by tourists and local residents alike, though most are unaware of the distinction between history and heritage, the distinction between industrial representation and industrial reality. Deriving a postmodern framework from her work and research in Dundee, Di Domenico concludes that heritage tourism has been good for Dundee, Scotland and Scots past, present and future. In fact, the work of Dundee's Heritage Trust has brought about a reassertion of local pride and an increased sense of local identity and community, alongside more national identification. This is *contra* modernist social theorist Anthony Giddens's (1990) suggestion that urban museums and heritage sites all contribute to a 'distancing' or 'disembedding' of local identity and community.

This theme – the commercialisation and politicisation of the past – is continued in 'Identity in the Making? National Museums in Scotland and Bavaria', the third chapter in this section. Here, Barbara Grabmann compares the museum construction of identity in two similar civil societies, both stateless nations. A museum is a repository of significant artifacts: an eighteenth century invention (Vergo 1997:1, Walsh 1992), the museum in the twentieth century is recognised by sociologists as a place no longer devoid of political, ideological and aesthetic agendas – be it a Gramscian establishment of a set of relations between state and people, Scotland and the Scottish in this case; or a Foucauldian ordering of things and people, from the siting of the Stone of Scone (Edinburgh or Scone) to the seating of Members of Parliament (Westminster or Edinburgh). Central to Grabmann's thesis is the idea that museums in Scotland and Bavaria are being used as a part of national projects of identity-construction. The musealisation of Scottish and Bavarian fashions, folklore and 'heritage' at the Haus der Bayerischen Geschichte and the new Museum of Scotland have, as part of their objectives, the aim to promote national and 'historical' consciousness amongst their visitors. This is done, according to the curators of these museums, by bringing the people into contact with the icons and symbols of the history of the nation, though they acknowledge that there are many versions of 'history' – or heritage – which can be offered. As organisations, institutions and providers of displays, Grabmann notes that these national museums foster a sense of national community by advancing the notions of political homogeneity alongside cultural diversity (from exhibitions about the Bavarian state and constitution, to exhibitions about twentieth century Scottish objects).

By the late 1980s, museums in Britain were opening at the rate of one every fortnight; many of them in Scotland receiving a visit from 35% of the local population every three months (McCrone et al 1995:2). This was to cater for the exponential rise in international tourism – between 1950 and 1994 international tourism increased 20-fold with expenditure increasing 30-fold, and by the year 2000 internal and external tourism has become the world's largest single economic activity. In Scotland, visitor expenditure totals £2.4 billion (5% GDP), with tourism employing up to 8% of the workforce, figures which rise to 20% of the workforce in the Highlands and Islands (Crop Ecology Group 1999). One increasingly significant tourism strategy investigated by Morris and

Gladstone has been the growth of farm tourism, 'farm-accommodation and agricultural heritage attractions' for visitors. Farm tourism makes use of the natural living and working landscape, one which predominates throughout much of Scotland, employing approximately 20% of Scotland's total workforce. Their final chapter in this section on tourism, heritage and community shows that when the 'Glasgow Cousins' (Kohn 1997:20), 'foreigners' and 'weekenders' take a break in rural Scotland, often staying in B&Bs, they contribute directly to the local economy, regenerating the local community as well as giving local community members a high level of control in their affairs. In their survey of accommodation providers in Perthshire, the Orkneys and South Ayrshire, Morris and Gladstone found that locals were more interested in meeting different visitors and giving them an appreciation of farming than supplementing their farming income: in 1996 the average profit from farm tourism per 'farm' was £1000, much of that ploughed straight back into upgrading the accommodation on offer.

As Valene Smith and William Eadington (1995:3) remark in the opening of *Tourism Alternatives*, 'alternative tourism' can be broadly defined as forms of tourism consistent with natural, social and community values. They go on to add that both the hosts and the guests should enjoy positive and worthwhile interaction and shared experiences. Whether enjoying urban or rural attractions – national museums, industrial heritage centres or rural farm breaks – each of the chapters in this section shows that though boundaries and symbols of Scotland and Scottish identity are erected, like a low-brow cognitive Hadrian's Wall, their diverse contents can be enjoyed and appreciated by all. Scotland then is a mental and physical region of both unity and diversity; a region where groups of people (inhabitants of Dundee, Glasgow, Edinburgh, the Orkneys; farmers, curators and other employed groups) share many characteristics from history and heritage to language and outlook – *amongst* each other and sometimes *between* each other. A community-imagined civil society composed of civic and rural groups, Scotland's future in the next century could be one of pride and tolerance, of nationalism with social inclusion, of economic growth and political satisfaction; or it could be a future of religious and linguistic divisions, of racist and nationalist tensions, of class and capitalist competition. It is to the former rather than the latter vision of Scotland – an enlightenment future – which Scottish academics and critics of Scotland of the past and the present have been, and are, writing and working towards.

References

Barth F 1969 Ethnic Groups and Boundaries. Oslo, Universitetsforlaget

Bloch M 1977 The past and the present in the present. MAN, 12:4, pp278–92.

Boskovik A 1995 William Robertson Smith and the Anthropological Study of Myth. In: Johnstone W (ed) William Robertson Smith: Essays in Reassessment. Sheffield, Sheffield Academic Press, pp303-10

Charsley S 1986 'Glasgow's miles better': the symbolism of community and identity in the city. In: Cohen A (ed) Symbolising Boundaries: Identity and Diversity in British Cultures. Manchester, Manchester University Press, pp.171-86

Cohen A 1987 Whalsay: Symbol, Segment and Boundary in a Shetland Island Community. Manchester, Manchester University Press

Cohen A 1989 The Symbolic Construction of Community. London, Routledge

Crop Ecology Group 1999 A Rural Policy for Scotland – Tourism. University of Edinburgh, http://meranti.ierm.ed.ac.uk/teaching/gr/homepage/tour.html

Giddens A 1990 The Consequences of Modernity. Cambridge, Polity Press

Kohn T 1997 Island Involvement and the Evolving Tourist. In: Abram S, Waldren J, Macleod D (eds) Tourists and Tourism: Identity with People and Places. Oxford, Berg, pp13-28

McCrone D 1992 Understanding Scotland: The Sociology of a Stateless Nation. London, Routledge

McCrone D, Morris A, Kiely R 1995 Scotland – the Brand: The Making of Scottish Heritage. Edinburgh, Edinburgh University Press

Macdonald S 1997 Reimagining Culture: Histories, Identities and the Gaelic Renaissance. Oxford, Berg

Skinner J 1995 Orientalists and Orientalism: William Robertson-Smith and Edward W. Said. In: Johnstone W (ed) William Robertson Smith: Essays in Reassessment. Sheffield, Sheffield Academic Press, pp376-82

Smith V, Eadington W 1995 Introduction:The Emergence of Alternative Forms of Tourism. In: Smith V, Eadington W (eds) Tourism Alternatives: potentials and problems in the development of tourism. Chichester, John Wiley, pp1-12

Trevor-Roper H 1992 The Invention of Tradition: The Highland Tradition of Scotland. In: Hobsbawm E, Ranger T (eds) The Invention of Tradition. Cambridge, Canto, pp15–42

Vergo P 1997 Introduction. In: Vergo P (ed) The New Museology. London, Reaktion Books, pp1–5

Walsh K 1992 The Representation of the Past: Museums and Heritage in the Post-modern World. London, Routledge

Civil Society, Civic Community:
Breaking the Rural-urban Continuum in the Global Age?

Graeme Morton and Angela Morris

The importance of civil society comes from the realisation that Scotland's national identity has been institutionally sustained rather than culturally led. This is not to deny all that is distinctive about the Scottish character and nation, its heritage, myth and history, but the everyday understanding of what Scotland got out of the Union with England in 1707 was its Presbyterian variant of Protestantism, its legal system centred on the principles of Roman not common law, and a tradition of education which has emphasised breadth and maintained its own (religious) ethos. Where we educate our children, where we worship our God or bury our dead, and where we dispense our justice, shapes our everyday culture as much as our state will ever do. In Scotland these institutions have their roots in civil society, from that we cannot escape. Nor should we wish to; Scottish national identity has not been missing, but has, for good or ill, been sustained in civil society in the centuries since that Union (Morton 1998a).

Civil society has been the arena from which the governance of Scotland has emanated in the modern period (since 1707), and is the basis from which we wish to develop our argument here. Our concern is to construct an understanding of civil society at the level of the community. We wish to delineate Scotland's governance through civil society in two contrasting communities. Edinburgh, as the capital city of Scotland and the second of its two most urban centres, and Orkney, its capital Kirkwall, and its influence on the islands which make up its archipelago. These will be our case studies, one national the other regional, one urban, one predominantly rural. Our key will be the boundary between the urban and the rural worlds as governed by the local state. Our hypothesis is that it is at this boundary that we can see the negotiation between different civil societies. The custodian of the boundary is local government and this will be our primary concern. How has local government managed different civil societies within Scotland? Our study will in part be historical as we search for our understanding of this process, but our contemporary concern is the challenge of globalisation to these communities.

Over-flexibility has been a justifiable criticism of the concept of civil society (Kumar 1993: 383). Yet we retain the notion that more than one civil society exists in the United Kingdom, and this is far from controversial. We wish to maintain an argument that goes one stage further. Not only do we accept that Scottish civil society has been stronger and more relevant than a notional British civil society, but we wish to suggest that its strength stems from the localities.

It is probably fair to state that discussion around the concept of civil society has focused on its intellectual traditions and its sociological worth as much as its very definition itself. The debates between Bryant (1994) and Kumar (1993) are the most instructive here. Ironically, this debate on the value of the concept has been prompted by attempts, particularly by British and US organisations, to recreate or even invent and impose civil society in newly liberalising states in Eastern Europe, Africa and Latin America (Morris 1998; Suhrke 1992). Seligman (1992: 102) is the clearest exponent of the view that civil society is ultimately a definition of citizenship, so its attractiveness to Western liberalism is clear. In contrast, Alexander (1998) and the contributors to his edited collection *Real Civil Societies*, question how ready theorists are to deal with the everyday contradictions which make it 'difficult to institutionalise the highly universalistic, often utopian norms and structures of civil societies (p 13). Here, then, the focus is on the control of access to the state for the populace or for minorities. Citizenship rights are rights of access to the government or the state, in terms of franchise or employment. Ethnic rights are similarly structured, argues Garcia in his study of urban relations (1996: 7-8). Yet civil society, its theorists tell us, is embedded in non-state associations and structured in communication networks and the formation of 'public opinion'. In essence, civil society is not about access to state power. One of us has therefore argued for a definition of civil society 'that includes the inhabitants and infrastructure of a physical space' and is not restricted by franchise nor ethnically particularistic in the granting of 'citizenship' (Morton 1998b). Civil society is structured and is operationalised around a community. That the community is in communion with the state is undenied. Our hypothesis is that the local state of the community mediates between civil society and the central state. The local state acts as a formal extension of associational or communicative networks, the two dominant structures of civil society, by providing status as well as empowerment through legislation. Yet there is a more fundamental administrative aspect of this mediator role. The survival and relative independence of civil society in the face of state centralisation and wider socio-economic processes is negotiated through the local state.

Civil Society as a Boundary

Our focus then is on civil society at the boundary as it is defined by the local state. We are working with the concept of boundary in two senses: as an administrative area and a symbolic construct. Anthony P. Cohen's work on the island of Whalsay in the Shetland Isles offers such a definition, while emphasising its cultural meaning:

> The boundary is thus more complex than its physical, legal or administrative bases; more complex than the ethnic, racial, religious or linguistic differences which it may enclose. Many of the elements which constitute the boundary may not be objectively apparent at all but, rather, exist in the minds of their beholders. Like other symbols, the boundary does not entail given meanings. Rather, it provides people with forms which they may then invest with meaning. But to say that community boundaries are often symbolic in character is not only to suggest that they imply different meanings for different people. It also suggests that boundaries perceived by some may be utterly imperceptible to others (1987: 14).

We too wish to develop the symbolic meaning of boundaries in our final section, but we also wish to explain the physical, legal and administrative bases of boundaries as determinants of unequal constructions of civil society. It is this concern which takes our focus to the boundary between the urban and the rural world.

The Rural-Urban Continuum

I t is a truism to point out that nations are made up of localities and regions as well as towns and cities. The national community is the next step up from a range of particular communities, its timing dependent on state and capitalist development (as Gellner 1983 and the modernists would argue). Yet regionalism is not ignored in constructions of the nation, and neither should it be in the construction of a national civil society. Important boundaries exist at the local level, particularly between the urban world and the rural world. The 'rural-urban' continuum is one of the fundamental models in sociology. It is an ideal type often used to structure our understanding of society. Clearly this continuum does not provide a complete or comprehensive description of either the rural or the urban sectors of any society. Rather, it is best thought of as a line running between two poles. The 'rural' pole stands for small, inward-looking, idyllic communities whose economy is mainly based on agriculture and whose primary relationships are essentially formed around an extended family. By contrast the 'urban' pole represents large, impersonal, cosmopolitan, industrial and commercial centres (Morris and Morton 1998: 12).

The work of the nineteenth century German sociologist, Ferdinand Tönnies has had most impact on the development of this binary model. Tönnies identified two contrasting ways of living: *Gemeinschaft* and *Gesellschaft*. Loosely translated, *Gemeinschaft* means community in the sense of community as 'communion'. It closely resembles the notion of a big family – of blood ties. *Gesellschaft*, in the words of Elias, represents a colder, unattached and more fragmented way of living devoid of cooperation and social cohesion. Instead of a sense of neighbourliness, people are isolated. *Gesellschaft* translates as association. Here blood ties are irrelevant and are replaced by a (monetary) contract. Associations are there for you to join, or to subscribe to, and above all to leave. *Gesellschaft* is much more impersonal and is much more characteristic of urban life than it is of the hamlet, the village or the crofting township (1974: 12–13). The associational structure which came to characterise it was a means of replicating what blood ties once provided. Hence the importance of civil society in the transition to modern society in the work of Adam Ferguson and the role of civic virtue to make it succeed

Edinburgh: Creating the Urban Boundary

To charge the concept of civil society with the analytical power we wish to make of it, it is necessary to take one step back to achieve progress. Civil society takes root in the promotion of social order and community in the world of *Gesellschaft*. We have proposed that civil society is by definition 'national' in its relationship vis-à-vis the state, yet its formation is rooted in the localities. Definitions of urban place in Britain can be rooted in the Roman invasion in 43 AD and Caesar's war correspondent Tacitus' classification of hillforts and *oppida*. Definitions of urban citizenship however are more usefully taken back to the medieval burgage plot and the burgers, particularly in the royal burghs, who were empowered with trading rights, wealth creation and tax collection. These elites self-selected their own local government. It was the transition of such oligarchies under municipal reform in 1833 which marks the point when citizenship of the vote matched citizenship of residence. Our concern is to emphasise the importance of residential citizenship to civil society.

We first wish to explain our ideas through an examination of the growth through legislation of the city of Edinburgh since 1833. That date, as we have pointed out, heralded a new version of citizenship. The franchise was more open than the parliamentary one upon which it was based (the ownership of property of a value of £10); it was to include women if they owned such property in their own name and it established the link between urban residence and urban government, so fundamental to statements of civic pride at this time. From this basis we are able to approach our first chosen example, the incorporation of either small amounts of neighbouring urban land or of the surrounding countryside into expanded municipal boundaries. Here the urban/rural boundary was changed. This, as one might expect, was a very formal process marked by a period of debate and petitioning by the relevant councils and landowners with the obligations of Edinburgh to its newly acquired territory being specified in careful detail in the empowering legislation. Edinburgh Town Council ensured that its newly expanded municipal electorate would receive the same rights and privileges in terms of matching the municipal and parliamentary franchise and tax burden and the conferment of paving, lighting, gas, electricity and policing (Morton 1998b). Municipal expansion, then, involved an extension of the electoral base, creating new wards and expanding the number of councillors. It also involved giving rights to residents whether they were entitled to vote or not. The argument for expansion was always that the districts to be annexed were as much a part of Edinburgh as the Royalty itself and that 'All who participate in the benefits, should share in the burden, and bear a part of the duties and responsibilities' (Macfarlane 1847-8: 1).

The process of municipal expansion involved the equalisation and the standardisation of infrastructure and taxation between the prior and the newly annexed lands. The citizens of Portobello, for example, were given new rights to sanitary and health provision following their amalgamation with Edinburgh City in 1896. Like the incorporation of minor lands into the city's boundaries, these less populated areas would then become entitled to the standard package of paving, lighting and other infrastructural provision upon reaching a particular density threshold. Not only were these residents given the vote to influence the town council of Scotland's capital city, they were immediately given infrastructural enfranchisement. This was the administrative underpinning of Edinburgh's civil society – one that was created in distinction to its rural hinterland.

With the amalgamation of Leith in 1920, Edinburgh created the last extension of the city boundaries upon which the post-war planning process, in town and county, was based. Edinburgh's appropriateness flows from the grand civic survey as an academic exercise begun with Patrick Geddes in 1915. In the post-war years, Edinburgh was the subject of a civic survey conducted by Sir Patrick Abercrombie, the third he carried out. His intention was to combine fact finding with planning, to produce results that could be adopted in full or in part under the 1947 Town and Country Planning Act (Abercrombie and Plumstead 1949: vii). The civic survey offered two interesting conclusions. The first was that the ultimate size of Edinburgh – as the capital city – should be a matter for national direction, not local interests. The capital city should be of a magnitude in balance with the actual size of Scotland's population – a balance to be confirmed by a boundary around the city of unbuilt-upon land. The second finding was that places of very high density within the city could be 'regrouped' within the city boundaries: 'there is no need for the creation of an external satellite or New Town to take the overspill of the denser parts' (1949: 2–3). This plan emphasised that the city should function as a self-contained and delimited entity, that it should not spread into the countryside, that it should not be serviced by satellite or new towns. It was to be in balance with the countryside, and this was to be achieved by creating internal balance within the city boundaries by the creation of 'precincts' (1949: 49). Precincts were to mark the internal structure of the city (residential zones, industrial, commercial and business, recreation and cultural zones, with a control over the height and architectural design of buildings). Both the internal and the external relationships of the city were to be balanced to achieve this civic plan – the organic city of Geddes was the clear analogy here. The role of this civic plan was to make Edinburgh, within its boundaries, infrastructurally self-sufficient.

Protecting the 'National' Countryside

The discussion of the legislative framing of Edinburgh as a municipal area within its county was centred on the levelling out of citizenship rights. Rather than a political definition, this definition of citizenship was a residential one. This was inevitably a binary relationship. The definition was the urban, the municipal area, something which was not the county, the rural area. The discussion of the Abercrombie report was to show how the city as a self-contained entity could be constructed with an internal and external balance. Our purpose now is to examine this binary relationship from the county perspective. Here the focus becomes the survival of the countryside from urban expansion. As a precursor to the need for national regeneration, Lord Justice Scott's 1941 Committee on Land Utilisation in Rural Areas established the philosophy and objectives which were to guide rural policy upon the cessation of hostilities. In 1946 the National Agricultural Advisory Service (NAAS) was created and became the Agricultural Development and Advisory Service (ADAS). To maintain the predominance of agriculture in the countryside the Agriculture Act of 1947 promoted food and timber production. The need to prioritise certain activities in the countryside remains well enshrined still in the Common Agricultural Policy, often controversially so. In Britain this immediate post-war solution was part of a holistic package. To control the spread of urban areas and industrial activity, the Town and Country Planning

Act of 1947 was passed and instead access to the countryside was managed and delimited. Complementing this Act, the National Parks and Access to the Countryside Act of 1949 was inspired by a vision of the countryside as an area to be preserved for all. This was partly in terms of the production of food and the extraction and processing of raw materials. But it was also part of an ideological vision of the land as national heritage (Rogers 1989; Allanson and Whitby 1996). The land had always been part of ours and most other nations' national psyche, our mother and/or father land, but now it was given a formal position through protection and promotion (McCrone 1997).

Again, as in the study of Edinburgh, the legislation has been framed to balance the rural–urban continuum. In this case changes in the consumption of leisure (by a primarily urban society) were added. Here we have the construction of locality from within the countryside. The legislation provided the framework for encapsulating the rural and the urban worlds, keeping them separate by controlling urban overspill and restricting access to the countryside.

What, then, has been the response from rural society when faced in recent decades with the process? The rural world and the global world are our final concerns and we now turn to our second case study, the Orkney Islands. Through this example we wish to move our thesis on by examining the rural world as it has existed in a time of increasing pressure on the coherence of the rural and the urban world.

Orkney Islands

The Orkney Islands have maintained a stable population in recent years despite much migration. Between 1951 and 1981 the population of Orkney fell by 10%, since then inward migration has countered the losses overall, despite depopulation in some of the outer isles (*Third Statistical Account* 1985: xi). In the 1991 Census the population stood at 19 328. Healthy as recent population figures may be, there remains a fear of depopulation from Orkney, and of the over-concentration of internal migration (and that from the mainland) to Kirkwall and Stromness. In 1968 the Orkney Council of Social Service commissioned Ronald Miller and Susan Luther–Davies of the University of Glasgow to study the causes and the effects of depopulation from Eday and Hoy. Part of their concern was to encourage meat processing on the islands, to stimulate local employment, rather than the export of cattle on the hoof. Their final conclusion was that

> ... probably the greatest single stimulus the outlying islands could have would be a conviction that their more fortunate neighbours on the Mainland and especially in Kirkwall were doing everything possible to share their higher standards with the islands (1969: 3-4, 91).

This was an economic case for positive intervention in Orkney as a whole, something which has not been lost in its marketing as a tourist destination. Here a carefully constructed Orkney Islands identity has been formed. From agricultural and cheese production, the Highland Park distillery to tourism, there has been a sense of unity. Diversity has still been stressed, the local nature reserve of Mull Head, the ornithological sanctuaries of Brodgar and Eynhallow, the twelfth century old-town structure of Kirkwall, the Churchill barriers and the military history of Scapa Flow. But this diversity has enhanced rather than fragmented the sense of place in and of the Orkney Islands. To explain this we can identify two processes. The first is an attempt to keep the economic, social and demographic balance of the mainland and remaining islands of the archipelago, especially those which are unattached. The second is a policy of spreading tourism around, rather than concentrating on any one feature.

The Orkney Islands Structure Plan (1993) makes clear the policy of maintaining socio-economic growth, and social unity, through the promotion of diversity. To this extent this Structure Plan was a return to the themes of the 1968 study and analogous to Abercrombie's civic vision of Edinburgh. The capital of Orkney, Kirkwall, is its largest urban concentration, and the Council had specified a range of policies to prevent the overall economy and its infrastructure from being further centralised there. If not a policy of dispersion, then one of balance has been followed. The North Isle has a higher proportion of the population aged over 60 and Kirkwall has the highest proportion of younger people, and this placed pressure on the provision of housing, clean water, waste disposal and on traffic congestion (1993: 7).

The Council identified the distribution of economic activity to areas and the islands outwith Kirkwall as a 'Key Issue' in its entire Structure Plan and attempts were then made to tackle this objective through a number of different policies (1993: 10). Urban sprawl and ribbon developments were to be actively discouraged and instead the focus was on existing nucleated settlements. The intention was to boost existing settlements to the level of critical mass great enough to sustain schooling, shops, leisure provision and the all the other facilities which encourage younger families to stay. The Council committed itself to the provision of new schools or extensions to existing provision (or closures) when a population rise or fall demanded, but also to 'give special consideration and support through a higher than average capital and revenue expenditure to under-used schools in isolated communities with low populations, particularly Graemsay, Egilsay, North Ronaldsay and Papa Westray' (1993: 41–2). The Council wanted to reduce the cost of the Stromness/Scrabster crossing which was then one of the dearest in Scotland per mile and to ensure that tariff levies were 'reasonable' to other routes, to develop new routes – including air travel – to rural areas and subsidise them when justified.

Linked to the Key Policy of economic redistribution was the conservation of the cultural and natural heritage of Orkney. And here it is tourism which is to be promoted in an attempt to increase the 120 000 who visit the many islands each year and who spend £24m. The plan was to increase their length of stay, especially on the outer Isles, with grants available for the erection and modernisation of visitor accommodation. The Orkney tourist brochure of 1995 described the islands as 'Other Voices, Other Worlds' by explaining that: '... though our 70 islands start just six miles north of the Scottish mainland, you'll discover that they're worlds apart. Only 20 are inhabited. Each has a distinct character, with its own set of attractions. Even if you were to visit them all, you'd have to start again to confirm your favourite'.

Diversification was not used just to describe the islands of Orkney, it was also used in a more technical sense, outlining what changes were needed in the economic activity for tourism to be promoted. Sponsored by the Scottish Tourist Board, Orkney Enterprise has instituted 'The Orkney Host Programme' for all who welcome visitors to the Islands, with workplace assessors able to gain Scottish Vocational Qualifications (SVQs). In reaction to government policy of the use of agricultural land, the emphasis has moved away from the expansion of food production to less extensive farming, the creation of woodlands and the provision of tourist accommodation (*Orkney Islands Structure Plan* 1993: 29–32).

> Farmers will be encouraged to refurbish vacant farm buildings for holiday lets especially on the North and South Isles through financial assistance devised by the Council and Orkney Enterprise (1993: 30).

Sustainable tourism is seen as one of the main saviours of rural areas. The Piper Alpha disaster of 1988, which reduced the supply of crude oil to Flotta, re-emphasised the importance of tourist-based employment, despite it containing many Cinderella industries precariously placed (Nurminen and Robinson 1985: 32–3). Tourist-based employment dates only from the 1980s in Orkney, and is usefully contextualised in a contemporary comparison with Ireland. There, a pilot programme for an attempted integrated rural development (IRD) had as its objective: 'to improve the employment opportunities, earning potential, quality of life and sense of community identity among people in rural areas' (O'Malley 1992: 5). Of the projects set up in this pilot, by far the most were based around tourism (28%) with primary agriculture (6.3%) ranking alongside 'heritage' (6%). Clearly the plan was to create a sense of community from the 'bottom up', by 'fostering viable private and community enterprise, based on full utilisation of the abilities and talents of local people' (1992: 1). Schemes like this benefited from the reform of European Community Structural Funds in 1988 to assist farm diversification and reform to the Common Agricultural Policy in 1992 which removed support away from production-centred agriculture. This was confirmed by the Uruguay Round Agreement on Agriculture which marked the end of the over-production of single foodstuffs, while promoting a wider means of farm diversification (Morris and Gladstone 1999). The most international of farming policies, then, has placed new emphasis on the diversity of the rural potential in the localities rather than the mono-crop production which marked the notorious butter and cereal mountains of the 1980s. Like the civic plan of Edinburgh in the post-war years, the Orkney Islands Council has seen its future development tied to a holistic civic identity. It is one where the farmer and the fish worker are as much part of the tourist creation of the Orkney experience as he or she once was essential to survival in a less prosperous and less connected world.

Globalisation

Has the impact of the on agricultural production therefore re-emphasised the locality? This will be our final concern as we consider new ways of fostering the conditions for civil society to flourish. Globalisation is about international economics and levels of interaction never previously seen. It is about companies with extensive supply change networks and an international division of labour, companies whose market value may be greater than the GNP of many small nations. Globalization is also about a new level of interaction across time-zones, bringing new communities of users to our terminals. It is argued that the real significance of the process is in its stretching, deepening and re-ordering of space and time and of our political and social experiences. The result, Giddens argues, is that 'locales are thoroughly penetrated by and shaped in terms of social influences quite distant from them' (1990: 19).

This talk of breaking free of the constraints of time carries a certain glamour. It is wrapped up equally closely with cross-national standardisation of culture and material goods. The phrase 'McDonaldisation' was coined by George Ritzer (1996: 1) as a means of analysing how 'the process by which the principles of the fast-food restaurant are coming to dominate more and more sectors of American society as well as of the rest of the world'. The phrase is also indicative of core-nation acculturation, in this case American-led. Take the example of the old man nursing a cup of tea in a cottage on Papa Westray in the 1970s. A cottage from which his father and grandfather had gone down to the sea, swapped Orkney tales over Orkney beer and listened to Orkney fiddle music. A cottage where now the old man sat watching the 'bump and grind of a Las Vegas showgirl' on TV (Linklater 1995: 12). We cannot deny the cachet that Hollywood, Disney and other similar brand-names possess, the cultural values they inculcate. The success of Reebok and McDonald's in the nations of Eastern Europe are cases in point. But as commentators such as Hall have pointed out, globalisation may destroy the nation-state, but equally it may not (1992: 300). Hirst and Thompson (1996) have even gone as far as to suggest that little has in fact changed and that the concept lacks value. Indeed, 'transnational relations are not merely 'post-modern': they have always undercut the sovereignty of all states' (Mann 1996: 298; Hall 1992: 299; Wallerstein 1989). Those who see the persistence of national boundaries as containers for specific cultures, argue that globalisation offers the opportunity for local or ethnic particularisms to be magnified – 'the globalization of culture is not the same as its homogenization', despite being its initial impetus (Appadurai 1990: 307). Mike Fetherstone has pointed out that 'one of the consequences of these changes is that more and more people are now involved with more than one culture' (1990: 8). This polarity of local and cosmopolitan may cause problems of interculture communication, he argues, but 'the variety of response to the globalization process clearly suggest that there is little prospect of unified global culture, rather there are global cultures in the plural (1990: 10). That capitalism thrives on difference and that cultural difference sells is a point made by Rutherford (1990: 11): 'It's no longer keeping up with the Joneses, it's about being different from them'.

The draw of the locality and the influence of a transnational world have both impacted on Orkney Islands society. In the 1950s it was noted 'that time was when Orcadians kept a small boat so they could go to the cuithes with a view to supplanting their diet: now racing dinghies and yachts are more characteristic' (*Third Statistical Account of Scotland* 1985: xi). This change was also noted by George Mackay Brown at the end of the 1960s, yet he still kept a window open on the uniqueness of the Orcadian:

> Monday is the market day in Kirkwall, and the farmers come in from the parishes in their cars. There is no longer a typical farmer or farmer's wife; year by year they tend to look more like the town people. But you can see an old countryman in Kirkwall on a Monday morning; he has red polished cheeks, he looks awkward in his best suit, he speaks in a slow rich wondering lilt, the sentences rising and breaking off at the crest: a good language for narrative and dialogue. In Scotland when people congregate they tend to argue and discuss and reason; in Orkney they tell stories (1969: 19).

The Orkney Islands council has long prioritised the transport networks between its islands and the Scottish mainland. The introduction of ro-ro ferries has done much for the connectivity of the Orkney economy. Telecommunications have also been important: most notably BBC Radio Orkney helped shape a distinct identity along with the efforts of some hardy entrepreneurs such as the Hoy Telecottage. Despite the inevitable lag experienced by isolated communities when waiting on telecommunication companies to connect less economic areas – a problem identified by the Council – the Orkney Tourist Board has not been slow to exploit the potential of the internet to promote what it describes as a 'virtual visit to Orkney' and its seventy islands (http://www.orkneyislands.com/). The World Wide Web (WWW) is used to advertise some of the commercial tourist facilities on Orkney such as boats available to charter and, on a cultural level, the Orkney Arts Review is now on-line, replicating the printed edition, but with plans to '... develop its own identity, with input from Orkney's rich seam of artistic activity.'

The Networked Community: New Identities

The rural community has most to gain from new types of communication which break the relevance of their geographical isolation. Satellite and cable television companies offering banking, telephoning, home shopping, film hire and the inevitable galaxy of TV channels are already in many homes. Modems and links to the WWW are becoming common, although most use the Web at their place of work or at internet cafes or public libraries. Sitting in front of a terminal is one of the most privatised and anomic experiences of the modern age, but it also opens up the opportunity for new levels of communication and, in particular, of information processing. This translates our sociological understanding of the community into one free from physical boundaries. It also creates new interactions in a way the traditional urban community of 1950s Bethnal Green or the highland rural idyll of 1980s Ford could never have hoped to match. The general anonymity of relationships conducted over the internet are matched by their frequency, ease of use across time and space and, in many cases, their continuity. These new networked communications are reminiscent of Wirth's associational response to the anomic city, but at a level which has broken the constraints of physical locality and time (Morris and Morton 1998: 130).

We saw in the work of Stuart Hall (1992) the view that globalisation is likely either to lead to the end of the nation-state or, in effect, if not the opposite, then a new sense of place. Regional identity it was argued is one of the most likely beneficiaries as the new idyll or 'golden past' as bounded societies cling to continuities in a time of accelerated change. Our research has tended to confirm a reinvigoration of sense of place, of regional identity, but one sustained on the foundations of the global economy and global society. As Ash Amin observes:

> One of the most striking features of most cities today is their character as a set of spaces of juxtaposed fragments and contrasts, where diverse relational webs might coalesce, interconnect or disconnect. The city does not possess a unitary identity or homogeneous spaces, perhaps it never has (1997: 131).

It appears that the societies that most embrace these changes do best. What our discussion of globalisation has contributed further, is that we should expect the hybridity of national identity to continue: 'Daily the "global village" is flagged, and this banal globalism is supplanting the conditions of banal nationalism' (Billig 1995: 132). The local and global coexist and can even be beneficial in comparison to cities lacking such a pull from the outside. It may be a 'good thing' to experience what Amin calls urban social fragmentation and hybridity (1997: 134–5).

Hybridity was apparent for one part of Orcadian life when it was claimed 'their ancestors would be ... stunned to learn that in 1983 a party of Orcadians could fly to Stockholm to support an Aberdeen football team' winning a European trophy (*The Third Statistical Account of Scotland* 1985: xiv). But this is merely symptomatic of the flexibility of boundaries under the challenge of modernisation, a process with a long history but perhaps one that was gaining pace. George Mackay Brown saw progress as the new religion – it was preoccupation with material concerns and a 'shower of good things'. The old stories had gone and were replaced by regurgitated news from the night before: 'Word and name are drained of their ancient power. Number, statistic, graph are everything' (1969: 28–9). The process is not new, neither is the reaction to it.

Conclusion

What we have tried to do in this chapter is to set out the framework for an analysis of the role of local government in the promotion of what is clearly civic identity, but which we would also like to argue was the framework for distinct civil societies. Our final discussion of globalisation has suggested that the promotion of the locality identity is more likely to increase rather than decrease, with the WWW removing the isolation of many rural communities. What we have not done is explain the workings of civil society in each community: the voluntary activity and associations, the cooperatives, the social groupings and the channels of power through which community decisions are formed and elites emerge. That is the job for other work. We have tried instead to stress the importance of local government to construct civic identity through administrative means, redistributing their populations, economic activities, transportation links and the many other parts of town and county infrastructure: the rural–urban boundary is the key point of contrast. Our conclusion has been that recent trends in the globalization process have emphasised the particularism of the locality and that this has added to the link between civic identity, the civic community and the maintenance of civil society.

Acknowledgements

Graeme Morton's research for this paper was funded by an ESRC Research Fellowship (H52427005694); Angela Morris's research was funded by Scottish Office Agriculture, Environment and Fisheries Department (SOAEFD) core-funding.

References

Abercrombie P, Plumstead D 1949 A Civic Survey and Plan for the City and Royal Burgh of Edinburgh. Edinburgh, Oliver & Boyd

Alexander J C 1998 'Introduction. Civil Society, I, II, III: Constructing an empirical concept from normative controversies and historical transformations'. In: Alexander J C (ed) Real Civil Societies: Dilemmas of Institutionalisation. London, Sage

Allanson P, Whitby M 1996 The Rural Economy and the British Countryside. London, Earthscan

Amin A 1997 'Placing Globalization'. In: Theory, Culture and Society, 14, 2

Appadurai A 1990 'Disjuncture and Difference in the Global Cultural Economy'. In: Theory, Culture and Society, 7, 2-3, June

Billig M 1995 Banal Nationalism. London, Sage

Brown G M 1969 An Orkney Tapestry. London, Victor Gollancz

Bryant C G A 1994 'A further comment on Kumar's "Civil society". British Journal of Sociology, 45, 3, September

Cohen A P 1987 Whalsay: symbol, segment and boundary in a Shetland island community. Manchester, Manchester University Press

Elias N 1974 Foreword In: Bell C, Newby H (eds) The Sociology of Community: a selection of readings. London, Cass

Fethersone M 1990 'Global Culture: an introduction'. Theory, Culture and Society, 7, 2-3, June

Garcia S 1996 'Cities and citizenship', International Journal of Urban and Regional Research, 20, 1, March

Geddes P 1915 Cities in evolution: an introduction to the town planning movement and to the study of civics. London,Williams & Norgate

Gellner E 1983 Nations and Nationalism. Oxford, Blackwell

Giddens A 1990 The Consequences of Modernity. London, Polity Press

Hall S 1992 'The question of cultural identity'. In: Hall S, Held D, McGrew A (eds) Modernity and its Futures. Cambridge, Polity Press

Hirst P, Thompson G 1996 Globalization in Question. Cambridge, Polity Press

Jones G E 1973 Rural Life: Patterns and Processes. London, Longman

Kumar K 1993 'Civil society: an inquiry into the usefulness of an historical term'. British Journal of Sociology, 44, 3

Linklater M 1995 'Globalization of the Media: the impact on national cultures'. In: Fladmark J M (ed) Sharing the Earth: Local identity in global culture. London, Donhead

Macfarlane, R Esq. 1847–8 Report on the Edinburgh Municipality and Transference of Police and Paving Bill', Local Acts - Preliminary Inquiries, 9 & 10 Vict., c.106, PP 1847-8 XXXI.1

Mann M 1996 'Nation-states in Europe and other countries: Diversifying, developing, not dying'. In: Balakrishnan G (ed) Mapping the nation. London, Verso

McCrone D 1997 'Land, Democracy and Culture in Scotland'. The Fourth McEwan Lecture on Land Tenure in Scotland, Rural Forum: Perth

Miller R, Luther-Davies S 1969 Eday and Hoy: a development survey. University of Glasgow

Miller R (ed) 1985 The Third Statistical Account. The County of Orkney. Edinburgh, Scottish Academic Press

Morris R J 1998 'Civil Society and British Urban History, 1750-1900. Urban History, Vol. 25, No. 3 December

Morris A, Gladstone J 2000 'Farm Tourism, Agricultural Heritage and the Social and Economic Regeneration of Farm Women', in this volume

Morris A, Morton G 1998 Locality, Community and Nation. London, Hodder & Stoughton

Morton G 1998a 'What if? The significance of Scotland's missing nationalism in the nineteenth century'. In: Broun D, Finlay R, Lynch M (eds) Image and Identity: the making and remaking of Scotland through the ages. Edinburgh, John Donald

Morton G 1998b 'Civil society, municipal government and the state: Enshrinement, empowerment and legitimacy. Scotland, 1800-1929'. Urban History, Vol. 25, No. 3, December

Nurminen E, Robinson G 1985 'Demographic Changes and Planning Initiatives in Scotland's Northern and Western Isles'. Research Discussion paper, 20, University of Edinburgh

O'Malley E 1992 The Pilot Programme for Integrated Rural Development, 1988-90. Dublin, The Economic and Social Research Institute

Orkney Islands Council, Department of Planning and Museums 1993 Orkney Islands Structure Plan: Written Statement

Orkney Tourist Board 1995 Orkney: Other Voices, Other Worlds

Ritzer G 1996 The McDonaldization of Society. (Revised edition), California, Pine Forge Press

Rogers A 1989 'A Planned Countryside'. In: Mingay G (ed) The Rural Idyll. London, Routledge

Rutherford J 1990 'A Place Called Home: Identity and the cultural politics of difference'. In: Rutherford J (ed) Identity: Community, Culture, Difference. London, Lawrence & Wishart

Seligman A 1992 The Idea of Civil Society. New York, Free Press

Suhrke A 1992 'Migration, State and Civil Society in Southeast Asia'. Working Paper M 1992: 4, Chr. Michelson Institute, Programme of Human Rights Studies

Wallerstein I 1989 The Modern World System. New York, Academic Press

Re-imaging the City:
Heritage Tourism Strategies for Regeneration in Dundee

MariaLaura Di Domenico

'At best the heritage industry only draws a screen between ourselves and our true past' (Hewison 1987: 10).

Place 'boosterism' is becoming increasingly popular in Britain and has been a focus of development in those Scottish cities that suffered most from post-industrial decline such as Glasgow and more recently Dundee. Re-imaging policies are often used to build on a city's positive image or counter a negative one by building up an identity based around distinctive qualities such as its industrial or commercial legacies. Whether the city was formerly perceived as a traditionally historic place or as an industrial centre, it is not surprising that local authorities have capitalised on the economic and political potential of local histories and heritage sites. The diverse past histories of cities are being restructured in order to save the present and ensure future prosperity. The aim of this endeavour is to attract to the city both visitors and income, as tourism demand has been consistently shown as potentially expanding. Many local officials regard tourism as an important means to promote their city. It is used as a way of generating jobs both directly and indirectly. Ashworth and Tunbridge (1990) give two economic reasons for the development of what they call 'the tourist-historic city'. The first stresses that demolition and rebuilding may actually cost more than preservation or renovation. The second emphasises the importance of the promotion of cities to potential investors, residents and visitors. Gold and Gold (1995) also observe that cities throughout the world are selling themselves partly through their cultural heritage attractions. Dundee, following in Glasgow's footsteps, has jumped on this particular bandwagon.

Dundee's local authorities have welcomed the challenge of urban regeneration. For the moment, it is still a relatively efficient and cost effective investment, compared to that required in other sectors of the economy. Through tourism, urban authorities can create employment in areas that have few other alternatives and revitalise the city economically and physically (Ashworth and Tunbridge 1994). This also implies both political and social elements in planning. For example, many local policy makers have the objective of getting their city on the 'tourist trail' or 'tourist map' (Hughes 1992). This may present a conundrum for new arrivals on the 'city booster scene' for, with an increasing number of local authorities making this choice, the task is likely to become more challenging in the future for all of them and especially for the latecomers such as Dundee. It becomes increasingly difficult to attract the 'post-tourist' who is selecting in a more careful and discriminatory way than before when 'consuming places' (Urry 1995). It is necessary for each city to present a unique and different face, and constantly revitalise it, in order to attract visitors. Former industrial and commercial cities such as Glasgow, and especially Dundee, may not be be able to keep up with this continuous challenge in the future. Can Dundee, presenting itself as a historic industrial city, remain different once the novelty aspect for the tourist has worn off?

The research described in this chapter is based on an analysis of recent changes connected to the heritage tourism industry which have taken place in Dundee. This is considered against a late 1990s backdrop of the evolving face of its city centre. Further development of the heritage tourism industry in Dundee would appear important as part of the urban regeneration programme of the city. This research describes a particular case study, presenting views on developments, and placing the analysis within a broad theoretical account of the heritage tourism industry. A research focus in this study is on the work of the Dundee Heritage Trust. The two attractions run by the Trust are Discovery Point and Verdant Works. The former is now a well-established tourist attraction that has been open to the public for more than five years. It features Captain Scott's ship 'The Discovery' that was originally built in Dundee. It is through the images, which the concept of 'discovery' paints for the public, that the city has been able to build a new identity in this new era, although based on a 'pastiche' of former identities. The strategy in the city is to make the title 'City of Discovery' synonymous with Dundee. In contrast, but with similar intention, Verdant Works is a restored jute mill, having been converted into a museum as a symbol of Dundee's industrial heritage. It was first opened in September 1996, the second phase was completed in September 1997, and it is still undergoing further development and on-site expansion. Both heritage museums are important in demonstrating the attempts being made in Dundee to repackage and market the city more attractively, directing efforts towards what is being interpreted as the needs and perceived desires of today's tourists as well as its residents.

As a researcher from a tourism background, the basic role of 'ethnographer' was adopted throughout the research process. Analysis was conducted using direct observations, interviews, and documentary materials. Discovery Point and Verdant Works, and the tourists and residents who visited these heritage attractions, were observed in detail over the summer period from mid-June until the beginning of October 1997. Participant observation in this period involved the researcher working as a 'Guide Friday' tour guide with the tourists and residents interviewed being consumers of these tours. In-depth interviews with twenty tourists and twenty residents were conducted during this main summer research period. Prior to this period, a pilot investigation was conducted in the summer of 1996 when the researcher was first employed by 'Guide Friday' as a tour guide. Research continued after the study date with repeated visits to the attractions being made until February 1998. Interviews with present and former members of the Dundee Heritage Trust as well as with professionals in the tourism and academic sectors in Dundee, especially at the University of Abertay Dundee and the Tayside Economic Research Centre, were conducted until December 1997. Thus, conclusions are arrived at by weighing up the sometimes more biased perspectives of tourist professional practitioners with those of a cross-section of the recipient visitor population and also with those perhaps more balanced views of academics.

During the course of the research, assumptions were examined and certain questions asked about the urban industrial heritage industry. For example, it was considered whether it is appropriate, in terms of the regeneration of Scottish cities such as Dundee, to present recent history as part of a heritage industry for commercial ends. Is the industrial urban heritage industry an attempt to preserve the past and local identity and to help us understand our recent past or is it simply the commercial exploitation and commodification of our history and culture? It is important when conducting research to question the status and ethical implications of a heritage industry which has transformed historical interpretation into a consumer product which has been refined for the new mass-produced twentieth century industry which is tourism. The heritage industry tends to be selective in its use of the past. It may be that to generate as much money as possible from the past, popular marketable areas are exploited and significant historical themes are pushed aside. For example, in Dundee it was found that the discussion of recent historical events such as the closure of the TIMEX factory in the city was actively discouraged among the 'Guide Friday' tour guides. This was thought to be too recent and painful an occurrence for inclusion and consequently not 'good for business'. Is this ethical? Is it truthful? In the race between places, truth may no longer be seen as significant as long as the tourist is exposed to stimulating and interactive heritage delights. Are real places and events being colonised by the heritage industry and preserved in a way that makes it difficult to change the narrative in the face of conflicting evidence? Do Dundonians have the same view of Dundee's recent past as the image which city officials and tourism and heritage organisations wish to project? Are other aspects of their history being neglected? This history appears to be very much alive in the minds of generations of Dundonians. Do they see their own history portrayed in the heritage industry as being a positive or negative development for both themselves and for their city?

Dundee's History and Setting

What history of Dundee is being used? Dundee is presented as an interesting example of an industrial city in Scotland that has been going through numerous changes throughout its history in terms of a physical environment influenced by a variety of social, political and economic factors. It did indeed grow from a medium sized town in the eighteenth century to Scotland's fourth largest city in the twentieth century. This was due first of all to its location at the mouth of the river Tay, looking out to the North Sea and with land suitable for building docks that encouraged the transportation of goods. Secondly, it was due to the Industrial Revolution, causing Dundee to become steeped in an industrial culture that can be traced back to 1763. From this date the flax and linen industries began to expand and develop with exports being sent as far afield as the American colonies. By the late eighteenth century the manufacture of coarse linens was the stable occupation in the city and encouraged its prosperity. Jute grew to pre-eminence in the nineteenth century when Dundee's title as 'Juteopolis' or the jute capital of the world became its dominant one (Walker 1979). The subsequent immigration of workers to Dundee resulted in a growth of the population. The jam and journalism industries followed later to give the city the three Js – jute, jam and journalism. However, 'though Dundee had industries other than jute, it was the single element of jute that dominated the life of the city from the 1840s to 1914 and beyond' (Checkland 1984: 46). Britain's colonial possessions had encouraged the manufacture and trading of jute as the plant is found in abundance in Eastern India and the present Bangladesh. The importance of jute to the development of the city may be likened to the importance of tobacco to the development of the city of Glasgow. Both were based on raw materials and trade with the colonies. In 1905 'Dundee had an almost complete monopoly of British jute manufacture – and indeed consumed about a third of the jute imported into Europe. Its greatest days had been in the 1870s, but its magnates often owned and managed its Calcutta rivals' (Harvie 1981: 3). The various uses to which jute was put along with an exhibition of the workings of jute and the roles of jute workers in Dundee is shown in the Verdant Works exhibition. There is also a feature on the cultures of the British Empire in the Indian sub-continent and the 'Calcutta Jute Wallahs' (Stewart 1998). The image of Dundee's jute days when it was a 'single industry' city has in this way been kept alive and it has not yet died in the memories of its citizens.

The remains of the overcrowded, smoke-laden 'Juteopolis' are also still evident throughout the city. Hundreds of tenement blocks throughout the city add to the panoramic view from the top of 'The Law', the highest hill in Dundee. The atmosphere of the industrial era still prevails. At that time, as featured also in Verdant Works, Dundee's working population lived in crowded and unhealthy conditions. Their diet was extremely poor when compared to the mill owners. This, combined with poor educational standards and bad public health care provision, resulted in higher than average mortality rates. However, the mill owners or 'jute barons' did provide a number of public buildings such as libraries as well as parks that still remain and counteract the dark industrial heritage embodied in the mills and tenements of the city. Verdant Works also shows how Dundee continued to suffer economic hardship during the First World War due to the decline in the jute industry and its over-dependence on that one principal industry. This continued after the war and consequently population growth slowed down in the period between the wars. Dundee had been over-dependent on a narrow industrial base and this was reflected in an economic, social and employment structure that was not in balance. The Depression of the 1920s and 1930s devastated the city, as there was less demand for its products due to the global recession. Added to this, advances in technology in India along with the availability of cheap labour, resulted in the further decline of the jute industry in Dundee. India's role was crucial in that the raw jute mainly arrived from there in order to be processed in Dundee. Following India's Independence and the development of its own jute industry based on lower costs and wages, the post-war period saw a further rapid decline in this industry. Shipbuilding also declined due to diminishing demand for transportation of goods. Dundee, burdened by outdated technology, failed to adapt to the changing conditions of the time or to diversify and produce goods for new markets. After the Second World War, there was a brief economic boom reflecting national economic growth and the reflationary measures of the post-war Labour Government. However, soon more city-centre traditional industries such as those associated with jam closed down reflecting the city's long-term steady decline, and residents began to move out leading to a further population downturn. At that point, Dundee, the city of jute, jam and journalism, had to change its image.

Since the 1960s a process of industrial and corporate restructuring has taken place. Throughout the 1970s and 1980s Dundee suffered from a steady contraction of its manufacturing base. By this stage most of the traditional industries had closed down bringing also a decline in other industries. This resulted in high unemployment. The service sector began to increase in relative importance and the social composition of the city began to change, reflecting the changing economy. There was also a simultaneous movement of the population from Dundee to other areas with better employment prospects. The population's size, distribution and density were severely affected and these later began to have implications for the quality of Dundee's urban environment. Indeed, the relics of the overcrowded, smoke-laden 'Juteopolis' are still evident throughout the city today. Factories, which stand unused in the city centre, are deteriorating rapidly. There are still hundreds of tenement blocks throughout the city, which once housed the workforce. They have now lost much attraction as residences, although adding to that atmosphere of the industrial era, which still prevails throughout the city. Dundee's inner-city decline up till the 1980s was accompanied by a corresponding decline in its accessibility and transportation network. It was at this point that a 'myth' of Dundee as Scotland's forgotten city began to emerge. A few new industries were set up in the post-war era such as one that manufactures jute's replacements, man-made textiles such as polypropylene. The last bale of jute was delivered to Dundee in 1998 with the only remaining mill being Verdant Works, the heritage museum. However, jute has not completely died with the mills as the attitudes and society of Dundee still derive very much from that industry (Ogilvy 1993).

In recent years, projects such as the 'Dundee Partnership' that link private and public organisations have encouraged new thinking and introduced a greater vitality into the city centre. There has been an expansion in tourism and teaching as well as technology. As the city centre is being improved and revived, attempts are being made to bring back shopkeepers, residents, tourists and other users. Some city centre streets are being pedestrianised and some abandoned buildings are being converted for teaching uses and into residences, reclaiming spaces that were once used mainly for industrial purposes. One of these spaces has been developed into Verdant Works, the heritage centre for people to use and experience the sensation of stepping back in time. From the industrial use of the city and its surrounding area, the development of the built environment and the docks as a tourism area has taken place in accordance with the city's changing needs. Today, heritage tourism has developed in importance in Dundee city centre and, from its past, a heritage tourism industry is in the process of emerging. Can Dundee be successful in its attempt to use nostalgia for the past to benefit the future? 'The question is not whether we should or should not preserve the past, but what kind of past we have chosen to preserve' (Urry 1990: 109). In Dundee's case it is the industrial urban past. The idea of developing and constructing a present identity from the industrial past of Dundee is one that is in the process of taking physical shape and this in turn may help to redefine the city for its inhabitants and for those who visit.

Scottish Culture and Industrial Heritage Tourism: Glasgow as an Example for Dundee

In Scotland there is a distinct shared value system which, defined as 'Scottish culture', includes Scottish history, heritage and tourism. 'Heritage' covers a range of subjects, acting as 'a vital source of legitimatory iconography' (McCrone et al 1995: 5). Scottish 'industrial heritage', equally representing and strengthening national and cultural identity, like 'cultural heritage' is concerned with the conservation and restoration of the past, preserving an important version of Scottish identity and history. This is reflected in Dundee's once thriving jute and shipbuilding industries. Industrial museums draw attention to an industrial past deemed worthy of preservation. 'Industrial heritage tourism' focuses attention on the reciprocal influences between tourism and industrial heritage. Industrial heritage tourism, reflecting the recent history of many urbanised Scots, has to rely, like heritage tourism generally, on the role of nostalgia in order to have an impact on people. A selective remembering of aspects of history and the romanticising of reality appears to be as powerful a factor in creating an interest in urban-industrial Scotland as in the more traditional tourist destinations. Dundee is actively exploiting its manufacturing past and competing with other cities for the opportunity to act as a 'honey pot' in the provision of a diverse range of cultural services. The 'heritage re-imaging effect' and 'urban regeneration' are important aspects of this attempt, involving the conservation of old buildings, including factories, mills, warehouses and docks and their conversion into apartments, leisure centres and for other uses. The conserved urban environment has to be turned into a set of 'townscapes', presenting the city as a cultural or heritage centre. Dundee is now symbolised by the ship, 'The Discovery', which dominates the dockland area.

'In the post-industrial world, cities must compete to attract new activities to replace those they have lost' (Law, 1993: 98). The spirit of Scottish urban regeneration and re-imaging began in Glasgow, which has acted as a symbol of hope to other cities like Dundee. Like Dundee, Glasgow, a one-time giant of trade and industry, rose to eminence partly based on the city's location with an 'empire *ad mare* and *ad terram*, each part of the other' (Checkland 1984: 38–9). Glasgow's role has been important as an example in that it was the first Scottish city to diversify its local economy from traditional industries based on engineering and shipbuilding towards other sectors in the service areas. For Dundee, like Glasgow, which has been branded as the 'City of Culture', tourism, urban regeneration and economic diversification go hand in hand. Glasgow now uses this industrial and commercial heritage as a resource and to 'invent' attractions. Glasgow was one of the first of the former British industrial cities to implement such strategies and in this way provides an object lesson for other cities like Dundee. Glasgow embraced and used its past as part of a strategy to exploit commercially all available resources, which could be used 'against all odds' for urban regeneration. It is said by many to be an excellent example of how well the re-imaging of a city can work if this innovative approach to 'culture', the city's current buzzword, is used. Glasgow makes clear just how powerful a marketing message can be if it is strongly reinforced.

It was in the 1980s when Glasgow embarked on the campaign that radically changed its reputation into a postmodern city of culture. Change was brought to the city by its response to the need to adapt to a programme of economic restructuring with a shift of strategic objectives away from the social and political concerns of the 1970s towards economic and regeneration concerns. 'The cultural dimension of the re-imaging process' came with the launching of the "Glasgow's miles better" campaign in 1983. Part of the city's policy sought to draw Glasgow's considerable cultural heritage to the attention of the wider public. The opening of many museums along with participation in festivals helped to promote the new image of Glasgow as a postmodern city of culture, fashion, arts and cultural tourism' (Gold and Gold 1995: 184). Glasgow fully initiated its re-imaging strategy in 1983 with the slogan 'Glasgow's miles better' and with the symbol of 'Mr Happy', a yellow smiling face which had the objective of attracting the public's attention to the city's improvements. Supporters of the city's achievements emphasise that 'what is important and defining in the character of Glasgow is the way in which the city has been able to continue undaunted on the path of reinventing itself as a modern, post-industrial complex of people and jobs looking forward to the new millennium rather than back towards the ghosts of its industrial glory.' (Gibb 1998: 64).

In an earlier publication, Gibb commented that 'it may be that Glasgow is fated to spearhead the exploration of yet another path of urban development, however unasked-for or forbidding, as the downward spiral of de-industrialisation continues.' (Gibb 1983: 150–1). Other views on what has happened to Glasgow have not been even so positive. Pacione strikes a note of warning when he points out that 'while many influential figures, including the Prince of Wales, have cited Glasgow as a model of urban regeneration, Glaswegians are too canny to be carried away by such hyperbole. While the heart of the city is being physically remade the problems affecting large parts of the working-class areas of the city have not gone away' (Pacione 1995: 250–1). This is also true of Dundee. It may be that in the cultural politics of the 1990s, image has replaced reality. The city could be said to be using poetic licence, moulding itself into any form that could secure it economic prosperity. In the 1990s the city grasped the opportunity to promote its cultural organisations and what they had to offer in order to develop a new cultural strategy to try to become a truly European city with a strong cultural identity. Through the vehicle of culture, the city hoped to attract more economic investment and further nominations such as the one as City of Architecture and Design 1999. Despite all Glasgow's successes and the undoubted energy of her citizens, negative perceptions of the city appear difficult to banish completely. 'The city has been rebranded and made over: It has celebrated style and culture. It has tried to be fashionable and been game for anything. Yet the thought remains: Glasgow is dying.' (Ian Bell in *The Scotsman* 20 Feb 1999: 15). In this way Glasgow could also be a standard bearer for Dundee.

The rebranding of Glasgow illustrates the way that Scottish culture and heritage have evolved into branded and idealised images, especially in relation to the heritage industry. The potential consumer is presented with typical themes or 'brands' of the city. Gold and Gold (1995) examine the representation of Scotland to the outside world in tourist-promotional literature and related media, examining the selling of industrial and urban Scotland through the promotion of heritage. The end result of 'imagining Glasgow ' or Dundee may be far removed from actual events or happenings. However, it is perhaps this imagining which gives history and culture its critical appeal to the tourist, and indeed the Scot, in search of a culture and identity. In the era of Scottish devolution, urban industrial heritage, like memory for the individual, presents a narrative that can be continually interpreted and re-interpreted. This allows a development of themes and explanations which are ever more necessary in a rapidly changing world, re-injecting into Scots a feeling of pride and identity in our cities and attracting visitors from home and abroad. The idea of developing and constructing a present identity from the industrial past of Dundee is one that is in the process of taking physical shape and this in turn may help to redefine the city for its inhabitants and those who visit.

The current status of many post-industrial cultures within the consumerist western world may be termed as changing from 'modern' to 'post-modern' with a dissolving of boundaries between different cultural forms such as tourism, heritage and education. Ryan (1995) emphasises that heritage tourism can be perceived as the example 'par excellence' of the products of the post-industrial society. It 'problematises the distinction between representations and reality' (Urry 1990: 85). The increasing links between peoples through 'high-tech' forms of mass communications has influenced cultures transforming the tourist's focus. Modernity, concerned with the possibilities of representing reality and defining truths, differentiates between real and inauthentic experience. In postmodern society, representations are increasingly less distinguished from reality. 'Tourism is prefiguratively postmodern because of its particular combination of the visual, the aesthetic, and the popular' (Urry 1990: 87). History and heritage become flexible, able to be manipulated or even reinvented. Tourists and residents endow their experience with authenticity in their own views and 'have little impetus or competence to go beyond self-reference.' (Errington and Gewertz 1989: 46). 'The heritage centre ... can be a way of telling the people's story, and of helping to make sure that it will be heard.' (MacDonald 1997: 175). A tourist quests the authentic attraction and real experience (MacCannell 1989: 55). However, despite this individual quest, all places, experiences and histories are in fact 'staged' and presented even when 'history' and 'heritage' are projected to the public as undoubted social truths. Such constructs are subject to subtle changes, alterations or reinterpretations over time and the past is often 'tailored' to meet the demands of the visitor as well as the resident.

Some Official and Media Views:
Tourism in Tayside and Dundee and the
Work of the Dundee Heritage Trust

Tayside is a popular tourist area immediately recognised by tourist professionals and members of the public alike. However, Perthshire as a tourist destination is better known than urban Dundee, despite marketing initiatives aimed at attracting visitors to the city through heritage and culture. Successful competition with other locations depends on taking new initiatives. As Alan Rankin, the Marketing Manager of Dundee Heritage Trust stressed when interviewed: 'It is essential to create a product such as the east-coast trail, in order to compete effectively with tourist 'honey-pot' zones ... I view this as the biggest single challenge for Dundee and Tayside in becoming a major tourism player'. Despite a history of boom and decline, officers of the Dundee Heritage Trust and other policy makers in Dundee are hoping for a future prosperity partly based on an industrial heritage tourism industry. With the decline of traditional industries, they state that Dundee is committed to an urban regeneration programme focused on making tourism a dominant economic force. The past is to be portrayed from the vantage point of the present, with a view to future needs. The city's industrial heritage is being used to develop 'sustainable year-round growth in tourism by maximising the experience of visitors to Tayside, through the development and integration of existing resources ...' (The Tayside Tourism Strategy, 1995). Early response indicators for changes introduced to Dundee have proved favourable showing a steady upward trend in visitor numbers. The enthusiastic local press note that 'the Scottish Tourist Board figures ... suggest that attractions in Angus and Dundee have enjoyed an increase in visitor numbers which is way above the national average – 26% as opposed to the countrywide average of 13%.' (*Courier & Advertiser*, 23 July 1997).

There has been a huge shift in the economy's employment structure away from manufacturing towards an expansion in services in order to create jobs. As pointed out by several respondents at the heritage museums, one of the arguments against using tourism to boost a flagging economy is that it is often perceived as providing low-paid, seasonal jobs. The aim of the museums was to provide year round attractions. It was also felt that while many jobs within tourism may be low skilled, this could be an advantage to an area such as Dundee where there is a strong reserve of unskilled labour. As Jonathan Bryant, a former Chief Executive of the Dundee Heritage Trust pointed out in a telephone interview, tourism should not be used in isolation to further urban economic regeneration. He affirmed that 'other important industries and sectors in the city should not be ignored such as the many 'hi-tech' industries, and the institutions of higher education'. Also, he added that it might prove challenging to maintain demand levels in the longer term as the recent 'proliferation of centres and attractions ... are all competing for people's free time and disposable income. This sector of the industry has become supply rather than demand led which poses a risk to attractions such as Discovery Point and Verdant Works'.

Tourist professionals at the heritage museums and at Tayside Economic Research Centre pointed out that there are many external influences affecting tourism levels in Dundee. Competition to gain revenue from tourism is rapidly increasing along with growth in international travel and exchange rates that make foreign holidays appear cheaper. According to respondents, tourism in Dundee must be examined within the context of Scottish tourism as a whole and Scotland is often perceived by both international and domestic tourists from 'south of the border' as being a distant location. It was also pointed out that tourists, who have higher expectations than before, are unwilling to go out of their way unless a location has 'a unique selling point'. A crucial issue affecting Dundee's success, according to those interviewed, is the quality of its attractions and services. It was pointed out that Scotland is often perceived as expensive which means that its products need to be seen as high in quality with customer service being as important as the actual standard of the facilities themselves. This is of some importance to Dundee with its relatively small catchment area and proximity to a number of apparently more significant visitor destinations such as Perth, St. Andrews and Edinburgh.

The tourism 'product' provided by Dundee can be defined as a 'range of city type attractions – museums, shops, leisure centres, parks' (Dundee Tourism Strategy 1995). As for the future, a new Dundee Contemporary Arts Centre was recently opened in March 1999 with projected visitors of 110 000 per year. Plans are also underway for a Dundee Science Centre and a Contemporary Dance Centre to be financed by lottery money. Combined with the development of interactive heritage centres such as Discovery Point and Verdant Works, according to respondents, the initial steps have been taken towards a much larger-scale plan of total urban renewal. This, they feel, would allow both visitors and residents to enjoy a more pleasant urban environment, a broader cultural base, and encourage them to become more aware of the heritage of the past.

Dundee Heritage Trust and its operating subsidiary, Dundee Industrial Heritage Limited, were formed in 1985 as a direct result of community concern for the 'exceptional industrial heritage' of the area and with the objective of preserving and presenting Dundee's heritage to the public. Trustees are drawn from all sectors of the community – business, local government, the Universities, trade unions and individual citizens. The Trust's primary role was summarised in an interview by Gill Poulter, the Heritage Officer of the Trust, as 'an educational one in that it provides an informative public service ... The Trust has other long-term responsibilities as being the guardian of important historical and cultural objects, equipment and arte-facts'. She added that 'jute, jam and journalism once popularly described Dundee, but now does little justice to the city's achievements or its character combining a complex industrial heritage with a vision of future prosperity based on tourism, teaching and technology'. Trust officials said that they had this in mind when deciding its policy, electing to concentrate on Tayside's maritime links and textile history by restoring the Royal Research Ship Discovery and by establishing Verdant Works as a living museum of textiles.

At present, Discovery Point is Dundee's main visitor attraction. Nevertheless, it may only be categorised as a medium-scale attraction due to the relatively low level of tourist numbers that it currently caters for. According to the marketing literature and brochures available, the tourist experience of this attraction is intended to be clearly interactive involving 'spectacular exhibits and special effects' which recreate 'the historic voyages of Captain Scott's Antarctic ship, Royal Research Ship Discovery'. The tourist is invited to 'absorb the sights, sounds and smells of the shipyard. Cheer as she is launched. Then sit back and enjoy "Locked in the Ice", a dramatic presentation on three giant screens showing how Discovery was blasted free from the crushing pack ice. Across the quayside you can board and explore Discovery herself, probably the strongest wooden ship ever built, now restored as she was on her last great adventure ...'

Verdant Works, purchased by Dundee Heritage Trust in 1991, is similar to the Discovery in that it is essentially a themed and restored heritage attraction, in this case a re-created jute mill. Various national press reports commented on the changes taking place in Dundee following the opening of Phase II of Verdant Works. For example, one newspaper succinctly summarised what the attraction symbolises for the city. Verdant Works, it was noted, 'epitomises the change that's coming over Dundee and Scotland. From 1830 onward it resounded to the clack of jute processing and weaving. Restored, it is attracting tens of thousands of locals ... Jute is a distant memory. Almost 2000 textile jobs have been lost to Dundee in a decade while 3450 more people are employed in hotels and catering' (*Scotland on Sunday*, 6 Nov 1997: 5). Further heritage attraction concept proposals now being considered 'include extending the themes to encompass journalism and jam' (Dundee Visitor Attractions Strategic Review 1996: 22–3). Indeed, it was felt by Trust officials that the large site of some 50 000 square feet has room for further developments that could reflect the city's industrial heritage.

Views from Tourists and Residents on Dundee and the Dundee Heritage Trust

The visitors to the city can be categorised as either overseas or domestic (British) tourists. Most of the tourists, including the twenty respondents interviewed in-depth, were domestic visitors. The average holiday period was a five-day stay in Scotland with one to two days in Dundee. Overseas tourists were more likely to be on holiday than domestic tourists. None of the overseas tourists interviewed had planned to visit Dundee and the maximum length of stay in the city was one complete day. This reflects Dundee's tourist situation at present as an 'accidental' rather than a planned destination. Respondents were equally divided between males and females. The majority of respondents appeared relatively affluent with more than one-third being retired.

Few overseas visitors had been encouraged to visit Dundee which they saw as 'out of the way'. A representative observation was made when an older American couple remarked that 'upon entering Scotland we headed immediately for the capital city. However, we then went to the tourist information centre there and noticed a leaflet about Dundee. We asked about excursions to the city and were met with the response of "Oh! Why on earth would you want to go there?" But, we decided to come anyway ... and we haven't been disappointed as the heritage attractions are so interesting and everyone is so friendly here'. The overwhelming consensus of the domestic visitors interviewed was, as one put it, that 'there is a lack of marketing about Dundee, despite there being so much to see and do, such as museums, shops and places to dine'. There was a widespread surprise at the actual range of facilities available in the city and the extent to which it had changed aesthetically in recent years. Many were familiar with the negative images and associations of the city's past, in terms of manufacturing, poverty and large-scale industry.

In terms of the two main attractions, overseas visitors were particularly impressed by Discovery Point as holding 'wide and varied interest', whereas some typically felt that Verdant Works 'is maybe too theme-specific which holds little of interest for those who are not particularly motivated by the jute industry'. Respondents expressed great interest in the plans for the jam and journalism stages of the development. Equal appeal was generated by Discovery Point and Verdant Works, and few detrimental comments were made about either attraction. Indeed, domestic visitors who enjoyed the history and information about the jute industry showed more appreciation of Verdant Works. They paid compliments about the attractive and true-to-life presentations. Visitors from other parts of Scotland also identified with the themes presented and enjoyed the nostalgia. The only identifiable distinction was one of gender, as it appeared that more women were specifically interested in Verdant Works, while men were more motivated by Discovery Point. This may have been because of the association of women workers with the jute industry, whereas ship-building has more masculine connotations.

Twenty Dundee residents were also interviewed in-depth in order to gain an understanding of the perceptions held of the changes which have taken place in their own city. Residents were of all age ranges and were evenly selected from both sexes. Their number included a few former jute workers. Some of these Dundee residents said that tourism was a necessary 'evil', which would generate revenue for a city where traditional industries were in decline. However, the general view expressed was that both Verdant Works and Discovery Point are greatly beneficial to the city, being also useful for entertaining, and taking visitors to, including visiting family members, as well as friends and children. Indeed, there appeared to be interest in greater community involvement in the development of the heritage centres. Residents did not remark on any specifically harmful effects of tourism, but were aware of the positive impacts on the city, including the conservation and encouragement of local arts and crafts which would aid in reviving the economy. They were keen that others should appreciate their own cultural heritage. They were aware that the attempt to attract tourists could result in the improvement of facilities and of the urban environment generally. Verdant Works was described generally as 'interesting, informative, but difficult to find'. Discovery Point was seen as 'entertaining for all ages, with a good central location'. Residents, like visitors, enjoyed visiting and comparing the two attractions as they felt that they obtained a more comprehensive picture of their own city in this way.

Both visitors and residents appreciated the educational value of the attractions. This was reflected in the interest and excitement that was shown by them. Older residents and the young alike were proud that Dundee was reflected 'so gloriously' in the two heritage centres. The older people enjoyed the nostalgia whereas the young appreciated the knowledge obtained through the interactive techniques used in both attractions. 'It was fun' was a common response about both attractions from children and adults alike. Thus, both overseas and domestic tourists as well as the residents appear to be positively supportive of the tourism developments and re-imaging of the city. Residents did, however, complain about the cost they have to bear if they take their visitors and friends to the attractions and contrasted the entry fee with the free entry to other museums in the city. Despite this, there is definitely community support, pride and involvement in the whole enterprise and much debate and even argument among the locals and visitors alike about what was shown. This was especially the case in the new phases of the Verdant Works exhibitions portraying working class life-styles in comparison with those of the managers and the jute barons. A comment that was made was that numbers of visitors are still few. This supported the comments made by the Trust officials who were trying to get word out about the attractions to other Tourist Information Centres in Scotland and elsewhere. Poor assistance with marketing and a lack of support of Dundee's efforts by other cities reflect the keen competition between urban areas in Scotland

Conclusions: the Way Ahead?

The very essence of tourism research is a deep fascination not only with places but also people, in an attempt to describe, understand and explain the reasons for behaviour. Heritage research involves the added analysis of how the conservation of history is turned into a modern commodity, a heritage product for contemporary consumption. Heritage has been identified as a mixture of 'history, ideology, nationalism, local pride, romantic ideas or just plain marketing' (Herbert 1995: 56). The present research was undertaken in Dundee, which over the last decade is undergoing dramatic restructuring and like other Western cities has 'adapted to new economic, social and political realities.' (Hubbard 1996: 26). Heritage tourism in Dundee has been increasingly recognised as an identifiable sector and one of the city's recent growth industries. Thus, the research focused upon the evaluation of the urban-industrial tourist experience, seeking to explore the relationship between tourism and urban-industrial representation. Respondents, including not only the tourism planners but also certain residents, view tourism activities as generally beneficial for Dundee. Revenue can be generated through tourism for a city in which traditional industries have declined. Thus, planners and other local interest groups are beginning to see tourism as a significant element within the urban economy making use of the very traditional industries which are themselves dying. Heritage was seen by the respondents to be one component in the revitalisation strategy leading to economic regeneration in Dundee in order to benefit both tourists and residents. The theme of the branded tourism product is important for the city in initiating redevelopment and tourism. The 'brand image' is the self-proclaimed 'City of Discovery', which had great appeal for tourists and residents, even though the latter had some reservations.

It has been important firstly to place the analysis within a broad theoretical account of the industrial heritage industry and also to compare Dundee with Glasgow, which has been used as an example of successful industrial and urban re-imaging. The heritage industry and the nostalgia it exploits may reflect a fragmented culture which may be characteristic of the postmodern era which in itself represents a reaction to the uniformity of culture encouraged by the earlier process of modernisation in Britain. Thus, the preservation of distinct local identities may help direct future purposes with post-industrial cities such as Dundee marketing a distinct identity of place. The collapse of the industrial base of many of our cities has led to the exploitation of the urban industrial heritage industry almost to its full potential in order to fill an economic gap.

It is clear that local authority and tourism officials in Dundee now recognise the economic, social and political potential of a focus on urban industrial heritage tourism as part of Dundee's culture and history. It is claimed, with some support from this research, to provide an increased sense of pride and awareness of identity for residents who still remember their own or their family's involvement in Dundee's industries. History in the form of urban industrial heritage is being actively developed and used by the authorities to attract visitors and their money to the city. However, as McCrone et al (1995) show, the heritage industry provides information mixed with entertainment or 'infotainment' rather than history. Much can be learnt if research is conducted from the perspective of particular case studies such as this one into the re-imaging of cities and the industrial heritage industry that is being built up in former industrial cities such as Dundee. It is necessary to obtain views from those involved in such developments. The development strategies, which are being planned by local authorities, should be reassessed, as should the viability of the focus, which is now being placed on the possibilities offered by tourism, and especially the industrial urban heritage industry. Competition with other cities must be taken account of. On a positive note, we can join the majority of our respondents in hoping that the aim of Dundee in this new era of its development will be to make sure that the 'future is good for Scots past.' (Wojtas 1998).

References

Adams G. 1995 Access to Nations Assets: Challenges for Scottish Tourism Policy. In: Fladmark M (ed) Sharing the Earth: Local Identity in Global – Culture. London, Donhead

Ashworth G, Tunbridge J 1990 The Tourist-Historic City. London, Belhaven

Ashworth G J, Larkham P 1994 Building a New Heritage. London, Routledge

Checkland S G, Checkland O 1984 Industry and Ethos: Scotland 1832–1914 London, Edward Arnold

Errington F, Gewertz D 1989 Tourism and Anthropology in a Post-Modern World. In : Oceania, 60, 37–54

Fladmark J M (ed) 1995 Sharing the Earth: Local Identity in Global Culture. London, Donhead

Fraser M (Ed) 1998 Essential Scotland. London, Agenda Publishing Limited in Association with Scotland the Brand Edinburgh

Gibb A 1983 Glasgow – The Making of a City. Kent, Croom Helm

Gibb A 1998 Glasgow 1999 U.K. City of Architecture & Design. In: Fraser M (ed) Essential Scotland London: Agenda Publishing Limited in Association with Scotland the Brand Edinburgh, pp 64–7

Gold J R, Gold M M 1995 Imagining Scotland: Tradition, Representation and Promotion in Scotland since 1750. Aldershot, Scolar Press

Harvie C 1981 No Gods and Precious Few Heroes: Scotland 1914-1980. In: Wormald J, Barrow G W S, Smout C, (eds) The New History of Scotland Series 8. London, Edward Arnold

Herbert D T 1995 Heritage as Literary Place. In: Herbert D T (ed.) Heritage, Tourism and Society. London, Mansell, pp32–48

Herbert D T (ed) 1995 Heritage , Tourism and Society. London, Mansell

Hewison R 1987 The Heritage Industry: Britain in a Climate of Decline. London, Methuen

Hubbard P 1996 Re-Imaging the City. In: Geography, Volume 81 (1), 26–36.

Hughes G 1992 Tourism and the Geographical Imagination. In: Leisure Studies, Vol.11, 31-42

Law C M 1992 Urban Tourism and its Contribution to Economic Regeneration. In: Urban Studies, 29, 3/4, 599–618

Law C M 1993 Urban Tourism: Attracting Visitors to Large Cities. London, Mansell

MacCannell D 1989 Edition with a New Introduction to the 1976 Edition The Tourist - A New Theory of the Leisure Class. New York, Schocken Books

MacDonald S 1997 A People's Story: Heritage, Identity and Authenticity. In: Urry J Touring Cultures. London, Routledge, pp. 155-175

McCrone D, Morris A, Kiely R 1995 Scotland - the Brand: The Making of Scottish Heritage. Edinburgh, Edinburgh University Press

Ogilvy G 1993 The River Tay and its People. Edinburgh, Mainstream Publishing

Pacione M 1995 Glasgow: The Socio-Spatial Development of the City. Chichester, John Wiley and Sons

Ryan C 1995 Researching Tourist Satisfaction: Issues, Concepts, Problems. London, Routledge

Stewart G 1998 Jute and Empire: The Calcutta Jute Wallahs and the Cultures of Empire. Manchester, Manchester University Press

Urry J 1990 The Tourist Gaze: Leisure & Travel in Contemporary Societies. London, Sage

Urry J 1995 Consuming Places. London, Routledge

Urry J 1997 Touring Cultures. London, Routledge

Walker W M 1979 Juteopolis: Dundee and its Textile Workers 1885-1923. Edinburgh, Scottish Academic Press

Reports

Dundee Tourism Strategy 1995-2000: Final Consultative Draft. August, 1995 The Dundee Partnership: Dundee

Dundee Visitor Attractions Strategic Review: Final Report. January 1996

Industrial Heritage Tourism in Scotland: A Review. March, 1996 Produced on Behalf of Scottish Tourism Co-ordinating Group by the Scottish Tourist Board, Edinburgh

Scottish Visitor Attractions Review. 1997 Edinburgh: The Scottish Tourist Board with Highlands and Islands Enterprises and Scottish Enterprise

The Tayside Tourism Strategy. 1995 Dundee: Scottish Enterprise Tayside

Newspaper Reports

Bell I 1999 'By the Wayside'. In: *The Scotsman* Edinburgh: 20 February

Scotland on Sunday 6 Nov 1997 Edinburgh

The Courier & Advertiser 23 July 1997 Dundee

Wojtas O 27 Feb 1998 Future Is Good For Scots Past. In: *The Times Higher*, London

Leaflets and Brochures

Discover the Secret (1996/7) Angus & Dundee Holiday Guide/Accommodation Register

Discovery Point: Dundee (1997) Brochure

Dundee Art Galleries and Museums (1997) Guide

Dundee City of Discovery (1996/7) Visitors' Guide

Dundee Our Future (1997) Pamphlet

The Accent: Discover Dundee's Arts and Heritage (Spring, Summer and Autumn, 1997)
Dundee: Dundee Arts & Heritage

What's On (June, July & August, 1997) Angus and City of Dundee Tourist Board

Guide Friday Information Sources

Explore Dundee (1996) Edinburgh: Guide Friday Guidance Notes

Explore Dundee (1997) Edinburgh: Guide Friday Guidance Notes

Guide Friday Training Course and Notes Taken During Training (Summer, 1996)

Identity in the Making?
National Museums in Scotland and Bavaria

Barbara Grabmann

The Current Situation

Observing political debates throughout the European Union over the past few years, it becomes apparent that European regions are increasingly relying on a sense of collective identity as a political strategy. Some of these regions are often referred to as strong, mainly as a result of their relative prosperity and economic strength, for example Catalonia or Lombardy. However, they also look back on long histories and memories of bygone sovereignty, two notable examples being Bavaria and Scotland. As the future role of the nation-state is being questioned with the progress of continuing European integration, the political environment has changed compared to the context of the regionalist movements of the 1970s. Even though, in some cases, they argue in genuinely political terms, many European regions appear to define themselves as culturally distinguished entities, thus staking their claim in the wider political framework of the European arena.

These observations present nothing particularly new. Still, the construction of identity in cases like Scotland and Bavaria is determined by a number of characteristics often overlooked in nationalism-research. At the same time, there are amazing discrepancies in the amount of research about both countries. A review of the comparatively abundant sociological and political research on Scotland over the past twenty years reveals a shift from finding political explanations to the constitution of Scottish identity in the 1970s towards a rather more culturalist approach in the 1990s. Bavaria, though, and even more so Bavarian identity, has received very little attention in social science research. However, by drawing from a detailed review of existing research findings in Scotland and by comparing these with phenomenological observations in both countries, four characteristics which distinguish the constitution of identity in both cases can be singled out. 1. Imagined cultural homogeneity coexists with experienced cultural fragmentation; 2. Cultural and political strategies determining a sense of distinctiveness interweave in a particular type of cultural policy; 3. Identity-construction hinges on territoriality, manifest as a sense of place in spatial and territorial debating strategies; 4. Conflicting interests and strategies result in a double-bind-situation for social actors. (For phenomenological observations on Bavaria see Mintzel 1991, Roth 1994; for Scotland – as a choice of examples – Nairn 1977, 1997, Kellas 1989, McCrone 1992, 1998, Marr 1992).

Thoughts on Identity-Construction

This section presents a few theoretical ideas, based on the need to find explanations for the characteristics listed above. These thoughts will be explored further in the following sections, which focus on the example of musealisation as a strategy of identity-construction and case studies of national museums in Scotland and Bavaria.

In general sociological terms, identity-construction in 'historic countries' is a form of social construction of reality as defined by Berger and Luckmann (1967). I propose to use the term 'historic countries' to refer to both Scotland and Bavaria. Following McCrone (1992), Scotland was increasingly refered to as a 'stateless nation', whereas Bavaria used to be termed 'regional state'. Yet for historical reasons these terms fit awkwardly. Other suggestions, for example, Ethno–region (Gellner 1983) or territorial identity (Goetze 1994), put too much emphasis on either ethnic or territorial elements of the construction, whereas the term 'historic nations' would do justice to the historicity of the construction but lends itself to confusion with modern concepts of the nation-state. Therefore, I have adopted the term 'historic countries': it communicates a notion of historicity with reference to the construction, or according to Heckmann (1997) its genealogical character, its historicism (and implicitly its ethnic character) as well as its territoriality. Identity would thus appear as a 'humanly produced, constructed objectivity' (Berger and Luckmann 1967: 78). While this reflects on the systematic properties of identity, the aspect of identity-construction as a process of social action also needs to be taken into account. We can consider it as a process of structuration according to Giddens, ie to 'study the ways in which that system, via the application of generative rules and resources, and in the context of unintended outcomes, is produced and reproduced in interaction' (Giddens 1979: 66). As a consequence, the construction of identity encompasses two very different components: an institutional element, drawing on symbolic repertoires, history, tradition, culture and heritage; and an element of strategic conduct. These elements form part of a constant circle of producing and reproducing shared concepts of collectivity, such as ethnicity, territoriality, community and identity. These, in turn, establish an institutional basis for representing the relations of the collectivity with time and space.

The making of these concepts represents a case of symbolic construction of notions of community as understood by Cohen (1985). The construction of identity is an active process of producing meaning. Meaning arises from the transformation of symbolic repertoire by acts of quotation, interpretation and invention, whose symbolic validity is the result of a process in which social actors negotiate and assert meaning. Meaning also depends on the context of its production. The very nature of symbols depends on the ability to take on different, even contradictory meanings. As a consequence, symbolic systems are invested with a degree of variance, even incoherence. Still, the process results in the construction of institutional concepts of collectivity which require a minimum of uncontested validity over time.

'Historic countries' have a sense of community in time and space, thus dialectically depending on ethnicity and territoriality. 'Historic countries' differ from both nations and regions. I refer to the concept of ethnicity as in Barth (1969) and his followers which incorporates amongst belief in shared cultural characteristics and notions of shared history the idea of these concepts taking on forms of political organisation (Barth 1969: 34). Concerning the concept of nation, I am fully aware of the problem of referring to 'the' nation as if the concept was unequivocal. However, for the sake of brevity, this cannot be discussed here. Suffice it to say that nation in this case stands for a western European model of the nation, constituting a sovereign nation-state. Nations are not necessarily identical to ethnic groups, even if constituted round an ethnic core (Connor 1978). This is obviously true for 'historic countries'. Within Scotland and Bavaria cultural, historical and political differences between distinct groups of the population, in other words ethnic differences, do exist. Nevertheless, nations are constituted as imagined communities (Anderson 1991). Only secondarily, territoriality constitutes the nation via the idea of homeland (Smith 1991). Regions, by contrast, define themselves via imagined territory. In this case, the borders of the territory are secondarily determined through common cultural characteristics and therefore ethnic dissociation.

'Historic countries' alternate between both construction modes. This is not as paradoxical as it seems: although they lack state sovereignty now, the constant remembrance of being a sovereign state in times past is a decisive element of their symbolic repertoires, which enables constant oscillation between both possibilities. They are moving on sliding scales between ethnic and civic nationalism, between regional and national construction modes of identity. I am grateful to Dave McCrone for this insight of Scottish nationalism sliding amongst other options between ethnic and civic strategies. Construction of identity can be characterised here by a constant shifting between homogenisation and fragmentation, ethnic and civic modes, ethnic and territorial strategies and debates that oscillate between anti-unitarian or federalist versus centralist arguments, according to the framework of the situation.

Referring again to identity-construction as a form of strategic conduct, this situation of ambivalence needs to be managed. Several forms of strategy or of reproducing the validity of institutions such as ethnicity, territoriality and identity don't mix or alternate. However, we can distinguish between strategies of ethnicisation and politicisation.

Musealisation as Strategy

Looking at one of the core strategies of identity construction based on ethnicisation – the exploitation of culture and cultural difference – the fields of heritage and tourism appear to be good examples for investigation. The development of Scottish heritage as a readily identifiable heritage brand was documented in detail by McCrone et al (1995). Part of this expanding market is a steady increase in heritage centres and museum numbers (from just above 100 in 1968 to currently circa 400), the most prominent and recent example being the building of a new Museum of Scotland in the centre of Edinburgh. Commenting on the economic and symbolic power of heritage in Scotland, McCrone et al state: 'To be sure, Scotland did not create the heritage industry, but it can be taken as an excellent example of the genre' (1995: 205). Austria might serve as an intriguing parallel in this field. Austria is in many ways comparable to Bavaria, although there is no space here to discuss the similarities in any detail. We can point out, though, that they are similar in terms of history, demographic, geographic and economic structure, size, popular culture and political interest. In more general terms, this also applies to Scotland. As Jagschitz (1997) points out, there are six possible strategies to deal with a quest for identity in the European context: musealisation, folklorisation, colonisation, economisation, peripherisation and building European partnerships.

Jagschitz describes musealisation and folklorisation as strategies of harnessing culture:

> The tendencies towards the marketing and the sale of history are growing stronger. Economic power is shifting abroad, the economy can ever less be influenced by Austrian factors and interests. The Austrians are left with the task to offer the country, its art, its culture and folklore like museum wardens. (...) Homeland, traditions and peculiarity serve as a base for marketing. Austria is depicted as a country of quaint customs, of rugged and natural life, where people dress themselves up rather oddly and wear *Gamsbärte*, briefly, as a place of European exoticism. The aim is to create a kind of alpine Disneyland that could be readily consumed as tourist fast-food. (Jagschitz 1997: 178-9).

My translation from the German original. A *Gamsbärt* is an adornment made from the hair on the back of a chamois, worn with traditional hats in all alpine regions These quotes convey the sense that culture, traditions, folklore, art, history etc are adapted and put to use, being transformed in the quest for identity.

Both musealisation and folklorisation are strategies for the commodification of the symbolic repertoire transforming it according to the demands of the marketplace. The Highland-myth with its tartanry or 'tartan monster' is a well-documented case (see eg Nairn 1977, McCrone et al 1995, Rosie 1992, Trevor-Roper 1983). The Bavarian parallel would be the development of the alpine/Upper-Bavarian repertoire of popular culture including some form of an alpine ghost in lederhosen. Such strategies of commodification promote a commemorating attitude within cultural production (Bleicher 1990). Within Scotland and Bavaria they represent processes of integration. Fostered mainly by economic opportunity related to mass tourism in this century, but originating in the romantic movements of the last, folklorisation became so successful a strategy that the distortions of Highland culture and alpine/Upper-Bavarian culture respectively were transformed into powerful symbolic structures, representing Scotland and Bavaria as a whole, in particular from outsiders' perspectives.

Yet, strategies of musealisation encompass several strains. They contain subtler forms of folklorisation, reflected above all in a boom in local history museums. They embrace enlightening attitudes to produce 'authentic' images of the past, together with an educational mission and employment of scientific methods. In terms of cultural heritage, they demonstrate excellence in order to legitimise aspirations to the national and international importance of their country's history. Because heritage can exist in the form of current objects and events, it is available for use as a resource in a wider sense than history or tradition. It lends itself to marketing, consumption, instrumentalisation and ideologisation (McCrone et al 1995). It is accessible for everyday experience and in that lies its power as a medium of identity-construction.

Investigating Museums

Museums, in particular those with a national remit, are important organisations concerned with the production of heritage as such and are simultaneously institutions where ethnic and civic elements of identity construction converge. They offer the link between cultural politics and the making of heritage. Owning heritage as a symbolic construction based on ethnicity is a quality of the nation.

Museums are places of identity-construction. This indicates that they should reveal the characteristics of identity-construction. At the same time, they act as framing places where symbolic contexts are produced and finally, they are the keepers of national heritage. For the purpose of investigation into the museums' part in the construction of identity we must concentrate on both the process of production and visible products. More precisely, we have to look at the organisational, the institutional and the presentational aspects of museums, the defining power of the actors and the agency as a whole, the mission of the national museum and finally at the symbolic construction produced and transmitted by the displays (see Figure 1).

To link this perspective on museums to the considerations on identity-construction in 'historic countries' above, we can draw again on the four characteristics mentioned before. We could try to investigate whether these issues occur in any topical way within the museums. Concentrating on cultural homogeneity as an example, one way of producing an impression of it is to provide historical accounts, a constant stream of historical information conceived as an account of one country's comprehensive history. In that respect national museums are obviously among the most interesting cases. Referring to Scotland and Bavaria, the most intriguing parallels can be drawn between the *Haus der Bayerischen Geschichte* (House of Bavarian History, hereafter referred to as HdBG) and the new *Museum of Scotland* (hereafter referred to as MoS). The case studies, the following material and analysis are drawn from a wider investigation of four case studies in my doctoral thesis: the Haus der Bayerischen Geschichte (House of Bavarian History), The Bayerisches National museum (Bavarian National Museum), the National Museums of Scotland and the National Galleries of Scotland. Material analysed in this thesis includes amongst other interviews with senior staff, laws, Acts of Parliament, publications by the museums such as annual reports, advertising and campaign material and documentation of displays.

Case Studies: Haus der Bayerischen Geschichte and Museum of Scotland

Concept and Institutional History

Both organisations were originally conceived as historically comprehensive and decidedly national museums. They should both provide an account of the respective country's complete history with an educational impetus,

Figure 1 Investigating Museums

museums as places of identity-construction

characteristics of identity-construction

places for the production of symbolic contexts

keepers of heritage

process of production "from ideas to images"	subject of investigation: organisation	subject of investigation: institution	subject of investigation: presentation	product "visiting the images"
	internal organisation and hierarchy	normative conditions	themes	
	connections and dependencies: finance, directives, tasks, interests, decision-making	history of the institution	interpretations	
	invention of themes and concepts for displays/exhibitions	motivations and expectations of the actors	type of collections	
			contexts	
	defining power of actors	mission	symbolic construction	

but an account that could be read in many different ways. In the case of the HdBG, there is a directive defining the operational terms for this organisation provisionally set down in an official notice, thus marking the official date of birth for the organisation as 1 January 1983. Official notice by the Bavarian Minister-President, 16 December 1982 (Franz Josef Strauß StAnz.Nr. 51/1982) and directive by the Bavarian State Government according to art. 43 of the Bavarian Constitution, 11 May 1985. My translation of the task list, identical in both legal documents:

> The house of Bavarian history has the obligation 1. to provide access to the historical and cultural variety of Bavaria for all social classes, in particular for the Bavarian youth, in all parts of the country, 2. to portray the Bavarian state in its totality as well as the development of state and society up to the presence in a historical-political-cultural framework, 3. to promote historical consciousness and to enhance it in order to thereby use the historical heritage for the benefits of the future of the Free State of Bavaria within the German and European framework. These tasks will be fulfilled predominantly through exhibitions in all parts of the country, publications, public lectures, film documentaries and the development of a photography archive on Bavarian history.

It will be shown in further detail below that the HdBG does not correspond to the conventional idea of a museum, but rather constitutes a virtual museum.

A very similar idea of comprehensiveness lies behind the conception of the Museum of Scotland. The description of the National Museums of Scotland remit in National Heritage (Scotland) Act 1995, Part 1 states very similar objectives. This can be seen, for example, in the mission statement engraved in the foundation stone, stating the main task for the new museum. Looking towards the Royal Museum of Scotland (which houses the national collections in general social, technical, natural, art and decorative art history and there-fore represents the international part of the holdings) one faces towards the inscription 'THE WORLD TO SCOTLAND'. Looking the other way, towards the MoS, the inscription reads 'SCOTLAND TO THE WORLD'. Scotland will – according to one of the campaign leaflets – 'at last have a museum dedicated to telling its unique story'. The leaflet continues:

> Over the years Scots have made their mark. Their achievements have touched the lives of millions of people throughout the world. Yet Scotland has never had a museum

to tell the story of this country and people. NOW HISTORY IS IN THE MAKING. A new museum is being built in the centre of its capital city. When the Museum of Scotland opens in 1998, it will present a unique portrait of the nation. Capital letters in the original. Leaflet issued by the Museum of Scotland Campaign, Chambers Street, Edinburgh EH1 1JF, under the title 'Nothing would be a more *fitting* TRIBUTE to our PAST than to GIVE IT THE FUTURE it deserves, 1994.

Apart from suggesting the narration of a unique – thus distinctive and in some way consistent – story, this short paragraph also reveals the twofold character of historical construction: it relates to the provision of a historical account, that will ideally be produced by the succession of displays while it also describes the historic achievement that lies in the building of a new national museum itself.

This is a reminder of the fact that museums themselves form part of the national history, their emergence expressing civic achievement, often manifesting itself in the architecture of the building and the organisational set-up, again taking its toll on the conception of displays and exhibitions. Here the institutional history of the HdBG is again a good example. Originally, after the experience of the Second World War, the idea was to create a comprehensive historical museum, to counteract public ignorance about the country's history, to deliver an educational service and to prevent any further nationalist catastrophe. Similar to the plans for the MoS, there should have been a cleverly designed museum that could provide historical account based on scholarly study and expertise. For a number of mainly political reasons the planning was delayed for several decades. The planning and conceptualisation of this museum became entangled in political debates and conflicting perspectives making Bavarian Government support unlikely for decades. The HdBG existed as a small task force, based at the Bavarian national Museum, staging historical exhibitions while the prospective ground for the constructoin of the HdBG was allocated to the building of the new State Chancellery. By the early 1980s however, the HdBG task force's exhibitions proved to be so successful in terms of public interest that the then Minister-President Strauß, himself a professional historian, personally took care of the project, reinventing the HdBG. It was established as a governmental department, an institution without permanent building or collection but as a sort of governmental provider of substantial historical exhibitions. At the time, the underlying ideas for the HdBG were to cater for the diverging Bavarian regions, to be entirely free to choose whatever historical period and topic for the big annual exhibitions, and to borrow objects (with a privileged status) from all public museums. These conditions were seen as a major advance on the original idea. It was assumed that over the years a much more comprehensive historical account could be established than would have been possible with a permanent collection and (semi-)permanent displays.

The institutional history of the MoS, albeit different in outcome, is a similarly long one and planning, as in Bavaria, could only go ahead when it became politically suitable and sustainable to pledge sufficient funds in 1989. The Government provided £30 million for the construction of the building with the National Museums of Scotland (hereafter referred to as NMS) spending £17 million over eight years to develop the project. The cost of fitting out the new museum and installing the exhibitions was estimated at £14.5 million, of which half was granted by the Heritage Lottery Fund, and half had to be raised through donations and sponsorship.

The curators and keepers of the NMS were faced with the task of designing a succession of displays that would provide a repertoire of various possible accounts of Scottish history. However, the meaning of national heritage, and therewith national identity, represented in the displays needs to be discussed. This does not only involve negotiation between groups of museum staff and other agencies involved, but also to find a balance between public expectation and the way museum staff see themselves and Scottish identity. Interviews with curators involved revealed among other contentious issues that not only the general public, but the curators themselves, see a problem in most of them – ie the curators – not being Scottish. Nevertheless, most of them regard the task of offering a version of Scottish history that strongly conveys its Scottishness as paramount. The identity of the interviewees cannot be revealed due to the request by some of them to remain anonymous. In all four original case studies, interviews with 10–12 senior members, including directors, keepers and senior curators were conducted by the author. To exemplify this with quotes from an interview – I had asked whether the interviewee had the feeling of having a particular task to fulfil – the answer was:

But that in a period when people are interested in their history, they will be brought into contact with the icons and symbols of their history and of the nation. ... So I hope that people who go through here can get a feeling for ... Scotland, that they get a feeling for difference and regional variation, and perhaps pride in... you know, culture, and nationhood and so forth, history. And also obviously, that people coming from outside, get a very strong feeling for Scottish history as well. ... I mean, I have always been aware, having travelled round the continent a great deal, that if you say where you come from, they say, 'ah, yes, English'. And we, I think, would like to say, 'well no, this is Scotland, we're Scottish and we were a separate nation once and we have a separate culture in many ways, yes, it has much in common with Europe, but yet we are actually right on the edge of Europe and that leads to all sorts of interesting traits of character and traits of culture and this is what they are and so on'.

This is a typical answer not only for the NMS, but if one replaced the references to Scotland with references to Bavaria just as typical for the Bavarian museum investigated. It indicates the strong educational impetus, the strive for enlightening 'the people' and at the same time the urge to convey a sense of nationhood through displaying national history. The wish to conjure up pride in national culture, nationhood and history is an indicator of the deliberate attempt to provide a sense of identity. This is also revealed in the very beginning of the passage quoted linking it to the present political situation.

Organisation

Depending on the respective institutional histories, the present organisational and institutional situations the museums find themselves in are negotiable, as are notions of nationhood. The MoS is part of the NMS. These are governed by a Board of Trustees, whose members are appointed by the Secretary of State for Scotland. The Trustees determine general policies and all major decisions in consultation with the museum's management board, consisting of the director and senior staff members. The museum was also directly responsible to the Secretary of State concerning financial matters and planning strategies. The role of the Department of

226

Education and Industry Arts and Cultural Heritage Division in these matters is the supervision of good practice in delivering a public service. However, the organisational shake-up as a consequence of devolution also brings about changes in museum management. Thus the NMS is responsible to the Scottish Parliament and to the Scottish Executive. The interviewees expressed an awareness of rising expectations towards the new museum, with its final realisation and opening taking place at the same time as devolution and increasing general interest in all matters Scottish. They also expected the generation of rising political interest in national identity, together with growing awareness of Scottish history, to increase interest in the museum as a heritage institution.

As regards internal organisation, the MoS is an integral part of the NMS. The NMS organisational structure consists of several service and conservation departments, the latter headed by keepers and employing several curators. As far as planning for the MoS displays is concerned, there have been four different teams, according to the sections of the new museum. The teams are headed by keepers or senior curators with specialisms in Scottish material culture. The teams and team members work in flexible arrangements subject to discussion. Concerning curatorial decisions the interviewees in general appreciated the opportunity to work independently. Restrictions much lamented, though, come from a source seen as external. The museum as a new building is regarded as an architecturally important achievement. The architects see themselves having an important role not only in designing the building as a shell for displays but also as an integral part of the display and therefore being able to determine part of the display designs. This situation leads to clashes between some architectural and curatorial interests.

The organisational situation for the HdBG is slightly different and might represent possible future relations between the NMS and a Scottish Executive. The HdBG is currently a Department of the Bavarian State Chancellery in contrast to all other state museums that are governed and administered by Bavarian State Ministry for Education, Culture, Science and Art. Constitutionally, this is an important difference: whereas the Minister at the head of the State Chancellery is responsible to the Minister–President, other Ministers are directly responsible to Parliament. With the State Chancellery growing in size and political weight, in particular during the past few years, the balance of political power is shifting towards the Minister–President. The HdBG and its Director are thus answerable to the Minister-President and have to work to his/her directives. According to the interviewees, in practice, the organisation functions independently. Permanent tasks, such as administration, publication, public relations, archive, education etc, are divided between five departments, each with a small number of permanent staff. All projects, mainly historical exhibitions, are developed and realised by separate project groups working relatively independently.

Still, the interviews also revealed a number of informal restrictions. Due to the comparatively short institutional history of the HdBG, current practice is highly dependent on senior staff and the 'founder myth' they are part of. History in this case began with a 'catastrophe': though the two exhibitions the HdBG task force staged before it came into existence in its present organisation were extremely successful in terms of visitor numbers and scholarly response, they were a financial and organisational disaster. Part of the HdBG myth is to emphasise the necessity of avoiding similar project outcomes at all costs, or face abolition. There is a strong sense of being dependent on political fortune and the interests of the Minister–President. Therefore, the interviewees felt the need to pre-empt the political need for the consideration of certain themes and events, be it an important anniversary, an important state visit, representation of a particular part of the country or a certain view of Bavarian history. The following quotes from interviews with HdBG staff substantiate these points (The translation cannot reflect the subtleties of the use of Bavarian dialect in these quotes, but it is an attempt to provide as truthful a translation of the way of expression and contents as I am able to give).

... that we, in principle, concerning our existence, can still be the plaything of whatever political interests.

... whereas the scope for planning, well, it changes, too, well, the scope was slightly larger in the past, well, at this moment we are a little more tied up, well, we are able to do a lot of, or a large amount of what we really want to do. One has to present that well, with good arguments, but obviously we also do things that are wanted.

This is simply part of the hierarchy; ultimately, the big plans go through to the Minister–President and he probably wouldn't authorise themes he didn't like at all, but it isn't much, really, that is prohibited or authorised, because most things have been discussed beforehand anyway.

Well, restriction to Bavarian themes in as much as we have to take care of covering all regions in Bavaria, more or less, and this certainly is also a political precondition, then, that certain controversial themes aren't tackled, that one, well, restricts oneself to very conservative themes, themes where it can also be expected that there will be many visitors, but themes where it can also be expected that there won't be any political controversies or trench warfare.

The differences between both case studies concerning external administration are due to the respective organisations' institutional histories as shown above. These differences, though, also cause differences in the internal set-up of the museums' organisations. There are consequences not only for work organisation as such but also for processes of decision-making and, therefore, as a direct result, for decisions concerning themes and displays.

Themes of Cultural Homogeneity

I referred above to the constant sliding between versions of cultural homogeneity and fragmentation as a characteristic of identity-construction in 'historic countries'. Both MoS and HdBG were intended to deliver a comprehensive presentation of the respective country's history which in itself is a way of producing homogeneity. In the case of the HdBG this can only ever be achieved over a long period of time. The HdBG is not a conventional museum but a sort of museum on the road and governmental provider of historical shows. To measure the displays against cultural homogeneity or fragmentation, the investigation has to focus on the spectrum of topics covered by exhibition themes and on representation of culture within exhibition displays. Strategies to produce a sense of Bavarian cultural homogeneity typically either try to represent carefully the fragmented situation as an interesting cultural diversity integrated in the Bavarian state or to concentrate on the core of old Bavaria. In the case of the HdBG the choice of topics over the past fifteen years aimed at representing all the different regions within Bavaria, the different religious groups and a wide range of historic epochs. The HdBG tries to be comprehensive in putting on display a broad sweep of Bavarian history avoiding typical themes. Nevertheless, the emphasis is on the more unusual historic events, anniversaries and historic figures. Between 1983 and 1998 the HdBG staged fifty-six exhibitions, ranging from small displays usually chosen for anniversaries to the huge *Landesausstellungen* usually held annually, occupying large venues for several months and more compact exhibitions travelling round the country for up to two years. (The term *Landesausstellung* – meaning exhibition of/for the country – had originally been coined by the Austrian Ministry of Culture for their national historic shows held in the 1980s). At the same time, comprehensive representation is sought by choosing the location for exhibitions in relation to the themes. Only sixteen exhibitions were shown exclusively in the old core of Bavaria, fifteen exhibitions in two or more locations (max. forty-two), the remainder in the regions of Franconia and Suabia. The choice of topics also reveals a bias towards themes concerning the Bavarian state as a political totality (as stated in the directive quoted above). A number of exhibitions over the years related to the Bavarian constitution and the country's territorial changes. Another large group of themes circled around groups representing cultural and social cleavages: working class, trade unions, religious denomination, farmers, family, youth and most recently gender. Important examples were the three exhibitions concerning the history of working conditions and trade unions 'Aufbruch ins Industriezeitalter' (1985), 'Unternehmer - Arbeitnehmer' (touring exhibition, 1985-87), '8 Stunden sind kein Tag. Geschichte der Gewerkschaften in Bayern' (touring exhibition, 1997-99), the exhibition about the historic role of farming 'Bauern in Bayern' (1994), the exhibition about the constitutional history of Bavaria 'Bayern entsteht. Montgelas und sein Ansbacher Mémoire 1796' (1996) and the three exhibitions about the Reformation '...wider Laster und Sünde.' Augsburgs Weg in der Reformation' (1997), 'Geld und Glaube. Leben in evangelischen Reichsstädten' (1998) and 'Bürgerfleiß und Fürstenglanz. Reichsstadt und Fürstabtei Kempten' (1998). (For a comprehensive list see http://www.bayern.de/HDBG/hdbgaust.htm and http://www.bayern.de/HDBG/#Ausstellungen. The titles mentioned translate roughly as 'Departure for the Industrial Era', 'Entrepreneurs - Employees', 'Eight Hours Don't Make a Day. History of the Trade Unions in Bavaria', 'Farmers in Bavaria', 'Bavaria Emerges. Montgelas and His Mémoire of Ansbach 1796', '"... Against Vice and Sin." The

Augsburg Way of the Reformation', 'Money and Faith. Life in Protestant Free Cities of the Empire' and 'Bourgeois Industry and Princely Splendour. Free City of the Empire and Princely Abbey Kempten'.) The image of comprehensiveness and thus cultural homogeneity is upheld by a strategy of representing Bavaria as a culturally diverse but territorially and politically unified totality.

Yet, this aim is very difficult to achieve. The public does not travel as much throughout Bavaria as would have been thought, and the catering for educational interests often results in sacrificing scholarly sophistication. At the same time, the organisation is chronically prone to attempts to political influence. It therefore tries very hard to represent the political centre ground thematically, not always daring to challenge received views of Bavarian history.

The strategy of presenting cultural homogeneity for Scotland within the MoS is slightly different. Due to the MoS being a conventional museum, it has decided to present a comprehensive chronological overview of Scotland's cultural history. The museum's conceptional structure is based on presenting the best and most important elements of Scottish history in order to link the different Scottish regions and historic epochs. Therefore, the museum is structured vertically according to historical chronology, starting in the basement with geology, prehistory and early peoples, continuing with the history of the sovereign kingdom from c. 800 AD to the Union, followed by the political and social transformations of the eighteenth and nineteenth century, concluding at the top floor dealing with the twentieth century. Each historical section is divided up according to prominent themes of the respective period. Thus, a number of different itineraries are available for individual exploration. For example, themes such as religion, power, genealogy etc could be followed through time; the same is true for different kinds of material or objects. However, the structure of the institution as a permanent building with permanent displays only allows for a limited number of different story-lines with reference to comprehensiveness as a form of representing cultural homogeneity. Whereas conceptions of museum displays for prehistory to the nineteenth century only offer visitors an opportunity to develop their individual views on Scotland's culture, the twentieth century displays present an exception in offering a greater variety of interactive museum-visiting than all other sections. Traditional museum display within the NMS, if regarded as 'permanent', has an average lifetime of twenty years. The twentieth century section presented a problem for the developing team for precisely that reason. To present it in a sanitised academic version of official national history in a permanent display for the next twenty years seemed, if not impossible, at least inappropriate. Therefore, the decision was to create something more temporary involving Scottish people's own views on their own past. The idea was for the general public to choose objects to represent the Scottish twentieth century. So the museum issued a leaflet asking people to suggest an object standing for their individual views. The team also chose a number of Scottish personalities and celebrities to ask, such as for example Kirsty Wark, Sean Connery, Donald Dewar, Ally McCoist, Lulu and the Queen Mother, mainly to inspire as many people as possible to take part. A limited number of objects is presented, together with short descriptions of the individual persons and their reasons for the particular choice of object. All other suggestions are accessible through a computerised interactive database where future visitors could also add their own views and suggestions.

The idea of presenting Scotland as a culturally and socially diverse but nevertheless comprehensively identifiable entity is very similar to the idea of comprehensiveness within the vast range of possible themes for the HdBG. However, the choice is more limited. Museum staff have to make a number of choices when drawing up the list of Scottish celebrities to ask, involving decisions about Scottishness. The same is true for the choice of objects to be put on display. Apart from practical limitations, the most difficult choice appears to concern the need to convey a distinctive Scottishness through twentieth century objects while avoiding mere tartanry and instantly recognisable icons, as opposed to the more general displays on twentieth century culture throughout the neighbouring Royal Museum of Scotland.

Conclusion

This brief examination of the topical issue of cultural homogeneity in the MoS and HdBG demonstrates how it can be traced through the three different aspects of museums outlined at the start, namely as organisations, institutions and as providers of displays. Representing cultural homogeneity in turn, is an aspect of constituting ethnic difference and therewith an element or criterion for identity-construction. As mentioned above, museum displays and therefore the museum as institution, can only provide offers of possible versions of identity based on a limited number of accounts of history and displays of material cultural heritage. The museum delivers props for the visitors' imagination. To investigate the museums' part in identity-construction in Scotland and Bavaria, one would have to focus not only on the three aspects considered in this chapter but also to concentrate on the visitors' own construction of meaning. Still, it is possible to demonstrate the strong initiative museums represent in the making of heritage and identity, in particular in 'historic countries'.

Acknowledgements

I wish to thank my referees for their kind advice and comment and I am particularly indebted to Antonia Dodds for her invaluable observations and help with revising my sometimes clumsy English.

References

Anderson B R 1991 Imagined Communities. Reflections on the Origin and Spread of Nationalism. London/New York, Verso

Barth F (ed) 1969 Ethnic Groups and Boundaries. Bergen, Universitetsforlaget

Berger P S, Luckmann T 1967 The Social Construction of Reality. Garden City, Doubleday

Bleicher J 1990 'Die kulturelle Konstruktion sozialer Identität am Beispiel Schottlands.' In: Haferkamp H (ed) Sozialstruktur und Kultur. Frankfurt a. M, Suhrkamp

Cohen A P 1985 The Symbolic Construction of Community. London/New York, Routledge.

Connor W 1978 'A Nation is a Nation, is a State, is an Ethnic Group, is a ... .' Ethnic and Racial Studies 1, 4: 379–400

Gellner E 1983 Nations and Nationalism. Oxford, Basil Blackwell

Giddens A 1979 Central Problems in Social Theory. Action, Structure and Contradiction in Social Analysis. London/Basingstoke, Macmillan

Goetze D 1994 'Identitätsstrategien und die Konstruktion sozialer Räume: Eine spanische Fallstudie.' In: Lindner R (ed) Die Wiederkehr des Regionalen. Frankfurt a. M./New York, Campus

Heckmann F 1997 'Ethnos - eine imaginierte oder reale Gruppe? Über Ethnizität als soziologische Kategorie.' In: Hettlage R, Deger P, Wagner S (eds) Kollektive Identität in Krisen. Ethnizität in Nation, Region, Europa. Opladen, Westdeutscher Verlag

Jagschitz G 1997 'Die Jagd nach dem Gamsbart oder Österreichs Suche nach seiner Identität.' In: Hettlage R, Deger P, Wagner S (eds) Kollektive Identität in Krisen. Ethnizität in Nation, Region, Europa. Opladen, Westdeutscher Verlag

Kellas J G 1989 The Scottish Political System. 4th Edition. Cambridge, Cambridge University Press

Marr A 1992. The Battle for Scotland. Harmondsworth, Penguin

McCrone D 1992 Understanding Scotland: The Sociology of a Stateless Nation. London, Routledge

McCrone D 1998 The Sociology of Nationalism. London, Routledge

McCrone D, Morris A, Kiely R 1995. Scotland - the Brand. Edinburgh, Edinburgh University Press

Mintzel A 1991 'Regionale politische Traditionen und CSU Hegemonie in Bayern.' In: Oberndörfer D, Schmitt K (eds) Parteien und regionale politische Traditionen in der Bundesrepublik Deutschland. Berlin, Duncker & Humblot

Nairn T 1977 The Break-up of Britain. London, NLB

Nairn T 1997 Faces of Nationalism. Janus Revisited. London, Verso

Rosie G 1992 'Museumry and the Heritage Industry.' In: Donnachie I, Whatley C (eds) The Manufacture of Scottish History. Edinburgh, Polygon

Roth R A 1994 Bayern. Eine politische Landeskunde. München, Landeszentrale für politische Bildungsarbeit

Smith A 1991 National Identity. London, Penguin

Trevor–Roper H 1983 'The Invention of Tradition: The Highland Tradition of Scotland.' In: Hobsbawm E, Ranger T (eds) The Invention of Tradition. Cambridge, Cambridge University Press

Farm Tourism, Agricultural Heritage and the Social and Economic Regeneration of Farm Women

Angela Morris and Joy Gladstone

Farm tourism is more than B&B with animals to pat and home-baking to consume. Important ingredients as these may be, a variety of elements combine to make up farm or agricultural tourism. The most useful and comprehensive definition is provided by Clarke (1996) and is shown in Table 1.

Table 1 Farm tourism elements

Attractions	Activities
Permanent	Horse riding/trekking
Farm visitor centres	Fishing
Self-guided farm trails	Shooting/clay
Farm museums	Boating
Conservation areas	
Country parks	**Accommodation**
	Bed and breakfast
Events	Self-catering
Farm open days	Camping and caravanning
Guided walks	Bunkhouse barns
Educational visits	
Demonstrations	**Amenities**
	Restaurants
Access (rural)	Cafes/cream teas
Stile/gate maintenance	Farm shops/roadside stalls
Footpaths/bridleways/tracks	Pick your own
	Picnic sites

Source: Clarke 1996: 19.

In April 1995 we obtained Scottish Office Agriculture Environment and Fisheries Department (SOAEFD) core-funding to carry out research into two of these elements: farm accommodation and visitor attractions with an agricultural heritage theme. The aim of our research was three-fold. First, to find out whether or not providing farm-based serviced accommodation benefited farm women. Second, to identify the range and popularity of agricultural-based visitor attractions throughout Scotland. Finally, we were also interested in the impacts both farm-accommodation and agricultural heritage attractions have on the local economies of rural Scotland.

Our main concerns in this study were the attitudes and experiences of those involved with the provision of farm tourism and agricultural heritage attractions. We were, however, also interested in how farm tourism accommodation and agricultural heritage attractions were regarded by the Area Tourist Boards (ATBs). To this end we attempted to interview a representative of each of the fourteen ATBs throughout Scotland. Although we decided to focus on three study areas (Orkney, Perthshire, and South Ayrshire) it was felt that it would be beneficial to acquire information about ATB attitudes towards tourism at the wider Scottish level.

From July to December 1996 interviews took place with representatives of the following ATBs: Aberdeen and Grampian; Argyll, the Isles, Loch Lomond, Stirling and Trossachs; Ayrshire and Arran; Dumfries and Galloway; Highlands of Scotland; Kingdom of Fife; Orkney; Perthshire; Scottish Borders; and the Western Isles. Interviews were not held with Edinburgh and Lothians Tourist Board or the Greater Glasgow and Clyde Valley Tourist Board because these authorities said that they did not have a great deal of information regarding either farm tourism or agricultural heritage. This is not surprising in view of the predominantly urban nature of these authorities.

The interviews with ATB personnel revealed that none of the ATBs treated farm tourism as a separate sector although Orkney, Ayrshire and Arran, Dumfries and Galloway, the Highlands of Scotland, Perthshire, and the Western Isles all recognised its importance in their areas. To quote the Chief Executive of Orkney Islands Tourist Board:

> Farming characterises the place. It's all about land and sea. It's a living, working, agricultural landscape. Orkney Islands Tourist Board has not set out to create an agricultural heritage. It's just there.

Kingdom of Fife; Argyll, the Isles, Loch Lomond, Stirling and Trossachs were more ambivalent. Edinburgh and Lothians, Greater Glasgow and Clyde Valley, Scottish Borders, Aberdeen and Grampian did not regard farm tourism as a particularly important part of tourism in their areas.

Farm Tourism in the UK

In the UK farm tourism has been the subject of research interest since the 1970s. Researchers have approached the subject from two distinct viewpoints: the agricultural economics perspective and the tourism perspective (Clarke 1993 and 1996). Agricultural economists have been interested in farm tourism as a category of on-farm diversification (see for example, Davies 1971, 1983, Dalton and Wilson 1989; Sale 1989 and 1997, Wilson 1990). Tourism researchers, on the other hand, have treated farm tourism as a form of rural tourism (Frater 1981, The British Market Research Bureau 1986, Denman and Denman 1990, Denman and Denman 1993, the Welsh Tourist Board 1986, and Clarke 1993 have all carried out studies of farm tourism).

It is our view that farm tourism should not be regarded simply as a form of on-farm agricultural diversification or as purely a sector of rural tourism. It is both. It was the important changes in rural and agricultural policy during the late 1980s and early 1990s which encouraged farmers to diversify into tourism. The reform of the EC Structural Funds in 1988 made funds available to:

assist infrastructure developments, to aid the diversification of farming (through policy instruments such as the Farm Diversification Grant Scheme of 1988, the Rural Enterprise Programme (REP) and the LEADER programme of 1991), to encourage the growth of small and medium-sized enterprises (Smells), to assist in training schemes and to conserve the environment (Sale et al 1997).

Farm tourism enterprises were well-placed to take advantage of Structural Fund support. Four years later farm tourism received another major boost following reform of the Common Agricultural Policy (CAP). The 1992 CAP reforms represented a move away from production-centred support for agriculture. They provided the opportunity for the commercialisation of the environment by introducing agri-environmental schemes and encouraging the development of recreational and tourist enterprises (Slee 1995). These reforms were reinforced by the 1994 Uruguay Round Agreement on Agriculture which reduced the likelihood of a return to policies with the capacity to encourage overproduction.

Farm tourism, in all its various forms, has been found to be important, not just to individual farm households but to the wider economy of rural areas.

A survey carried out by the English Tourist Board (ETB) in 1992 found that farm-based accommodation represented 3% of all serviced accommodation, 9% of all registered self-catering accommodation, and 4% of recorded visitor attractions. From these figures it was estimated that farm-based accommodation accounted for some £70 million of farm output and benefited the rural economy to the value of £115 million. A survey carried out in 1997 by Devon Farms Accommodation revealed that income from holiday accommodation is a vital support to 35% of farming enterprises in Devon. To quote Jackie Clarke:

> The tourist crop is accepted within the farming community, and the automatically assigned role of pin-money is redundant. In the 1990s, some tourism enterprises keep the farm (1996: 12).

There are no comparable figures for Scotland because apart from Clarke's 1993 report to the STB 'An Analysis of the Demand for Farm Tourism in Scotland' no research exists on farm tourism in Scotland from a tourism as opposed to an agricultural economics perspective.

Our research into farm tourism was carried out from neither an agricultural economics or a tourism perspective. We were aware of both the importance of tourism as a form of agricultural diversification which combines support for the economies of rural areas with custodianship of agricultural land, and the fact that in rural Scotland tourism is a major employer, providing employment for approximately 20% of the total workforce (The Scottish Office 1995: 70).

While farm tourism in Scotland remains under-researched we do know, however, that 15% of all Scottish farms have diversified into providing on-farm tourism accommodation (Denman and Denman 1993). In most cases it is the farmer's wife who is responsible for the management of the farm accommodation enterprise. One of the issues we wanted to address was to what extent has this opened up new opportunities for women on farms? The provision of B&B accommodation and self-catering facilities are the mainstay of farm tourism. They are not, however, the only forms that farm tourism can take. Apart from experiencing farmhouse hospitality tourists also want to be entertained. They want places to go for a day out, things to do on a budget, and somewhere dry to go if it rains. Some tourists, especially those rich in cultural (as opposed to economic) capital (see McCrone et al 1995) may feel that staying on a farm is the ideal opportunity to learn a bit more about agriculture in the area they are staying, especially how it has changed over the years. This is where agricultural heritage attractions such as agricultural museums and working farms can have an important role to play.

Farm tourism has close links with the heritage industry in that it is based on and helps to perpetuate notions of the rural idyll and a romantic, sanitised agriculture. We had originally hoped to build on previous work (McCrone et al 1995) and explore in detail the links between agriculture and the heritage industry. Unfortunately, due to time constraints we were only able to conduct a postal survey of agricultural heritage attractions which had a low response rate (42%). On the basis of this it is not possible to make any grand claims or draw too many conclusions about agricultural heritage in Scotland. Our survey does, however, throw up a few tentative suggestions and draw attention to issues and questions which need to be studied in more detail.

Sustainable Tourism

Any discussion of farm tourism has to be seen in terms of the debate over 'sustainable' or 'green tourism'. To quote the Chief Executive of the Scottish Tourist Board (STB) at the 1994 Robert Gordon University Heritage Convention:

> We also must ask ourselves the basic question: what is the Scottish tourism product? A dramatic landscape: a powerful sense of history: a reputation for friendliness? Yes, all of these, but traditional values can only be part of what we must sell. Current tourism trends favour clean, green, unspoilt destinations. That describes Scotland very well, but we will not reap the benefits, unless we can also offer good all-weather facilities and entertainment for families with children; unless we promote ourselves to appropriate markets such as the independent European market; and most particularly, unless we can develop our product in such a way that it does not damage the environment (1994:.x).

This latter point is particularly important, for tourism is dependent on the quality of the environment. Visitors are attracted to clean, green, places, precisely because they are clean and green. If they are spoiled by the careless disposal of litter from picnics and camp-sites, pollution from exhaust fumes, 'purpose built' holiday chalet developments, and unsightly caravan parks then they lose their attractiveness to visitors.

Much of the debate concerning rural tourism in the 1990s has hinged on the issue of 'sustainable tourism'. If tourism is to be sustainable it has, Denman argues, to satisfy the following criteria: (i) sensitive development appropriate to the local environment; (ii) support for conservation; (iii) support for the economy at a very local level; (iv) ecologically sound practice; (v) providing visitors with a genuine appreciation of the area (1994:216). Farm tourism fits easily with the concept of sustainable tourism. This is because, to quote Clarke 'the farmer has additional roles in the wider rural tourism product through provision for countryside access and maintenance of the rural landscape through farming activity' (1996: 19). Most farm tourism enterprises are based on existing, traditional buildings such as farm and croft houses, farm cottages, and byres. As these are important features of the Scottish landscape, tourism can provide an economic use for cottages and byres which might otherwise fall into a state of disrepair.

The Appeal of Farm Tourism

The growth in the short breaks holiday market; the increased demand for activity-based holidays; consumers reacting against mass tourism combined with an increased concern to protect the scenic and built heritage of rural areas has meant that farm tourism has become popular with a wide range of people. Denman (1994) found that 46% of British people were interested in using farm B&Bs, with 16% saying that they would be very interested: 'Farm tourism is not simply the province of *Guardian* readers in sensible shoes' (1994: 18).

Scottish farm holidays appeal to European visitors, particularly from Belgium and Germany where there are strong green movements. Jean Buchanan, Director of the organisation Scottish Farmhouse Holidays which was founded in 1982, stresses that: 'It is the unspoilt nature of the Scottish countryside that attracts these people in increasing numbers' (*Dundee Courier* 21 August 1995). A consequence of this is that the season has become extended at both ends. It starts around Easter and continues until the end of September. In Scotland approximately a third of farms offering B&B and self-catering accommodation are open virtually all year round (*Dundee Courier* 21 August 1995).

The Changing Nature of Farm Tourism

Farm tourism started to become popular in the 1960s, before the Development of Tourism Act of 1969 and the existence of national tourist boards aimed at encouraging the provision and improvement of tourist facilities and amenities. In the early days farm tourism was basic, budget tourism. It appealed to families and young people who wanted fun and fresh-air on a tight budget. One of our respondents started doing B&B in the Orkneys in 1970 when there was no requirement for B&B accommodation to be inspected. At this time she did not have a fridge and water still came from the well.

In view of this, it is hardly surprising that until the early 1980s the dominant image of farm tourism was of draughty barns and limited hot water. The development of grading and classification schemes by the national tourist boards in the early 1980s, combined with the growth of bodies such as the Farm Holiday Bureau and Scottish Farmhouse Holidays (1982) has done much to revamp the image of farm tourism and bring it into the quality accommodation sector.

Changes in the nature of farm tourism have meant that the market for farm tourism has become increasingly fragmented. It is no longer simply family tourism. Couples now form 50% of the B&B market; international visitors account for approximately 16%; business people approximately 10% and the over 60s roughly 25% (Clarke 1996: 21).

In the early days of farm tourism the trend was for guests to help out with farm work in order to gain 'hands on' experience of life on a farm. Mechanisation and an increased awareness of their insurance positions have discouraged farmers from letting visitors help with farm work. With the disappearance of the participatory element of farm tourism, the farm becomes simply part of a rural backcloth which is there to be appreciated quietly. An 'authentic' farm experience is created for example, by serving traditional farm food including home-made preserves and home-baking, by having piles of *Farmer's Weekly* in the sitting room and framed photographs of prize-winning livestock, and cups or rosettes, displayed on walls and in cabinets.

Encounters between farm host and guests invariably take on a staged quality. In farm B&B enterprises which offer an evening meal, the farmer's wife dresses up to serve dinner and greet her guests. The farmer is either hidden from view or allowed to make a guest appearance only when he has showered away all traces of the day's agricultural activity. Such interaction takes place in what Goffman (1973) calls the 'front' or public regions. Overalls, muddy boots, the farm dog, children, and the unshowered farmer are confined to the 'back' or private regions. Being a living tourist attraction of any kind can produce tension within the farm family. It is significant that 9% of our interviewees mentioned juggling the accommodation enterprise with family responsibilities as a potential source of conflict. The following comment by Dean MacCannell is particularly appropriate in this context:

> Conforming to the requirements of being a living tourist attraction becomes a total problem affecting every detail of life ... Any deviation from the touristic cultural ideal can be read as a political gesture that produces conflict not between groups but within the group (1974; p.179).

Our remit was the more practical one of identifying the benefits and impacts of farm-based accommodation and agricultural heritage attractions for farm women and on the local rural economy. Although the ideas of Goffman and MacCannell are relevant to farm tourism and agricultural heritage there was no place or opportunity to explore them further in our study without losing sight of the original focus.

The Farm Tourism Accommodation Survey

Brief visits were made to each of the tourist board areas in Scotland during the summer of 1995 to look at the extent and diversity of farm tourism accommodation enterprises and agricultural heritage attractions and to interview key members of ATB personnel. As a result of the visits we decided to complement the general overview with more detailed study of three areas: the Orkney Archipelago, Perthshire, and South Ayrshire, representing examples from the north, central, and southern Scotland respectively. Apart from their geographical locations, the three study areas were chosen because they contain different farm types. Orkney is predominantly cattle farming, Perthshire mixed agriculture, and South Ayrshire dairy farming.

Inventories of farm-based tourist accommodation were compiled for each of the three study areas, using the Area Tourist Board (ATB) accommodation guides. This was easily done because farm B&Bs and self-catering cottages attached to farms all display a tractor symbol. Of the three study areas Perthshire had the highest number of farm tourism accommodation enterprises (54). South Ayrshire had 19 and Orkney 15.

All farm tourism accommodation providers in each of the three study areas were surveyed by means of a face-to-face interview or a postal questionnaire. In each study area twelve accommodation providers were identified by a random sample and interviewed face-to-face using a semi-structured questionnaire. The remainder were sent the questionnaire through the post. In view of the small numbers involved the results of the face-to-face interviews and the postal survey were treated as one and the results of the three study areas were combined, giving an overall sample size of 88. The respondents who were to be interviewed face-to-face were contacted in the first instance by letter. This was then followed up by a telephone call to arrange an interview. Face-to-face interviews and the postal survey took place during the winter and spring of 1997.

We were particularly interested in the following issues: (i) farm tourism accommodation as a source of additional income; (ii) the advantages of farm tourism; (iii) the disadvantages of farm tourism; (iv) farm tourism and the regeneration of the local rural economy.

(i)   Farm tourism accommodation as a source of additional income

Our survey demonstrated that most farm tourism (accommodation) enterprises (81%) in Orkney, Perthshire, and South Ayrshire made a profit. The average profit in 1996 was between £1000 and £1500 p.a.

Much of this profit is reinvested. It is used to upgrade accommodation, furniture, and fittings, often in line with proposed Tourist Board recommendations for future grading and classification purposes.

While profit levels were relatively low, all respondents who made a profit appreciated the extra income and the sense of financial independence it gave them. In their own words:

> I value having my own money for the kids growing up.
>
> I can now afford to take my family away on holiday.
>
> I like my own independence.

A minority of respondents (11%) said that they did not make a profit. One respondent did not know if she made a profit. This question was not answered by five respondents.

(ii) The advantages of providing farm tourism accommodation

The most striking finding to emerge from our survey was that farm tourism is a source of intrinsic satisfaction for accommodation providers. Most respondents (68%) said that while they appreciated the extra income from farm tourism it was not the only, or even the most important, reason for doing it. Respondents felt overwhelmingly (99%) that the biggest advantage of farm tourism was that it enabled them to meet interesting people. In remote or geographically isolated areas this was particularly important, as in the case of the respondent in the Orkney Islands who said that she did farm B&B simply because she liked doing it. She did not know how much profit she made, or even if she made a profit at all!

Just under half the total number of respondents (47%) felt that an important advantage of farm tourism was that it prevented buildings from deteriorating. This is an aspect of farm tourism which receives tourist board approval. At the time the fieldwork was being carried out Orkney Tourist Board were encouraging the renovation of traditional agricultural buildings for tourism purposes rather than purpose-built new ones.

For a significant number of respondents (36%) farm tourism was ideal because it enabled them to work but be based at home. As one respondent in the South Ayrshire study area said: 'I'm tied to the farm anyway so this is something which can be done'.

Another advantage of farm tourism specifically mentioned by respondents was that the work involved was 'interesting work'. Furthermore, for one respondent, farm tourism was the ideal way of giving farming some good publicity. This particular respondent used her tourism enterprise as a way of presenting farming in a more favourable light: 'It lets people see the truth about farming - it's not as grim as the TV/media paint it at present'.

(iii) The disadvantages of providing farm tourism accommodation

The intrinsic satisfaction that farm tourism offered our respondents was reflected in the fact that 18% of respondents could not think of any disadvantages at all. Other respondents mentioned several disadvantages of being involved with farm tourism which affected them at an individual level.

The disadvantage most commonly mentioned by respondents was the hard work that farm tourism entailed (20%). Related to this was juggling the tourism enterprise with farm work and family responsibilities (9%). It is interesting to note that these were two of the major causes of stress among Scottish farmers (McGregor et al 1995).

Other disadvantages took the form of minor niggles rather than major grievances. Bad behaviour by a minority of visitors had been a problem experienced by 8% of respondents. For 7% of respondents being tied to the house for the summer was seen as a nuisance, while 6% of respondents resented the lack of privacy. Other disadvantages of being involved with farm tourism which were specifically mentioned included the fact that it was time consuming (3%); the extra wear and tear on the house (2%); that it reduces the availability of homes for local people (2%); that there was no income during the winter (2%); having to put on a welcoming manner at all times (1%); being hard on children (1%); being unable to take a summer holiday (1%).

The Agricultural Heritage Attractions Survey

The second part of our study focused on visitor attractions with an agricultural heritage theme. Given the closeness of the tourism-heritage relationship we were originally keen to explore the links between farm tourism accommodation and agricultural heritage attractions. We found that in reality no such relationship exists. Farm tourism accommodation and agricultural heritage attractions exist independently and as separate entities.

Within a short time of starting our fieldwork it became increasingly apparent that the term 'agricultural heritage' is something of a misnomer. Agricultural heritage has to be seen as part of a wider rural heritage which is predominantly regional in flavour. In attempting to draw up an inventory of agricultural heritage attractions, using the STB's *Scotland Groups Guide* (1997) we found ourselves including time and time again, attractions which are more accurately described as rural than agricultural, for example, Culzean Castle and Country Park, Barwinock Herbs, The Atholl Country Collection, The Shetland Museum.

It was comforting to discover that we were not the only ones to find the term 'agricultural heritage' misleading. The Scottish Agricultural Museum at Ingliston is in the process of moving to a site outside East Kilbride and changing its name to the Museum of Country Life. The current curator feels that it is more relevant to see agricultural heritage against the wider backcloth of rural change.

After much deliberating we identified a total of 86 agricultural heritage attractions throughout Scotland. In March 1997 a postal questionnaire was sent to each of these attractions. The number of questionnaires returned was 36 (42%). Of these, three were uncompleted and one was excluded because it turned out to be a stately home, rather than an agricultural heritage attraction. This made the total number of returned and completed questionnaires 32 (37%).

In view of the low response rate and the ad hoc nature of our visits it is not possible to make any grand claims or draw too many conclusions about agricultural heritage in Scotland. Our 'results' do, however, throw up a few tentative suggestions and draw attention to issues and questions which need to be studied in more detail.

(i) Visitor numbers

Of the 32 agricultural heritage attractions which took part in our survey 30 had been opened after 1980. With half of Scotland's 400 museums having been opened since the late 1970s, this echoes the general trend for heritage attractions in Scotland (McCrone et al 1995).

Agricultural heritage attractions attract a significant number of visitors. Only three of the 32 attractions in our sample had less than 1000 visitors during 1996 while 11 attractions (4 country parks/estates; 4 farm parks; 2 museums; 1 rural craft/ trade), were visited by over 20 000 people during the same period. Nearly half (15/32) of the agricultural heritage attractions in our sample experienced increased visitor numbers during 1996 while for a third (10/32) visitor numbers remained the same. Just under a quarter (7/32) said that visitor numbers had declined during 1996.

(ii) Entrance fees and retail outlets

The majority of agricultural heritage attractions in our sample (18/32) had entrance fees of between £1 and £3 per head. An eighth of attractions charged more (between £3 and £5) and one attraction less than this (less than £1). An interesting finding was that a quarter of attractions (8/32) did not charge an entrance fee although they were willing to accept donations. These attractions were more likely to stress granting the public access to local agricultural heritage or preserving it for future generations as the reason they came into being, rather than filling a gap in the heritage/tourism market.

An interesting finding to emerge was that entrance fees were the sole source of income for a minority (4/32) of attractions. For half of the attractions in our survey the entrance fee constituted less than 25% of the total income.

Much more significant as a form of income were retail outlets. Nearly all of the attractions in our survey (28/32), had some form of retail outlet. Over two thirds (22/32) had a shop selling souvenirs, including booklets and gifts. Exactly half (16/32) had cafe/restaurant facilities. Just under a third (10/32) sold local craft produce. Other retail outlets included farm shops (3/32); an ice-cream parlour and tuck shop (1) and the opportunity to purchase animal feed (2); bric-a-brac (1); and take-away home-baking (1).

(iii)   Agricultural heritage as inheritance and enterprise

Even a small sample such as ours points to the existence of two distinct conceptions of agricultural heritage: as inheritance and enterprise. This was revealed by the reasons respondents gave for setting up an agricultural heritage attraction.

By far the most common was to fill a gap in the heritage/tourism market (14 mentions). Providing another form of income for the farm/estate came next (8 mentions). This was closely followed by enabling the public to benefit from local agricultural heritage (7 mentions). A diverse variety of other reasons were also given. They included: preserving local heritage for future generations (3 mentions); to make use of redundant buildings (2 mentions); diversification (2 mentions); conservation (1 mention); to offer a countryside facility (1 mention); to offer a community facility (1 mention); to educate the public about organic/non-intensive farming (1 mention); to display a collection of objects (1 mention); 'a germ of an idea that got out of hand' (1 mention).

The inspiration for setting up the agricultural heritage attractions in our survey also reflected the idea of agricultural heritage as both inheritance and enterprise. A total of 14 attractions were the inspiration of individual heritage entrepreneurs (12) and limited companies (2) tapping into a niche in the heritage/tourism market. These attractions represent heritage as enterprise. Heritage as inheritance is represented by the 8 attractions in our survey which were established by local community groups/trusts/preservation societies and the National Trust for Scotland (NTS). These attractions are dedicated to the preservation and conservation of agricultural heritage. The remaining 10 attractions were set up by local councils (7) and landowners (3). They are best described as representing a mixture of enterprise and inheritance.

Conclusion: Farm Tourism Accommodation, Agricultural Heritage Attractions and the Regeneration of the Rural Economy

Richard Denman's research into farm tourism (1990 and 1993) suggests that farm tourism benefits rural people and rural economies because farm tourism enterprises are developed by local people with local control.

Profits are made and retained in the local community. Visitors to farmhouse B&Bs, Denman found, use local pubs, restaurants, and shops within a five-mile radius of where they are staying. They spend, on average, £10 per head, per night (1993 figures).

Our survey of farm tourism accommodation in Orkney, Perthshire, and South Ayrshire supports Denman's findings. Like Denman we found that the provision of quality farm tourism accommodation brings tourists into an area and, once there, they spend money on local goods and services. It was beyond the scope of our study to survey the spending patterns of visitors to farm B&B accommodation enterprises although specific mention was made, by our respondents, of visitors to their B&B establishments going out for meals to local hotels, restaurants, and pubs; spending money in local shops, making use of local leisure centres, and visiting local heritage attractions. As our survey of agricultural heritage attractions demonstrated, many of these attractions have a retail outlet, even if they do not charge an entrance fee. This is rural regeneration in the conventional economic sense used by policy makers and politicians.

At this point we would do well to consider the older, and arguably more important, meaning of the word 'regeneration'. This is regeneration in the sense of 'breathing new and more vigorous and spiritually higher life into, (person/institution, etc) and bringing them into renewed existence' (The Concise Oxford Dictionary). For the women in our survey who felt overwhelmingly that the biggest advantage of farm tourism was that it enabled them to meet interesting people, farm tourism is as much about personal regeneration as it is about bringing extra money into the farm business or benefiting the wider rural economy.

Acknowledgements

Special thanks to the following: Joyce Willock (Queen Margaret College) for help with questionnaire design and analysis and for carrying out the Perthshire interviews. Sandra Stewart (SAC) for carrying out the Orkney interviews. Harriet Palmer (SAC) for help with the heritage attractions survey.

References

British Market Research Bureau Ltd 1986 Welsh farms: a report on the taking of farm holidays in Wales. Wales Tourist Board, 1986 (BMRB/RMH/95413)

Clarke J 1993 An Analysis of the Demand for Farm Tourism accommodation in Scotland. A report submitted to the Scottish Tourist Board in fulfilment of an STB Postgraduate Research Scholarship

Clarke J 1996 'Farm Tourism'. In: Insights. BTA/ETB, Jan 1996; pp 19–25

Dalton G E, Wilson C J 1989 Farm Diversification in Scotland (SAC Economic Report No 12)

Davies E T 1971 Farm Tourism in Cornwall and Devon. Some economic and physical considerations. Agricultural Economics Unit, University of Exeter, (184)

Davies E T 1983 The Role of Farm Tourism in the Less Favoured Areas of England and Wales. A physical and financial appraisal. Agricultural Economics Unit, University of Exeter, (218)

Denman R 1978 Recreation and Tourism on Farms, Crofts and Estates, Scottish Tourist Board

Denman R, Denman J 1990 A Study of Farm Tourism in the West Country. Ledbury, Tourism RMD

Denman R, Denman J 1993 The Farm Tourism Market, Research report for English Tourist Board and other partners

Denman R 1994 'Green Tourism and Farming'. In: Fladmark J M (ed) Cultural Tourism. Oxford, Donhead

English Tourist Board 1992 British Tourist Authority, Tourism Intelligence Quarterly 1994 Vol.15 No. 4

Frater J 1981 Farm Tourism in England and Overseas. MSc thesis, University of Birmingham

Goffman E 1973 The Presentation of Self in Everyday Life. New York, Overlook Place

MacCannell D 1974 'Staged Authenticity: arrangements of social space in tourist settings'. American Journal of Sociology vol.79, 3

McCrone D Morris A, Kiely, R 1995 Scotland The Brand: The Making of Scottish Heritage. Edinburgh, Edinburgh University Press

McGregor M, Willock J, Deary I 1995 'Farmer Stress'. Farm Management, Vol.9 No.2, Summer

Slee B 1987 Alternative Farm Enterprises. Ipswich, Farming Press

Slee B 1995 Market Led Provision of Environmental Goods in Agricultural Externalities in High Income Countries. Kiel, Wissenschaftsverla Vauk Kiel KG pp 53-67

Slee B, Farr, Snowdon P 1997 'The Economic Impact of Alternative Types of Rural Tourism'. Journal of Agricultural Economics Vol. 48, No.2, pp 179–92

The Scottish Office 1995 Rural Scotland: People, Prosperity, and Partnership

The Scottish Tourist Board 1997 Scotland Groups Guide

Wilson C J 1990 'Incomes from Farm Diversifaction in Scotland'. SAC Economic Report No. 25